THREE FIRST SONS
Love and Great Food Never in Short Supply

THREE FIRST SONS
Love and Great Food Never in Short Supply
A MEMOIR

PAUL "BIFF" COLALUCA

PB COLALUCA PRESS

For permissions please contact:
Paul Colaluca Jr. at PB Colaluca Press
email: pcolaluca@gmail.com

THREE FIRST SONS, LOVE AND GOOD FOOD NEVER IN SHORT SUPPLY

Published by PB Colaluca Press

Book design and cover by: Olga Singer / SimplyTwo Design

Library of Congress Control Number: 2022917854

ISBN 979-8-9869025-0-0

Copyright language: English

Printed by Ingram Sparks, Publishers Group West
Berkeley, California USA

First Edition: December 2022

DEDICATION

I dedicate this book to my grandfather, father, mother, and my wife. As I look back on my time with Raffaele, Paulo, and Loucille, I am humbled by the never-ending gifts of love and support they gave to this quixotic grandson and son and honored to be a part of the ongoing tapestry of their legacies.

Finally, to Karen, my beloved wife of forty-four years, who was my best friend and irreplaceable partner, there are no words to describe your North Star influence on my life. Thank you and rest in peace sweetheart. (August 8, 1945-April 20, 2022)

CONTENTS

INTRODUCTION

INTRODUCTION

This memoir is based on family stories told to me over the years about events that happened before I was born, events I experienced growing up, and a variety of documents, including family letters, interviews, military and Merchant Marine records, and a surprising treasure trove of family history contained in the Baby Book my mother kept on me for the first six years of my life. I have used family members' original Italian names versus the Americanized versions they adopted later, to avoid confusing the reader.

This is a work of creative non-fiction. It's my attempt to tell the story of three generations of first sons and, growing up in an immigrant Italian family, where love and great food were never in short supply. I offer it in homage and gratitude for the myriad gifts of guidance, wisdom, and love I have received over the years.

-- Paul "Biff" Colaluca

For me, writing is an act of reciprocity with the world; it is what I can give back in return for everything that has been given to me.

from ***Braiding Sweetgrass***
by Robin Wall Kimmerer
Milkweed Editions, publisher

CHAPTER ONE

THE BEGINNING 1878

My grandfather, Raffaele Colaluca was born in the small medieval village of Bugnara, Italy, on Monday, May 20, 1878. He was the first child and eldest son of Baron Venjenzo and Baroness Angela Colaluca. In the years that followed, his parents had four more children: Luigi, Augostine, Erina, and Panfilo.

His father was a landowner, who farmed and raised sheep on his estate.

As a youngster, Raffaele was well-known in the mountain community for his irreverent charm, and later for his clarinet playing and woodworking skills. He routinely played for community festivals, wedding receptions, family celebrations, and was a respected craftsman for his cabinetmaking.

Raffaele sometimes played in nearby villages such as Cauze and Sulmona, and after joining the Italian Army at twenty, he saw a great deal more of his Italian homeland playing in the Army Marching Band. Following his honorable discharge from the Army, he returned to the village of Bugnara.

Standing on the balcony of his family's home one morning, he saw a girl in the street below, walking in a line of novitiates on their way to church. She was beautiful.

"Buongiorno!" he called out impulsively. The young girls looked up and giggled, earning him a reproachful look from the Nun escorting them.

"Per favore, what's your name?" he said, pointing at the unknown girl. She glanced up, smiling shyly.

The Nun growled "Come girls!" and strode toward the church.

One of the novitiates called out, "Her name is Anna Maccarelli."

The Nun glared up at Raffaele over her shoulder.

At dinner that night, Raffaele related his encounter as his mother, Angela, listened, frowning.

Venjenzo, trying to suppress a smile, cleared his throat. "If you would like to meet this young lady properly, I will arrange an introduction. Let's have no more calling out in the street. Capisci?"

After their formal introduction, Raffaele was allowed to meet with Anna, who was only fifteen, with her mother serving as chaperone.

Raffaele courted Anna for the next two years, inviting her whenever he played in the village, and sometimes just for her alone. Slowly, and reluctantly, her dream of becoming a Nun faded, replaced by love for this persistent musician. They married on February 16, 1904, when he was twenty-five and she was seventeen. Raffaele wanted a civil ceremony, but Anna insisted on being married in the village Catholic Church.

*

After the wedding, Raffaele and Anna lived with his parents. Anna gave birth to their first child, Claudia (Clara), on December 13, 1905. The Christmas holidays were filled with even more happiness and gratitude than usual in the Colaluca and Maccarelli families, for the special gift of their new granddaughter.

The repeated eruptions of Mount Vesuvius in the spring of 1906 were a metaphor for Raffaele's growing disenchantment with what was happening in his country. Years of mismanagement of southern Italy's farmlands led to a decline in agricultural production, depressions, and a breakdown of the historically agrarian society. The resulting social unrest, combined with the rapid industrialization of northern Italy, fueled the migration of his countrymen to jobs and a better way of life in the north, and the emigration of Italians to America, which peaked in 1907.

Having served in the military, Raffaele was also concerned about the Italian government's colonial ambitions, military buildup, and the political unrest it was creating. He came to believe that the life he'd known was disappearing.

Raffaele's head strong, younger sister, Erina, left for America right after he married, and it broke his mother's heart. His childhood friend and fellow musician, Antonio went to America the next year.

Raffaele decided America was his chance for something different from his father's way of life. It took until the next spring, to first convince Anna, then to deal with his mother's tears and Venjenzo's deep sadness. Finally, his parents reluctantly gave their approval, on the condition that when he got to America, he live with his younger sister, who was living in Mahoning, a town near New Castle in western Pennsylvania. When Erina got his letter, she excitedly wrote back and said to hurry and come. Mahoningtown, Pennsylvania was a wonderful place to live.

Raffaele also wrote to Antonio and told him he was coming and would be living with his sister, and about Anna and baby Clara.

CHAPTER TWO

LEAVING 1906

"Where are you, Papa?" he said impatiently. Raffaele got up from the high-backed brocade sofa and walked to the arched, hand-carved double doors at the front of the house. Opening the door, he walked to the edge of the stone terrace, and looked out across the field for Venjenzo, who had asked to see him. Trying to block the late afternoon sun, Raffaele didn't see him, but knew his father loved being out among his workers.

Straightening his shirt collar, and smoothing his wavy black hair, he sighed and decided to look for his father. He ran his tongue over his teeth, turned his head to each side, breathed deeply, and shrugged.

Just as Raffaele started out, Venjenzo came in from the kitchen, carrying a pitcher of wine and two stemmed glasses. "Sorry I'm late." He sat on the matching couch across from where Raffaele had been sitting and set the pitcher and glasses on the marble-topped coffee table between them. "Wine?"

Raffaele sat down again and patted the dark inlaid wood on the upholstered rolled armrest. "Sure, Papa."

His father filled the glasses and handed one to Raffaele. "Here's to you my eldest son," he said, raising his glass.

Raffaele followed suit, took a drink, set his glass on the table, and leaned back into red upholstery. "Papa, I've decided. I am going to leave." His father ran his fingers through his thinning gray hair and put his palms together. "But you are my first son. You're supposed to be the next Baron Colaluca."

Raffaele looked at his father and shook his head. He lifted his wine glass from the marble-topped coffee table, took another drink, set the glass down, and said softly, "Papa, I don't want to be the next Baron."

"What of our lands and our people?"

Raffaele glanced up at the vaulted ceiling and back at his father. "Papa the soil and people are both poor. Everyday more tenants leave for factory jobs in the north. Soon there will be no barony."

The older man's shoulders sagged as he looked down at his hands.

"It's crazy here, Papa. The king demands more and more volunteers join the army. It's stupid." Raffaele stood. "I'm sorry."

His father gazed up at him. "There's nothing I can say to change your mind?"

"No, Papa. I need to make a different life for Anna and the baby. I can do that in America. I must do this."

His father stood slowly, and they embraced. Standing apart tears filled Venjenzo's eyes. "You're sure Anna is all right with this? Your leaving will be hard for her."

"We've talked. She cried at first but understands my reasons."

"She's a good wife for you. You be good husband in America."

Raffaele smiled. "I'm not wild anymore, Papa."

His father patted him softly on the cheek. "I know. I see your love for little Clara."

"Thank you for watching over my family until I can send for them."

"Of course. They will help dry your mother's tears about your leaving."

Two weeks later, just before dawn, Raffaele and Anna stood in the entrance hall. He pulled her to him. "Anna, don't cry." He held her face in his hands and wiped away the tears on her cheeks with his thumbs. "We'll be together soon."

Anna looked into his eyes. "America is so far away."

He straightened the collar on her bathrobe. "As soon as I find work, I'll send for you. I promise."

She searched his face. "But I worry you will—"

"Anna, stop."

"You are my wife. I love only you."

Raffaele stepped back and grinned. "How could I forget those soft brown eyes." His fingers disappeared into her hair. "Or these thick black curls." Pulling her into him, he added, "and especially this body."

She put a hand on his chest, pushed. "Raffaele, not here."

"What? I can't say loving words to my wife. Remember I'm a Baron's son."

When Anna blushed, then frowned, he raised his hands in surrender. "All right, my shy flower, I'll be more proper." He buttoned his suit coat. "I'm looking forward to seeing my little sister, Erina and maybe my friend, Antonio."

"Be careful your foolish friend doesn't get you into trouble in America."

"Foolish? You do remember he helped me serenade you in the piazza?"

"I remember Mr. Don Juan serenaded many young ladies in the piazza." Raffaele shook his head. "Not that many."

Anna stood on her tiptoes, flung her arms around his neck, and kissed him hard.

He smiled. "That almost makes me want to stay."

From the pocket of her bathrobe, she took a folded, white linen handkerchief, with tiny flowers embroidered at the corners and tucked it into his coat pocket.

"What's this?"

"Something to help you remember us in America."

"My little worrier. I would never forget you."

She nodded and gave him a brave smile, as Raffaele picked up his knapsack, opened both front doors, and took a deep breath. "It's going to be a good day."

Anna followed him across the terrace and down the path to the front gate. "Have a safe journey, my husband," she said through tears.

Raffaele blew her a kiss, and started down the street, a lump in his throat.

Seeing the tip of his clarinet sticking out of the knapsack, Anna smiled. He'd have his music in America. She watched as dawn came and he was out of sight.

Raffaele took the early morning bus from Bugnara to Naples. At lunchtime, as the countryside passed by, he ate the bread, cheese, and hard salami Anna packed for him. The sun was setting when he arrived at the harbor. The ship terminal was crowded and noisy. Many people looked like farmers, like those who worked for his father, standing in groups talking. Their scruffy children laughed and played next to women sitting on their belongings.

Raffaele waited impatiently in one of the long lines, watching an hour pass on the big clock above the ship's arrival and departure board, before he reached the counter.

He smoothed the coat of his brown wool suit and tipped his fedora. "When does the next boat leave for America?"

The clerk looked him up and down and said nothing.

Raffaele was not used to being ignored. "Excuse me—"

The beleaguered clerk pointed over his shoulder at the board. "They're called ships. Passport please."

Raffaele slid the dark red booklet to the clerk, "Is there a problem?"

"No, no problem, sir."

"Good. I must leave as soon as possible."

The clerk looked at the papers. "The SS Celtic leaves later tonight. Only steerage is available. First class is available on a ship that leaves tomorrow."

"What is steerage?"

The clerk rolled his eyes. "There are three classes of passengers on a ship." He held up his thumb. "First class," then his index finger, "second class." Pausing for effect and held up his middle finger…"or steerage, which is what is available tonight."

Raffaele stared at the dismissive man. "I'd like one steerage ticket then, if it's not too much trouble."

"150 lire, please." The clerk took Raffaele's money, filled out a ticket, stamped his passport, and handed it back.

"Thank you. Where do I—" The clerk, looking at a manifest, pointed to his right. "You board through gate four. Any more questions?"

"None you could answer, I'm sure."

"Then have a nice trip." He looked past Raffaele. "Next."

Raffaele moved out of the line turned and saw a large black 4 above a door at the far end of the terminal. He got in the shortest line, looked at the first date in the little red book and smiled. The entry read July 3. 1906.

On board, Raffaele discovered that third class passengers were packed into small stuffy cabins below deck, near the bow and stern of the ship. Two wooden bunkbeds in each cabin, were filled to overflowing with men, women, children, and whatever belongings they could carry. In his cabin, a family of four were settled in. A man and woman sat on the lower beds; their two children were cross-legged on the top bed above their mother.

"Good evening. My name is Raffaele Colaluca, I'm going to America," he said proudly. Self-consciously, adding "I guess you are, too."

The man extended his hand. "My name is Mario Gaetano. My

wife, Rosalina."

"Pleased to meet you, all of you," Raffaele said, looking at the boys on the top bunk. He reached up to take their hands as Mario said, "These are my sons. Carlo is six, Nicolo is eight."

"Do either of you snore?"

The boys grinned and shook their heads.

"Good. Then you'll be able to hear me when I do," he said, smiling back at them.

Raffaele put his knapsack on the empty upper bunk.

"May I ask, are you related to the Baron Colaluca in Bugnara?"

"Yes. He is my father."

"We're from Sulmona. Some friends who worked for him say he is good man."

"Thank you. He is a fair man and loves his land. Well, I've never been on a ship before. I think I'll look around."

Outside the cabin, were long communal tables where passengers ate their meals, cafeteria style. Aromas from the kitchen indicated the evening meal was being prepared. Next, he located the dank bathrooms, no showers, only toilets. As mealtime neared, the noise and crowding intensified. Needing fresh air and quiet, he went topside.

Raffaele spent most of the seventeen-day crossing on deck, to avoid the smell and commotion below, often sleeping outside on the cold, damp crowded deck covered only with the thin, gray blanket given to steerage passengers.

When they passed through the Strait of Gibraltar, the calm, blue waters of the Mediterranean became dark gray swells. Raffaele experienced his first seasickness.

The next morning, Pietro Grasso, a barrel-chested man in farmer's overalls, stood next to a hunched Raffaele, whose elbows where on the railing, his forehead resting on his fists, listening to the sound of water rushing down the side of the ship, and trying not to throw up.

Pietro said, quietly, "You don't look so good."

"Thanks."

"I can't believe how the people push and shove for that stuff they call food." Pietro continued.

Raffaele's queasy stomach lurched. "Please don't talk about food."

"Oh, sorry." Pietro looked out at the ocean. "I can hardly wait to get to America."

"Me, too," Raffaele answered, his eyes closed.

"I'm going to make a lot of money in America and go back home," Pietro said.

Raffaele looked at him. "Good for you, but I'm not going back." He gazed back down at the dark water that calmed his stomach a little.

"What?"

"I am not going back."

"Why not?"

Raffaele grasped the railing with both hands and straightened up. "Because what was is dying. I'm going to find a job, save my money, and send for my wife and baby."

"But Italy is our country."

"Not anymore. I want to be American."

"Not me. I'm going to own my own farm, marry my Sofia, and live like a baron."

"That's a nice dream."

"It's no dream." Pietro looked at him, shook his head, and moved away.

The queasiness returned, and Raffaele again concentrated on not throwing up.

When his stomach settled, he breathed in the salt air, smiling. Pietro had no idea about being a baron. "And I choose not to be one," he yelled into the wind.

A young woman, in a peasant headscarf, with a ship's blanket around her shoulders, cleared her throat and moved closer. "Are you alright?"

Embarrassed, Raffaele said, "Yes…I'm fine."

She leaned on the railing, quietly studying him with her hazel eyes.

Raffaele returned her gaze. "You don't need to be a baron to enjoy life."

"I see…and are you one?"

"I could have been." He looked at the early morning sky and felt the vibration of the ship's engines rumbling far below.

Raffaele arrived in New York, early in the morning on July 19, 1906. While being processed he showed the official a letter with Erina's address, who guided him to a train to Philadelphia. Once there, a ticket agent directed him to a train going to New Castle, and an Italian-speaking conductor gave him directions to Erina's. She let him unpack before stuffing him with food. Raffaele finally relaxed and slept well into the next day.

Erina's boyfriend, Antonio Erecco, worked for the railroad. She'd lived in a boarding house after coming to America and was enjoying managing one now that catered to men. She was not ready to get married.

For the next couple days, Raffaele walked around the town during the day, and listened to the men at night talk about their jobs on the railroad and in the tin mills, or their girlfriends. One day after dinner, he played his clarinet for the boarders and was invited to a party the next Saturday.

He told Erina that playing his clarinet again reminded him of the festivals in Bugnara, and his friend Antonio.

She went to her room, returned with a letter, and handed it to Raffaele.

"What's this?" he asked, reading the return address. It was from Antonio.

"It came before you got here. I never liked Antonio, Mr. God's gift to women," she said. "I knew you'd want to see him right away, and I wanted you to stay here with me."

Raffaele opened the letter. It read:

Dear Raffaele,
    Welcome to America. I am glad you decided to come.
Where I live is like our village back home, but not so many farms.
Many Italian people and businesses.
    I am in a marching band. We play in parades and festivals.
I like it very much. Raffaele, you could play in a band here, it would
be like old times. Please come for a visit. Give my love to Anna.
                       Antonio

Raffaele gave Erina the letter. Her expression hardened as she read. "Mahoningtown is not like Germantown," she said, "but it's a good place for me."

Raffaele hugged her. "I know Sis."

Two days later, he boarded a train for Philadelphia with a bag of sandwiches Erina packed for him.

Arriving at the Pennsylvania Railroad's Broad Street Station, Raffaele showed Antonio's address to a ticket agent, and was directed to the trolley north to Germantown.

The trolley conductor spoke Italian and dropped Raffaele off a block away from Antonio's address.

The minute Raffaele stepped off the trolley in Germantown, the neighborhood sights, sounds, and aromas, made him feel like he was back home.

When Antonio opened his apartment door, Raffaele watched his friend blink and stare at him a moment, before embracing him.

"You're here?" He held Raffaele at arm's length. "You got my letter?"

Raffaele frowned. "Erina didn't give it to me right away. She doesn't like you."

"She was the only girl I never got a kiss from," Antonio grinned. "Come in, come in," he said, pulling on Raffaele's arm.

Raffaele stepped into the small front room and took off his fedora.

Antonio motioned for him to sit on the worn sofa with faded floral upholstery.

"How's Anna and the baby? Clara's her name, right?"

"Yes. She and the baby are living with my parents. I'm going to send for them once a find work and a place to live." Raffaele leaned back into the sofa. "I'll be honest, Antonio, I already like Germantown more than Mahoningtown. It feels alive. I'm thinking about staying here. Do you know where I could get a room around here?"

"You can stay here! It'll be like old times," Antonio exclaimed.

CHAPTER THREE

GERMANTOWN 1906

I was so happy when I got your letter, Raffaele. I wasn't sure I'd ever see you again after you got married."

"It's not good in our homeland, Antonio, and I didn't want to be the next Baron Colaluca."

"I see. Well, good for you. Tell me about Clara."

Raffaele's eyes glowed. "She's beautiful."

"Like her mother. You're a lucky man."

"I know." He looked at the cluttered apartment. "And you? Have you married?"

Antonio burst out laughing. "Me? No—too many beautiful women in America."

"Still the playboy?"

"Of course, always."

Raffaele smoothed his black hair and looked directly at his friend.

"Antonio, I need to find place to live...and a job."

"The first thing is easy. Stay with me for as long as you like."

"I don't have much money left, but I'll pay you what I can."

Raffaele held out his hand to shake, but Antonio pushed it away and grinned.

"Pay rent after you find a job, Baron."

Raffaele returned the smile. "Thank you. Do you know of any jobs?"

"Ah, the second thing, jobs are not so easy to find. It took me a while, but I know someone who might help. Enrico, who owns the delicatessen up the street. He's been here many years and knows everyone.

Let's go have dinner so you can meet him."

When Raffaele hesitated, Antonio stood and said, "Come on, it's my treat. It's not every day a Baron's son comes to America."

"What kind of job did you find?" caused Antonio to mimic playing a trumpet.

"I couldn't find work, but Enrico knew I played and sent me to a band-master he knows. I've been playing in the band ever since. It's only part-time, but enough to live on, and a great way to meet the ladies."

Raffaele nodded. "I still play some."

"You were good. Maybe you could play until you find a job." Antonio pulled open the glass door of the delicatessen, making the bell overhead tinkle.

He bowed and motioned Raffaele inside. "You'll like Enrico and his wife, Rosetta. He used to play saxophone and is partial to musicians."

Raffaele stepped inside and stopped, causing Antonio to bump him from behind.

"Hey, what's wrong?"

Raffaele breathed in. "Nothing. This smells like my mother's kitchen."

Antonio laughed. "The boat didn't smell like this?"

"I don't imagine it did," said the rotund man behind the cold case, peering over his glasses. "Who is this, Antonio?"

Raffaele looked at the salamis and cheeses hanging on the wall behind the counter, when he felt Antonio's hand in the middle of his back, pushing him forward.

"Enrico, this is my friend, Raffaele, just arrived from the old country."

Enrico stepped from behind the cold case and held out his hand. He was taller than Raffaele, with salt and pepper hair, wearing suspenders that curved slightly over the front of his white shirt. "Welcome to America. It's a pleasure to meet you."

"Thank you. I'm glad to meet you."

"He's a musician, too. Plays the clarinet," Antonio added.

A slender, dark-haired woman, wearing an embroidered bib apron, came through the door behind the counter. "Who's this?" Her large hazel eyes crinkled when she smiled at Raffaele.

"Rosetta, this is my friend, Raffaele Colaluca. His father's a baron in Bugnara."

"Really? I'm from Sulmona. His father's name is known in our town." She said to her husband. "I was coming to get you for supper. Why don't we invite our new arrival…and Casanova here to dinner?"

Enrico nodded. "I'd like the chance to hear firsthand, how things are in Italy these days. Rosetta, why don't you take them back and I'll lockup."

The men followed her through the door behind the counter, into their well-appointed home behind the delicatessen.

The next day, Raffaele had an audition with the Sousa-type marching band Antonio joined after coming to America. The bandmaster was impressed, and Raffaele began playing clarinet with the band that weekend, pleased that one of his favorite pastimes would earn him money.

Raffaele and Anna exchanged letters. He told her he'd arrived safely, described his voyage and arrival, and about playing in the band. She said she missed him and wanted to know when he would send for her. He explained his band job was only part time until he could find full-time work but would send her money soon.

CHAPTER FOUR

CONCERNS 1907

As Raffaele continued to play in the band, weeks turned into months. He was handsome, talented, and loved playing. Every time the band appeared in Germantown the neighborhood wives noticed other women in the audience paying a lot of attention to him. Sometimes he'd wink back at them while he played, to acknowledge their smiles.

When the band took breaks, Raffaele often sat with his feet hanging over the edge of the stage, talking with audience members. In October, at a Friday evening concert in the park, a young woman with bleached-blonde hair and black eyebrows, pressed herself up against the chest-high stage in front of his music stand, and smiled at him every time she caught his eye.

When the band took its first break, she rested her crossed forearms on stage and cocked her head to one side. "You play very well, clarinet man."

Raffaele started to stand but sat back down. "Thank you. The band, it's playing good tonight."

"How long have you played the clarinet?"

"Since I was a boy in Italy." He smiled. "I love to make music."

"Have you been in America long?"

"No, just three months."

"Do you have family here?"

Raffaele sighed. "No, my wife is not here yet."

"Really. It must be lonely here all by yourself."

"Sometimes, yes."

"My name's Frieda." She extended her hand.

"Who is this pretty girl, Raffaele?" Antonio said, coming up behind him and reaching down to shake the woman's hand.

"Her name's Frieda," Raffaele looked over his shoulder. "She likes the band."

Frieda pulled her hand from Antonio's grip. She looked at Raffaele and smiled. "Maybe we can talk more later." Frowning at Antonio, she walked away.

"How do you do it? A beautiful wife is not enough for you?"

Raffaele scowled at his friend. "She just likes the music."

"Yeah, sure. I didn't get a smile." Antonio went back to his seat as other members of the band came back on stage.

Several of the Italian wives in the neighborhood witnessed the attractive young woman talking to Raffaele. He was getting more female attention than any of them thought a married man should.

That Sunday after Mass, the group approached Rosetta, the leader of the Altar Society, and voiced their concerns.

"You should have seen how the young women smile at him," one of them started.

"Yes," said another, "and one openly flirted with him."

"Does she attend our church?" Rosetta looked around the group.

The women looked at each other and then shook their heads. Several comments followed:

"I'm sure she saw his ring."

"He looked like he enjoyed the attention."

"Too much."

After listening to the group, Rosetta raised her palms. "So, what do you all think we should do?"

"He's a married man," said one.

"If his wife were here, he'd act like one."

"She needs to come as soon as she can, to protect her marriage."

Heads bobbed in agreement.

Rosetta gazed at each. "Thank you for bringing this to my attention. Marriage is a serious matter. Sometimes men can forget their responsibilities. Any man."

The women nodded.

"His behavior is not good for any of us."

Rosetta nodded. "No. Let me think about how we might help the two of them."

That evening after dinner, Rosetta sat down on the sofa with her husband.

"Enrico, when you talk to Raffaele, does he ever say anything about his wife?"

Enrico was reading the newspaper and didn't look up. "Sometimes."

"Does he miss her?"

"I suppose, why?"

Rosetta looked at the back of the newspaper for a moment. "Several wives came to me today after Mass, concerned that he's forgotten her."

Enrico lowered the paper, frowning. "What are you talking about?"

Rosetta shifted toward him on the sofa. "Women were paying a lot of attention to him at the concert Friday night."

"So."

"He seemed to be enjoying it a bit too much."

Enrico breathed out a long sigh. "Raffaele loves Anna. He told me he's saving money to send for her."

"How much can he really save just playing in that band?"

"I don't know, and it's none of our business." Enrico stared at his wife over the top of his spectacles. "What are you thinking, Rosetta?"

"I want him to act like a married man."

"And how are you going to do that?"

"I'm not sure." She stood, and went into the darkened kitchen, untying and putting her apron on the hook by the sink. Rosetta gazed out over the starched white café curtains at stars beginning to shine in the twilight sky.

"What are you doing, Rosetta?" he called.

"Just thinking about the sanctity of marriage."

"In the dark?"

"It's a beautiful night, Enrico. Maybe we could go for a walk?" She went to the front room and saw him standing by the doorway.

"You are such a romantic. A walk sounds nice."

They strolled hand-in-hand up one side of the block and down the other. Streetlamps glowed into brightness as they exchanged greetings with families enjoying the evening from their porches.

When they reached the delicatessen, Enrico embraced her. "So, what are you thinking my wife? I bet it's about Raffaele and Anna. What are you planning?"

She stood on her toes and kissed him softly. "You know me too well my husband," and hugged him tightly.

"Well?"

Rosetta sat down on the wooden bench that ran under the store's display window and patted the space next to her.

Enrico sat and relaxed against the back of the bench.

Rosetta rested her head on his shoulder. "I think I'm going to write to my family—Sulmona is only a few miles from Bugnara—and have them take a letter to Anna. It's such a small town someone will find her. I want her to know how important it is that a wife be with her husband, and long separations are not good for a marriage."

He looked at Rosetta and chuckled. "So that's why you never let me out of your sight."

She poked him in the ribs. They both laughed.

When Enrico turned to her, his face was solemn. "Like I said, I don't think it's any of our business. A marriage is between a husband and his wife. Raffaele is a good man. Let him work it out, Rosetta. And don't get your family involved. No letters please."

The next Sunday, Rosetta told the ladies in the Altar Society meeting what Enrico said, and she would not write a letter to Anna or get her family involved.

The wives shared and vented, about talking with their husbands.

An older woman huffed, "My husband thought he was just being friendly. Can you believe it?"

"Mine said the same thing," a younger member added quickly.

"His behavior sets a bad example in the community," another declared.

Rosetta touched the locket at her neck. "Ladies, your husbands are all good men. Giving someone the benefit of the doubt is an honorable trait."

No one spoke.

"Only Raffaele is responsible for his actions." She rubbed her chin, turned, and gazed at the ornately carved wooden cross hanging on the wall to her left.

"Let me think about what else we might do to help Raffaele change his behavior." She pointed at the ladies. "In the meantime, go home and tell your husbands you love them."

The Marching Band's season ended with the onset of winter, and with it the reason for the Altar Society wives concerns about Raffaele's public behavior. Though he sometimes played for the church and other private parties, he still had not sent for his wife. Spring was coming and the Marching Band would resume playing. With the lack of support from their husbands, the women's simmering frustrations came up at the April planning meeting for the May Crowning of Mary ceremony. Rosetta listened calmly.

Finally, a normally quiet matron raised her hand. "Rosetta, here we are planning a devotional ceremony to celebrate Mary, the mother of Jesus, and we have a husband who still has not sent for his wife who he left in Italy almost a year ago. She's a young mother who needs our support. Marriage is sacred. His behavior is a sacrilege."

"My husband," another woman added, "doesn't think we should get involved. That's a sacrilege too."

"I think all our husbands need to be reminded that marriage is a sacred bond," said a young woman expecting her first baby.

"I am as concerned as you are and am also dealing with facing my husband who does not want to get involved. My Enrico is a good man. I will talk with him again tonight and ask for his advice in how to help Raffaele. But now, Let's finish our planning for the May Crowning ceremony."

That night, Rosetta cooked Enrico his favorite meal, eggplant parmigiana. Holding the ends of the baking dish with dishtowels, she carried it to the kitchen table. "Dinner's ready, Enrico."

"Coming." He sniffed. "Eggplant parmigiana? What's the special occasion?"

"Nothing. It's been a while since I've cooked this, and I know it's one of your favorites."

"Everything you cook is my favorite." He smiled and motioned for her plate, putting a steaming helping on it.

Rosetta put her napkin in her lap, took her plate, and watched her husband serve himself a generous portion, then tuck his napkin in his collar and pick up his fork.

"Enrico? Will you say Grace tonight?"

He put the fork down. "Of course. Dear God, thank you for this delicious food my beautiful wife prepared."

Rosetta shook her head and crossed herself.

"And watch over our friends and their families. Amen. Okay?"

"Yes, except for the 'beautiful wife' part."

"Well, you are beautiful."

"I don't think God cares whether I'm beautiful or not."

"The Bible says he made us in his image, and isn't he perfect in every way? Then I think he likes to be thanked for the beauty he created."

Rosetta sighed. "Thank you. Eat your food before it gets cold, my philosopher."

After washing the dishes, Rosetta sat on the couch with Enrico. "I need to talk to you about something."

Enrico looked up from his newspaper.

"At the Altar Society meeting today, the wives were talking about the situation with Raffaele, but when they've talked with their husbands about his behavior, most of them thought he was just being friendly."

"So ..."

"They didn't like their husbands thinking Raffaele's behavior was innocent. They think it's inappropriate, and he's setting a bad example in the community."

Enrico shook his head as Rosetta moved close to him and put her hand on his arm. "Would you talk with him about his behavior?"

"What? No. I'm his friend, Rosetta, not his priest. You Altar Society ladies started this. Have Father Savona talk to him."

Rosetta sat back. "You're right. Our priest would council him about his marital responsibilities." She blew a kiss to Enrico. "How did you get so smart, my husband?"

"I'm not smart. I'm just tired of listening to husbands grumbling in my shop after their wives have talked with them."

"Who's grumbling?"

Enrico wagged his finger at her and touched his temple. "What I hear stays here."

"Really? We'll see about that." She kissed him on the cheek. "I will talk with Father Savona tomorrow, first thing in the morning."

CHAPTER FIVE

CONFRONTATIONS 1907

Two weeks later, after Sunday morning Mass, the elderly priest waited for Raffaele. Father Savona was the community icon for all matters spiritual during his thirty years at St. Vincent's. Soft spoken with close-cropped gray hair and piercing blue eyes, he could be direct. After hearing from the wives in his Altar Society, he knew this pastoral conversation was overdue.

A quiet knock broke into his thoughts.

A young man stood in the doorway, dressed in a suit and tie, his black hair combed straight back, and his fedora in both hands at his waist.

"Please," Father Savona motioned for Raffaele to enter, "Come in."

Raffaele stepped cautiously into the ornate, darkly paneled room.

Father Savona extended a hand toward one of the two high-backed chairs facing the large mahogany desk and went to sit next to him in the matching chair.

Raffaele chose the chair nearest the door, sitting on the red velvet upholstery.

A low round Victorian parlor table with claw feet separated the chairs, which were angled toward each other.

"May I call you Raffaele?"

"Yes, Father."

"Do you know why I asked to speak with you Raffaele?"

Raffaele shook his head.

"I understand you are married and have a baby daughter."

Raffaele sat up straighter. "Yes, Father," he said proudly. "My wife's name is Anna, and my daughter's is Clara. They will come to live here soon."

"So, I am told, and when would that be exactly?"

"I'm not sure. I send her money whenever I can."

"Do you love your wife, Raffaele?"

Raffaele blushed. "Yes, Father, very much."

Father Savona cleared his throat. "I understand you are an accomplished musician and play in a band. Is that true?"

"Yes," he replied in a barely audible voice, looking at the priest quizzically.

"Do you have a fulltime job somewhere," the priest asked, with an emphasis on the word fulltime, "to help bring your wife to America sooner?" Raffaele shook his head and sank back into the red velvet.

Father Savona leaned forward. "Raffaele, your friends are concerned you're enjoying your new life in America so much," he paused, "you've forgotten your family responsibilities. Could that be so?"

Raffaele stiffened. "No. They have a no right—"

"They have every right," the priest interrupted. "They are your friends. If you saw a friend stray from the righteous path in life, do something hurtful to himself or his family, would you not say something, reach out, help him?"

Raffaele looked down at the carpet and squeezed the brim of his hat.

Father Savona stood, studied Raffaele for a moment, and said, "Come, let me show you something." Raffaele followed the priest to the large picture window to his left. The eight-by-four-foot expanse of clear glass was topped by a stained-glass header of colorful floral designs and framed in dark crown molding. Thick emerald, green, floor-length curtains hung at both ends of the window.

The priest said, "What do you see out there, young man?"

"I see grass, some trees, flowers—and the church."

Father Savona gazed out the window. "What I see is beauty created by love. When we love something or someone, we take care of them, and that means being responsible. I feel that you love your wife and daughter. Are you showing that love by being responsible, Raffaele?"

The younger man bowed his head. Moments passed in silence. Finally, his eyes met Father Savona's. "No, Father. Not like that."

"When will you start being more loving to your wife and daughter?"

Raffaele sighed. "Soon, Father. Very soon."

"Excellent." The priest put his arm on Raffaele's shoulder. "Did you have a trade in the old country?"

"No, not really. My father was Baron Colaluca."

"Ah, I see. What else did you like to do besides play your clarinet?"

"I'm good with wood, working with my hands, carving," Raffaele answered, his voice becoming animated.

Father Savona nodded toward the outside. "Really. Woodworking is an honorable profession. You might start your search for a better paying job where they need good carvers."

The next week, Raffaele reluctantly quit playing in the band.

Enrico, with Rosetta's urging, let him rent the tiny one-bedroom apartment above the delicatessen, with rent due when he found work. His new home came with an ice box, coal burning stove, and electric lights. The furniture consisted of a squeaky Victorian style metal bed frame and mattress, a scratched oak highboy dresser, and a stained maple kitchen table. In the front room, a threadbare brown wingback chair sat by an un-curtained window with a view of the street below.

The day Raffaele moved out of Antonio's apartment was sad for them both. They hugged and were embarrassed by their emotions.

Antonio slapped him on the back as he walked out the door. "You be good, Baron Colaluca. If I hear of any jobs, I'll tell you."

Antonio took a step out of the door and added, "Let me know when Anna and the baby arrive. Okay?"

Raffaele nodded and walked up the street.

The following Monday, Raffaele came into the delicatessen, dressed in his Sunday suit and fedora. Enrico motioned him to a table from behind the counter, came around wiping his hands on his apron, and sat down.

"How's my new tenant this fine day?"

"I'm well, thank you. Today, I look for a job."

Enrico smiled broadly. "When you first arrived, you told me that you enjoyed woodworking almost as much as playing your clarinet. Is that still true?"

Raffaele nodded.

"Good. I talked to some friends last night. One, who works in maintenance at Wanamaker's Department store downtown said they're looking for an apprentice furniture restorer."

"What is that?"

"Someone who fixes broken furniture. Someone who likes to carve."

Enrico reached across the table and tapped Raffaele in the chest.

"Someone like you."

"You think so?"

"I think you should go and see."

Raffaele was hired as an apprentice furniture restorer and received his first paycheck from Wanamaker's after two weeks on the job. Enrico and Rosetta invited him to dinner with them to celebrate. After the meal, several other couples appeared at the door, were welcomed, seated around the dining room table, and served wine.

That was when Enrico's wife, sitting across the table from Raffaele cleared her throat. "Raffaele, we have something to tell you."

He put down his wine glass and glanced around the table.

"We wives," she nodded around the table, "asked Father Savona to talk to you.

Raffaele stared at his wine glass. "I know. Father Savona told me."

"Did he also tell you how much Anna misses you?"

He looked up and shook his head. "No."

"Anna was heartbroken when you left. As the weeks, and then months, went by, she thought she'd lost you."

"How do you know this?" Raffaele said, confused. "Her letters sounded happy, all about the baby."

"It's not what she told us."

Raffaele's eyes widened. He looked quickly at the other women, and back at the dark-haired woman across from him. "All of you?"

As the women nodded, Rosetta continued, "After you saw Father Savona, we wrote to Anna."

Raffaele bolted upright. His flash of anger at the subterfuge, melted into embarrassment as he put his elbows on the table, his forehead resting in his hands, and stared at the crumbs on the tablecloth.

"Family is the most important thing, Raffaele," Rosetta continued. "Anna and the baby need to be with you."

He lifted his head and looked around the table. "I know. Thank you. You're good friends. I love her very much."

Everyone around the table smiled at him and lifted their glasses. A boisterous round of "Welcome to America" followed. The women looked at each other and nodded, while the husbands came around the table, slapped him on the back, and mussed his hair. After many toasts and hugs the couples left.

After dinner, Enrico and Raffaele sat sipping amaretto.

"Wives, they're really something," Enrico said. He rested his head on the high back of his wingback chair. "When they get together, watch out."

Raffaele nodded. "I'm finding that out."

"Tell me, how did you meet Anna?"

"I first saw her from my balcony. She was a novice walking to church." Enrico stared at Raffaele. "She wanted to be a nun?"

"Yes, but she'd not said her vows. She was so beautiful."

"She was to be a Bride of Christ? To interfere is a sacrilege."

Raffaele clenched his fists. "Better my bride than a slave to priests."

Enrico watched his young tenant's hands slowly relax. He leaned forward. "You have a problem with the priests?"

Raffaele scowled. "They didn't keep their vows. It's a long story, Enrico. For another time, okay?"

"Sure. So, continue about Anna."

Raffaele beamed. "I called out 'Buongiorno' to her and asked her name. She said nothing, just looked straight ahead so I asked for her name."

Enrico grinned. "What did she do then?"

"Still nothing, but the girl behind her giggled and told me it was Anna Maccarelli. She looked up then with such a sweet, shy smile." Raffaele leaned back in the chair. "I went home and told my father I wanted to marry her."

"Just like that? What did he say?"

"My parents, especially my mother, were not pleased with my calling after her in the street. When I explained she was not just another girlfriend, my father said he would arrange for a proper introduction with her parents, and not to talk to her again."

"And?"

"My father was a Baron and her parents let me see her. I could see her in the evenings in the piazza, with her mother as a chaperone. We would walk around with her mother behind us, watching. She was only fifteen."

"What did you talk about?"

"She wanted to be a nun, and I wanted her to be my wife."

"What finally changed her mind?"

"I'm not sure. Maybe it was the stars or the music from the cafes. One night we sat by the fountain, and I played my clarinet for her. Perhaps it moved her heart." Raffaele smiled self-consciously. "After a while, I invited her, and her mother of course, to come when I played at our village festivals. I just would not go away."

Enrico chuckled. "Raffaele, you are a determined young man."

"My friends say stubborn." He shrugged then couldn't help yawning. "Thank you for dinner. Please excuse me. Favore, it's been a long day."

They rose, and Enrico embraced him. "See you at church on Sunday?"

"Maybe. Good night." He picked up his coat and fedora and left.

Upstairs, Raffaele stood at the front room window and gazed down at couples holding hands and family clusters moving along the sidewalks under the streetlights. He could hear the faint sound of music from somewhere.

He turned away from the window and sat in his only chair, leaned back and closed his eyes. "Anna I'm glad you're coming soon," he said quietly. His breathing slowed, and in a few minutes he snored softly.

CHAPTER SIX

WORK AND WAITING 1907

*E*very morning Raffaele took the trolley to his job at Wanamaker's wearing his navy-blue marching band suit, tie, and fedora. In a wooden briefcase he carried his carving tools, work uniform, and lunch. When the weather permitted, he walked the six miles home to save money. He worked eight hours Monday through Friday, a half day on Saturday, and earned ten dollars a week. After paying rent for his room above the delicatessen, buying groceries and trolley fares, he sent the rest to Anna for her passage and care of Clara, tucked into his biweekly letters.

When he got home from work after a cold and blustery mid-October walk, Rosetta stopped him with a letter from Anna in her hand. He sat down at one of the tables in the deli to read it.

> *Dearest Raffaele,*
>
> *Thank you for your letter with news from America. As always, I read it to Clara and shared it with your parents. I'm excited to tell you I have saved enough for our tickets to America and am thrilled to think of being with you again. I am also sad to tell you that my mother is ill with pneumonia. Clara and I are staying with my parents while I take care of her. I will come as soon as I can my sweet husband.*
>
> > *All my love,*
> > *Anna*

Raffaele sat back and read it again.

Rosetta came around from behind the counter. "Raffaele, is everything all right?"

"Anna finally has enough money for her tickets, but now her mother is ill, and she's taking care of her. She waited so patiently when I was in the marching band. Now it's my turn to wait."

Raffaele grinned at Rosetta. "Is this God's punishment for my foolishness?"

The next eight weeks dragged by as Raffaele wrote Anna letters, continued to send money, and waited to hear about her mother's slow improvement. Finally, a week before Christmas, Rosetta handed him a letter when he came from work, his overcoat dusted with snow. Tears ran down his cheeks as he read it.

Dearest Raffaele,

My prayers have been answered. My sweet mother has recovered. Clara and I will be leaving December 21, 1907, from Naples on the S.S. Canopic. We will stop in Portugal for a day and arrive in Boston on January 11, 1908. I am excited beyond words to be with you again in America. Your father and mother send their love.

Your loving wife,
Anna

Raffaele wiped his tears with the back of his hand, handed the letter to Rosetta, stood up and hugged Enrico.

"This is wonderful news," Rosetta said, embracing Raffaele.

Raffaele nodded, his throat tight with emotion.

"It calls for a toast," said Enrico, pouring three glasses of wine. He handed one to Rosetta, one to Raffaele, and then raised his, "To Raffaele, Anna, and baby Clara, together at last in America. Salute!"

CHAPTER SEVEN

ANNA ARRIVES 1908

Raffaele awoke before dawn, lit the coal-burning stove in the kitchen before walking to the window in the front room to see last week's snow almost gone. Back in the kitchen, he savored the warmth on his back as heat gradually filled the room.

"No work today. Not this Tuesday." Raffaele yawned and stretched before washing, shaving, and combing his black hair back. Dressed in his brown wool Sunday suit, he returned to the kitchen, cut himself a thick slice of provolone cheese and bread, and stood at the kitchen counter to eat.

Raffaele chewed and stared out the half-window above the sink, as the sunrise pierced the gray clouds. "It's a good sign, Anna. Today you bring your sunshine into my life again."

He read the piece of paper on which Enrico wrote the name of Anna's ship, the S.S. Canopic, and the pier where it would dock that afternoon in Boston.

When Raffaele went out, Enrico stopped sweeping the sidewalk in front of the delicatessen and said, "So, the big day has finally arrived."

The two men embraced. "Yes, my friend. I'm on my way to catch the train."

"You have my directions?"

"Right here." Raffaele patted the breast pocket of his overcoat.

Rosetta came out of the deli to join them on the sidewalk. "Here, this is for you."

He took the unexpected gift, a small cardboard box tied with string. "What's this?"

"Something to eat on the way. I knew you'd be too excited to think about lunch."

"Thank you," Raffaele said, kissing Rosetta's cheek as she hugged him. "Safe travels. See you tonight with Anna and the precious baby."

Nervous about changing trains in New York, Raffaele followed Enrico's directions exactly and found the right gate with plenty of time to spare. He hopped off the train the moment it arrived in Boston and almost ran, going directly to the harbor. In the crowded, cavernous terminal building, he waited all afternoon as the ship's passengers were processed. Finally, Anna came out a door, a suitcase in one hand, Clara clutching her other hand. In her long black coat with a black and red shawl framing her face, she was even more beautiful than he remembered.

He waved his arms over his head, yelling over the din, "Anna! Over here!" When she looked from side to side, he waved again. "Anna, I'm here!"

Finally, spotting him among the sea of faces, she softly said his name, put her suitcase down, stood, and started to cry.

"Excuse me, excuse me," he repeated, until he reached her, and they embraced. He murmured, "I love you, Anna."

"I've missed you so, Raffaele."

She kissed him again and again, until Clara started to cry.

Raffaele bent down, picked her up, and cradled her in his arms. "There, there, little one. Your father's here. You're in America now!"

Wiping Anna's tears with his fingertips, he said, "Anna, I'm sorry I didn't send for you sooner."

"Shhh," Anna said. "Were together now, that's what matters."

Going home the train's movement put Clara to sleep. Raffaele and Anna sat arm in arm in the dimly lit car, whispering like excited school children. The train's whistle wailed up ahead as it hurried through the night.

Anna awoke first the next morning, and lay next to Raffaele, watching him breathe. Kissing his ear, she said softly, "Wake up, husband. It's our first Wednesday together in America."

Raffaele pulled her close. "Good morning wife. I love you."

While he dressed, Anna made breakfast, fed Clara, and packed his lunch.

At the door they embraced and kissed.

Anna straightened his tie and smoothed the lapels of his suit. "You look very professional, my love."

"Thank you, my love. Enrico and Rosetta are right downstairs if you need anything. I will be back by six this evening." Raffaele kissed Clara, donned his fedora, collected his newly stained and lacquered wooden briefcase with his carving tools, work uniform, and the lunch Anna made.

Anna walked downstairs with him, stood at the front door, and watched until he was out of sight.

She lifted her long skirt and hurried upstairs where she surveyed the small apartment that needed a woman's touch, including a morning scrubbing, cleaning, and straightening. Anna put Clara down for a nap and went downstairs to the delicatessen.

Rosetta was behind the counter, dressed in a long black skirt and crisp white blouse, with ruffles at the neck and cuffs.

"Good afternoon, Anna." Rosetta said tying her apron behind her back. "And how are you this fine day."

"Good. Thank you for asking."

Rosetta scrutinized the younger woman's plain cotton dress, handmade apron, and scuffed brown oxfords. Her dark hair was pulled back under a scarf tied behind her head. "I heard you moving things upstairs. Cleaning today?"

Anna blushed. "I'm so sorry I disturbed you."

Rosetta waved her hand. "No, no. You didn't. Raffaele's a good man… but it's my experience that men don't really know how to clean."

Anna nodded. "Thank you again, for helping me come to America. I am so happy to be here with Raffaele."

Rosetta came around the counter and hugged her. "We're all happy you're here, Anna. Raffaele needed his family." She paused, "Raffaele told us you were studying to be a nun?"

Anna blushed. "Yes, but then I fell in love."

"Would you be interested in joining the Altar Society at our church?" Rosetta smiled, "I'm always looking for extra hands to help with the work."

Anna's hand went to her heart. "Yes. I would be honored."

"Good. Meetings are after Sunday Mass. The members are excited to meet you."

Anna looked at the table of vegetables. "Raffaele said he has an account here. If it's alright, I'd like to buy some things for a special meal I'm making for him tonight."

"Of course. What do you need?"

Anna bought potatoes, flour, spices, and tomatoes.

At six o'clock, Raffaele came up the stairs, setting his briefcase by the door. Anna went to him, and wiping her hands on a dishtowel, wrapped her arms around his neck, and kissed him. "Welcome home my husband."

He looked past her. "The apartment...looks nice."

"Thank you." She kissed him again and pointed to Clara in the wing-back chair playing with her ragdoll. "Go and meet Clara's best friend," she said, winking. "Dinner's almost ready."

As they sat down to eat, Raffaele touched the white, intricately cro-cheted tablecloth. "Is this ours from home?"

"Yes. I wanted something from our old home to start our new one." She served her homemade gnocchi, and before he could take his first bite, she said, "Tell me everything. From the moment you left this morning."

"Well, I took the trolley downtown, and went to my basement locker at work to change into my work overalls. They're tan with a Wanamaker's logo on the breast pocket."

Anna smiled at Raffaele's proud look.

"Today, I carved a new leg for a Victorian wingback chair. It was uphol-stered in red velvet...very beautiful." He went on to describe how big the store was, and all the other people in the furniture department. "When the weather's nice, I walk home, but took the trolley tonight to have more time with you and Clara."

After dinner, Anna put Clara to bed and snuggled with Raffaele on the dark blue sofa he'd bought at a second-hand store, the week before she arrived.

Anna listened intently as he described their new friends in America. Smiling to herself because she had what she wanted, her husband close to her again...at last.

When Anna began experiencing morning sickness in early March, Raffaele took her to Wanamaker's free employee health clinic where her second pregnancy was confirmed.

To be closer to medical care and have more room for two children, Raffaele rented a small house in south Philadelphia. 2744 Sears Street was eight miles from Germantown and their friends, but only two and a half miles from Wanamaker's. Their second daughter, Emma, was born

October 8, 1908.

Anna's friend, Franchesca, came from Italy to help care for the baby. She intended to return home, but met and married Paulo Marcellio, a handsome farmer, and stayed.

Two years later, Raffaele and Anna's third daughter, Angelina (Angie), was born January 8, 1910.

CHAPTER EIGHT

MORE BABIES 1912

From the kitchen sink Anna heard the front door open and felt a draft of the warm August air. "Welcome home, my husband."

"It's nice to be home." He put his briefcase in its usual spot next to the thrift store sideboard, hung his coat, and turned to see Anna coming from the kitchen.

As her arms went around his neck, his arms circled her waist. He pulled her close and she kissed him. "What's that for?"

"I'm glad you like it," she said, coyly.

"What I really like is being greeted like this," he said squeezing her.

"Raffaele, the children …"

He looked around, squeezed her again, and said, "I don't see any children."

"The girls are in the bedroom, and thank goodness their door is shut, otherwise, they'd be out here being spoiled by you." She stepped back. "Besides me, what else do you like about our home?"

He rubbed his chin. "Do you remember how crowded we were in our apartment?"

"I liked that little apartment. We were happy there."

"Happy, yes, but after Emma was born…I remember sharing our bedroom with the girls. We could barely turn around."

"Was it so bad, being that close?"

Raffaele grinned. "No, you know I like being close to you." Going to the front room, he spread arms. "I love all this space…our Sears Street mansion. A bedroom for the children, and a bedroom, just for us."

Anna blushed. "Raffaele."

"We have a front room, a real dining room table, and for you my love, a kitchen."

She went to him and cradled his face in her hands. "We have almost everything."

Covering her hands with his, he asked "Why? What else do we need?" She was silent with a faraway look on her face.

"Anna?"

"I went to see the doctor."

"The doctor? What's wrong? Are you sick?"

"No, I'm fine."

"What then?"

"We're going to have another baby."

Raffaele wrapped his arms around her, lifted her off the floor, and twirled her around.

"This is fantastic. I love you, my wife."

Anna put her forehead on his. "I know, my husband, I know."

He put her down gently. "When?"

"In the spring, the doctor thinks sometime in March."

"Maybe this time...a boy?"

Anna nodded. "It's in God's hands, but I'll pray."

When he snorted and shook his head, Anna looked at him sternly. "You should be thankful for God's grace. All three of our girls are healthy and beautiful."

"I am, Anna," he said in a quiet voice. "I am very thankful. Clara, Emma, and Angelina are gifts from heaven, but only a son will carry on our name."

Anna knew the importance of sons for men, especially for her son-of-a-baron husband. "I will pray, Raffaele. I promise."

After getting the girls into bed, Raffaele and Anna sat in the living room, he in his wingback chair. She sat on the couch across from him, embroidering one of the girl's dresses.

Raffaele sipped wine and said, "Maybe we should move to a bigger house."

"What?" Anna stopped stitching. "Why would we move? We have room for another girl here."

"What if it's a boy, Anna?"

"Let's not worry about moving until we know what God is giving us this time." Anna resumed to her embroidery and thought of their first year when Emma came so quickly. She gazed around the front room at the hand-me-down furniture from friends and thrift stores that they were slowly replacing with store-bought items. She patted the crochet doily on the arm of the couch—proud of their home.

"You think God will hear my prayers for a boy, Anna?"

"God hears everyone's prayers, Raffaele." With a grin added, "He may be surprised but delighted to hear yours, my husband."

Life continued routinely for the next seven months. Raffaele was promoted in recognition of his craftsmanship. Anna managed the house and children, he doted on his daughters. She continued her weekly Thursday evening English class at the church and volunteering for the Altar Society on Sundays.

On Saint Valentine's Day, Raffaele arrived home from work, and handed Anna a small, flat box wrapped in red paper.

"What's this?"

"A Valentine present." Caressing her burgeoning belly, "How's our baby today?"

She held her hand over his. "Can you feel that? He's been moving around today."

"That's my boy."

Raffaele tapped the box. "Open it."

Anna slid a finger under the wrapping. "Torrone! Thank you!"

"Your favorite, soft nougat. You better hide it from the girls."

"They can have some."

"I bought it for you, Anna."

"I know, but they've been extra helpful around the house lately."

"It's your candy, so whatever you want to do, my love."

Early Friday morning, March 29, Anna's contractions began. Raffaele called Enrico. Rosetta came to watch the girls.

Hearing Enrico's car, Raffaele went out to usher them in.

Rosetta patted Raffaele's arm. "Calm down. You've done this before. Have you forgotten when Clara, Emma and Angelina were born?"

"No, but this time is different. It could be—"

"A boy. Really. You men."

Enrico went to Anna, who sat on the couch with Clara and Emma on either side, and Angelina on her lap. The girls were still in their pajamas.

"Your chauffeur has arrived, Mrs. Colaluca. May I help you to the car?" Anna scooted Angelina into Clara's lap, took Enrico's offered hand, and said, "Raffaele, please bring my suitcase. Rosetta, the girl's breakfast is on the kitchen counter."

Rosetta hugged, kissed, and reassured Anna they would all be fine.

At the hospital, Raffaele helped Anna out of the car, got her suitcase, and led her to the entrance as Enrico called out.

"Call me if you need anything."

"Yes, of course. Thank you, my friend."

Enrico waved and drove away.

After check-in, a nun in a nurse's uniform escorted her down the hallway to her room.

Once Anna was settled, Raffaele was allowed a few minutes before being sent out to wait. Over the next several hours, he paced the waiting area, walked out into crisp winter air, and had a snack in the cafeteria. Late in the afternoon he went to the chapel.

Sitting in the last pew, he stared at the huge cherry wood cross on the wall behind the altar, then leaned forward, rested his elbows on the seat in front of him, and clasped his hands together. "God, you've blessed us with three beautiful daughters. Now please bless us with a son. I've never been upset with you…just some of your priests." He crossed himself, sat back, and heard someone behind him.

"You may see your wife now, Mr. Colaluca."

Raffaele turned and saw the nurse standing with clasped hands. "Is Anna, okay?"

The nurse nodded.

"What did we have?"

"Come and see."

The long hallway seemed longer and at the doorway he stopped, seeing a tired, but smiling Anna cradling a baby in each arm.

"Anna, the nurse didn't tell me. Twins?"

"Two boys, Raffaele. God must have heard your prayers."

He leaned over and kissed her. "Thank you, my wife." Tenderly touching each of the babies' foreheads with his fingertips. "What shall we name them?"

"They are a miracle. I'd like to give them saints names. Paulo and Vincenzo."

Raffaele nodded, and grinned. "Let's hope they behave like saints."

With the arrival of the twins, two-year old Angelina was moved fulltime into her older sisters' bedroom. Four-year old Emma took the change in stride, but seven-year-old Clara was not pleased with the intrusion.

"Why can't Angelina stay in your room? They're all babies," she said, sitting next to her mother on the couch.

"First, because she's no longer a baby, and second, she's a girl and they're boys," Anna explained, again.

Clara snorted and folded her arms across her chest. "It's just not fair."

Anna took her daughter's chin in her hand and looked into her eyes. "Clara, life isn't always fair. We can complain about it, or take what life gives us and make something better.

You're my oldest child. I expect the best from you. No grumbling."

Raffaele and Anna knew they needed to save for a down payment on a bigger house—and soon. Sharing their dilemma with friends, Paulo and Franchesca Marcellio surprised them.

"Come live with us," Franchesa said, one day after church. "Paulo has become a very successful farmer. He sells his special little tomatoes and peppers to markets in Philadelphia and now across the river in New Jersey."

Franchesca hugged Anna. "It will be like old times with baby Emma, remember?"

Raffaele looked at Paulo. "Thank you. I will pay you rent and—"

"We don't need your money. Stay and save enough for your down payment."

The large, three-story colonial house at 94 E Haines had more than enough space for both families and an uncle named Angelo. It was also back in Germantown, six miles and an hour trolley ride from Wanamaker's.

CHAPTER NINE

VINCENZO 1914

Over the next two years, Raffaele and Anna became pillars in the close-knit Italian community of Germantown. He helped provide music for local events, she continued her work with the Altar Society, and sewed for other families.

The Colaluca children thrived as well. Serious Clara became an "A" student, winning awards in spelling and essay writing. Emma, always the social butterfly, enjoyed the non-academic opportunities of first grade. Angelina helped her mother at home and tried to stay out of the path of the rambunctious twins, who were always in sight of each other.

A week after the twins second birthday, Anna took Angelina, Paulo, and Vincenzo to the park for a Friday afternoon outing. The last of the winter snow had melted, but the April weather was cold and windy. When they got home around four o'clock, Anna noticed that Vincenzo was flush and felt his forehead.

"You feel awfully warm, Vincenzo. Let's take your coat off." She took him into the bathroom, wiped his face with a cool washrag, and knelt. "I want you to lie down before dinner."

Vincenzo shook his head. "Wanna play...please," he pleaded.

"Okay." She kissed his forehead. "Go find your brother."

Vincenzo ate little dinner, and when Anna felt his forehead, it was warmer than before. Raffaele carried him upstairs to bed and took his temperature, which was high. Anna held cold compresses on his forehead until his fever seemed to break, and he fell asleep.

"I think he's alright," she told Raffaele. "Maybe he caught a cold at the park."

She went upstairs later to kiss Vincenzo good night and called to Raffaele. "He's burning up. We'd better call Dr. Conte."

Dr. Conte came quickly and asked, "When did the fever start?"

"He was warm when we came home from the park this afternoon," Anna answered. "And he didn't want dinner either."

She led him up to Vincenzo's bedroom, where Dr. Conte examined the boy, took his temperature, and listened to his heart. He took the stethoscope out of his ears and looked at Anna sitting on the end of the bed, with Raffaele standing behind her.

"Has he been around any other children who are sick?"

Anna shook her head. "No. None of the other children are sick." She rubbed Vincenzo's leg through the blankets and added, "He seemed fine until we came back from the park this afternoon."

Dr. Conte put the stethoscope in his black medical bag. "What did you do for the fever?"

Raffaele said, "When he didn't eat dinner and felt warm, I carried him upstairs. Anna put cold compresses on his head."

"After a few minutes, his fever broke and he fell asleep," added Anna.

"How soon did the fever return?"

"Maybe an hour. When I went up to kiss him goodnight," Anna replied, "he was hotter than ever, so I started the cold washrags again, and then the chills started." She reached for Raffaele's hand, then covered her mouth when Dr. Conte said, "There's fluid in his right lung. I think he should be hospitalized."

The doctor closed his bag. "We don't want it to become pneumonia."

Enrico, drove them to the hospital, Raffaele cradling Vincenzo in his arms.

Dr. Conte was at the hospital entrance. Vincenzo's fever spiked, so he ordered nurses to wrap him in cold towels. His fever broke again, and he slept.

Dr. Conte sent Raffaele home around midnight. "Vincenzo needs his rest and so do you. I'll call you if there's any change."

Anna's met him at the door with red eyes. "How's my baby? Will he be all right?"

Raffaele held her. "He was asleep when I left. Dr. Conte will call us if there's any change. He said for us to get some rest."

Early the next morning, Raffaele called to tell his boss about Vincenzo being in the hospital so he would not be coming in to work.

A short while later, Rosetta called Raffaele and said she would come stay with the children, so Enrico could take them to the hospital.

Dr. Conte was at there when Anna and Raffaele arrived. "His fever stayed down during the night, but he still has fluid in his lungs. Until that is resolved I want to keep him under observation. Please wear these whenever you're with him." Handing them each a white mask, he said, "I'll look in on him after my rounds."

Vincenzo was asleep, looking tiny in the oversized white metal crib. He wore a pale blue hospital gown, and was lying on his back, not moving. The overhead light was off, a rectangle of sunlight shone on the pale-green linoleum floor, from the only window.

Anna stood by the crib. "He looks so small. Is he going to be all right?"

Raffaele put his arm around her shoulders. "They're doing everything they can. Sit here," he said, pulling a chair next to the crib.

Anna sat, reached through the crib bars, and touched Vincenzo's arm.

Raffaele shoved his hands in his pockets, feeling helpless. "I'm going to walk in the hall."

She turned, her eyes moist, and mouthed "Okay."

At the door, he looked back and pulled his mask down. Anna's head rested against the crib railing as she prayed.

Raffaele walked toward the front of the hospital, eyes downcast on the green linoleum, his mind a blur. Glancing up, he saw an open door and read the lacquered wooden sign, the carved-out white letters shining in the corridor light—Chapel. Two nurses stopped talking as they passed behind him, seeming to propel him into the small, dimly lit room. The large cherry wood cross hung on the wall behind the altar, flanked by two tall, white ceramic vases overflowing with a rainbow of flowers.

As he did before, Raffaele sat in the last of the four pews, leaned forward, rested his forearms on the pew in front of him, and clasped his hands together.

He breathed in, let it out slowly, and then looked up. "God, the last time I was here you gave me two sons. Now Vincenzo's here and he's very sick." His throat tightened. "Please make him well again."

Raffaele's eyes welled, blurring the cross. He put his face in his hands, then sat back, wiped the tears with the back of his hand, stared at the cross again, nodded, and stood.

Raffaele walked to Vincenzo's room. Anna was in the same position, praying.

"Any change?"

"Dr. Conte took his temperature. It's up again, higher than before." She stood to look at Raffaele and started to cry.

Raffaele crossed the room, embraced her, gently kissing the top of her head.

A nurse came in holding a small glass beaker, partially filled with a watery white liquid. "Dr. Conte ordered more aspirin to bring his fever down. Mr. Colaluca, please put your mask on again. It's doctor's orders."

Raffaele pulled his mask up. "Sorry."

The nurse nodded and walked to the crib. "Would you hold Vincenzo while I give him the medicine?"

Raffaele reached over the crib rail and picked Vincenzo up. He was listless and his skin was hot to the touch.

The nurse squeezed an eyedropper of medicine into the boy's mouth. "Thank you," she said to Raffaele.

Anna kissed Vincenzo's hand, and Raffaele gently laid him back down.

The nurse touched Vincenzo's forehead, then she put her fingers on the side of his neck to check for a pulse. "The aspirin will lower his fever and help him rest. Have you two eaten this morning?"

Neither answered. "You need to keep your strength up. There's a cafeteria in the basement. We will come get you if there's any change. I promise."

Anna sat back down next to the crib. "I'm not hungry."

"I know, Anna, but the nurse is right. We must be strong for Vincenzo." Raffaele helped her to her feet and held her hand all the way to the cafeteria.

Distracted, she picked listlessly at her breakfast, her eyes on the clock.

Raffaele put his fork down and whispered, "There's nothing else we can do."

"We can pray, Raffaele." Her voice grew strong. "We can pray." She rose and walked away.

He watched her go out the cafeteria door and knew he'd find her by Vincenzo's bedside. If God heard anybody's prayers, it would be hers. He forced himself to eat a couple more bites, returned their trays, and went back to Vincenzo's room.

Anna sat by the crib praying quietly.

Vincenzo woke coughing in the middle of the afternoon. Dr. Conte was called, and after examining him, elevated the head of the bed, and ordered an oxygen tent.

He motioned Anna and Raffaele into the hallway. "We've controlled his fever, but the fluid in his lungs has increased, causing the coughing. I think he has viral pneumonia. Viruses are the most common cause of pneumonia in children. The oxygen tent will help him breath, and hopefully rest. A nurse will monitor his breathing every fifteen minutes."

Dr. Conte put his hand on Raffaele's shoulder. "You two have been here since early morning. Perhaps you'd like to go home and get some rest. I'll call you if there is any change in his condition." He squeezed Anna's hand and left.

She looked at Raffaele. "I'm staying."

"I know. I'll call to see how the children are and maybe go home for a while."

"That's fine," Anna said from her crib side vigil, her eyes never leaving Vincenzo.

In the waiting area, Raffaele stepped inside a phone booth, and dialed home.

"Enrico, it's me—"

"Raffaele? How's Vincenzo? Is he better?"

"His fever keeps going up and down, he has fluid in his lungs, and is having trouble breathing."

"I'm so sorry my friend. Hold on, Rosetta wants to talk to you."

"Raffaele, how's Anna?"

"Rosetta, she just sits by Vincenzo's bed and prays, refusing to leave the room. I don't know what to do. None of our children have ever been so sick. How are Paulo and the others?"

"They're fine. Enrico took them to the park. I made them lunch and put Paulo down for his nap. I've started dinner and will make sure they all have baths tonight."

"Do you need me to come home?"

"No. Raffaele, your job is to be Anna's rock. She's very afraid. One of her babies is in danger and she can't protect him."

"I can't protect Vincenzo either."

"Raffaele, that's doctor's job. Can you be Anna's rock?"

"Yes."

Rosetta's voice softened, "Raffaele, stay at the hospital with Anna and your little one. Tell Anna not to worry, that the other children are fine, *capisci?* Enrico will come pick you two up whenever you want to come home."

On the way back to Vincenzo's room, he was grateful how Rosetta stepped in and took charge of the children, the house, even Enrico. Through their friendship Anna had become like her, the center of their family.

When Raffaele walked in the room, he saw the nurse and the oxygen tent with a three-foot square hood hanging down over Vincenzo's upper body. The front panel was clear plastic, the sides and back were black. A hose ran from an oxygen tank next to the bed, up the pole supporting the tent, and into an opening at the top.

Anna stood, her hands on the crib rail, watching the small face inside.

Raffaele delivered Rosetta's message and saw a brief look of relief on her face.

Moving next to her, he looked into the tent to see Vincenzo lying on his back, eyes closed, chest rising with each breath. He glanced at the nurse.

"His breathing is more labored. I've called for the doctor."

Anna leaned into Raffaele.

Dr. Conte came in, motioned for them to step back, and lifted the tent. He examined Vincenzo and put the tent back down. He replaced his stethoscope around his neck and turned to face them. "His lungs are not clearing, making him work harder to breathe." He talked quietly with the nurse and left.

The next couple of hours dragged, Anna immobile next to the crib.

Raffaele walked down the hallway, to the front entrance, back past Vincenzo's room, to the end of the corridor, and back to the front of the hospital. He listened to murmuring sounds coming from other rooms. The nurses' evening shift change came and went. It seemed every other time he passed Vincenzo's room; a nurse was checking on him. Finally, he went in again.

He put his hands on Anna's shoulders, and said, "Come. Eat dinner, my love."

She reached up, covered his hand with hers, and said, "I'm not hungry, you have something." She looked at him with a sad smile and turned back to watch her baby.

Raffaele went to the cafeteria, got a steaming bowl of vegetable soup, and took it to a corner table. He stirred the soup, listened to hospital staff and visitors talk quietly at other tables. Finally, he sipped a little soup, returned his tray, and headed to the room.

He spotted Dr. Conte hurrying into Vincenzo's room from the other direction. As Raffaele came in, he saw the tent flap was up with Dr. Conte listening to Vincenzo's chest through his stethoscope, then rolling him on his side to listen on his back.

At the foot of the bed, Anna's hands gripped the crib rail. "He started wheezing."

Dr. Conte carefully rolled Vincenzo onto his back, put two fingers on the side of the boy's neck and felt his pulse. He motioned to the nurse, and they administered another dose of aspirin.

Dr. Conte put the tent back down. When he turned to Raffaele and Anna, perspiration covered his forehead.

He took a deep breath. "The fluid in his lungs is still not clearing." Dr. Conte took Anna's hands and said, "I've increased the oxygen to make it easier for him to breath. The nurse will stay in the room to monitor him, and I'll check on Vincenzo again in—"

"Isn't there anything else you can do?"

Dr. Conte looked at Raffaele. The only sound in the room was Vincenzo's wheezing. "We're doing everything we can, but children's bodies," he hesitated, "sometimes their immune systems can't fight off the virus."

Anna fell against Raffaele and sobbed.

Dr. Conte put his hands in the pockets of his lab coat and shook his head, "I wish there was something else I could do."

During the next few hours, Vincenzo's nostrils flared as his breathing became increasingly labored. His fever spiked repeatedly, followed by sweating and chills. Finally, he lapsed into unconsciousness and died a few minutes after midnight.

Vincenzo's death was difficult for everyone who had known the energetic little boy. Anna was devastated, blaming herself for his sickness and prayed for forgiveness every Sunday for a year. In the summer of 1915, with the saved down-payment money, Raffaele and Anna bought a small two-story, three-bedroom house at 2334 Watkins St. in south Philadelphia. Only two miles from work, but more importantly, Raffaele hoped the move would diminish the sad memories.

Anna got a job at Wanamaker's sewing silk and satin comforters. Clara, Emma, and Angie cleaned the house and did laundry, in addition to attending school. Paulo not yet school age, went to "nursery".

CHAPTER TEN

A SECOND CHANCE 1916

Anna hummed to herself at the sink. The April evening felt like Spring had finally arrived. Dr. Conte had confirmed her suspicions earlier in the afternoon and she couldn't wait to tell Raffaele her prayers had been answered.

When she heard him coming up the front steps, he was talking loudly to himself.

Anna stopped chopping tomatoes, wiped her hands on the dishtowel, and walked to the door. "Raffaele, what's wrong?"

He was silent as he set down his briefcase and put the grocery bag on the sideboard.

"Papa's home," Clara called out from the girl's bedroom.

The ten-year-old started down the stairs, with her younger sisters following.

"The King is a fool," he exclaimed.

"What King?"

"What's wrong, Mama?" Clara asked, almost to the bottom of the stairs.

Anna motioned for her to stop.

Clara paused and sat down, her hands clasped in her lap.

Seven-year-old Emma and five-year-old Angie sat on the stair behind her.

Raffaele's jaw clenched before blurting, "Vittorio Emanuele III, King of Italy."

Anna put a hand on her husband's chest. "Calm down. Clara, take your sisters, wake up your brother, and play with him for a few minutes."

Clara stood, turned, and motioned for Emma and Angie to go

back upstairs.

Anna watched until she heard the bedroom door shut, then said, "What are you talking about?"

"I stopped by the delicatessen to get the salami and cheese you wanted and looked at the Italian newspaper. The Italian Army is still bogged down in the trenches in this stupid war with Austria."

"I know it is." She sighed, touching his cheek. "I know."

"Anna, thousands of soldiers have been killed," his voice rising again, "and for what? Some ice-covered mountains. It's crazy."

She put a finger to his lips and hugged him. "Italy's far away. Be thankful America's not fighting. Let's sit in the living room."

Raffaele slumped into his armchair. "Men are being conscripted into the army every day." Head back, he let out a long breath and closed his eyes.

Anna brought a glass of wine and set it on the end table, then leaned over to kiss his forehead.

He opened his eyes. "Anna, life is precious."

"Yes, it is."

"To waste it fighting a war is—"

"A sacrilege."

His eyes flashed. "Leave religion out it. It's old men's vanity." Although almost two-years had passed since Vincenzo died, his anger raged.

Anna knew he blamed the doctor, God, and worst, himself, for his son's death.

Anna put the salami and cheese in the refrigerator, stood at the sink, and gazed out the kitchen window, looking at her blooming purple pansies and red tulips. With summer's heat, yellow marigolds would be arriving soon.

She needed to tell him her news. "Raffaele, I have something—"

"Mama, can we come down now, please?"

"In a minute, Clara." Anna turned from her flowers and went to the living room door where Raffaele motioned to her to have the children come down.

"Yes, your father wants your hugs." Her news would wait.

Emma and Angelina bounded down the stairs, followed by Clara, holding Paulo's hand.

Anna leaned against the doorjamb and watched the children fill

Raffaele's arms and lap, softening his face into a broad smile. He squeezed them. "I love you my little ones."

Clara sat up straight. "I'm big now, Papa."

He tousled her hair. "That you are and soon you'll be as tall as your mother."

Anna listened as the children's chattering voices erupted, spilling over each other, their love pulling her grieving husband back from the past.

The next morning, Anna and the children went to church. After mass, as she always did, she knelt and lit a candle under the statue of Jesus for Raffaele, and one under the Blessed Virgin Mary for herself.

When she stood, Rosetta came up. "Anna, it's good to see you."

Anna turned and the two friends embraced.

"It's good to see you, too."

Rosetta held Anna at arm's length. "Don't forget the Altar Society meets this afternoon."

"I know, but I must talk with Raffaele today about something. I'll come if I can."

"Is he still upset about the war?"

"Yes, but this is something else, something important."

"About him not coming to church?"

"He comes when he can, Rosetta."

"Anna, I'm sorry. I didn't mean to—"

"Rosetta, he's still hurting about Vincenzo, but I never stopped praying, and God gave us a miracle that might get him to return to church."

"A miracle?"

Anna whispered, her hands on her stomach, "I'm going to have a baby."

Rosetta hugged her again. "That's wonderful. When did you find out?"

"Yesterday. I haven't told Raffaele yet. Please don't tell anyone."

Rosetta nodded. "I won't."

"Not even Enrico, okay?"

"No one, I promise. Don't worry about the meeting."

Anna motioned to the children sitting in the first pew. "It's time to go."

"What were you whispering about with Rosetta?" Clara asked on the way home.

"That's between Rosetta and me. You'll find out soon enough. No more questions, Miss Curious."

At home, when Anna heard Raffaele singing in the basement, she knew it was a good time to tell him. She sent the children upstairs to change out of their good clothes and called down into the basement, "Raffaele?"

"Anna, come see what I'm making."

She held onto the wooden railing and started down.

Raffaele came part way up the stairs, took her hand, and led her to his workbench. "It's walnut," he said, wiping some dust off with a rag.

Anna rubbed her finger in the smooth scrollwork of the headboard. "It's beautiful."

"It's for you, my love." He looked down. "Anna, I'm sorry about yesterday."

She took his face in her hands and kissed him. "Come upstairs, I have something to tell you and the children."

"Let me put my tools away."

"I'll be waiting."

Anna sat on the couch with her hands in her lap, patted the cushion next to her, and said, "Please sit here."

She took his hands, "I understand about yesterday. The war is terrible, and the loss of life is senseless." She added, "Just like Vincenzo's death. His dying made no sense either. I blamed myself."

"Anna, you did nothing wrong."

"And neither did you or Dr. Conte."

Raffaele pulled his hands free and looked down. "There must have been something else he could have done."

Anna lifted his chin with her finger. "Dr. Conte couldn't, but God has."

Raffaele stared. "What has God done?"

She took his hand and placed it on her abdomen. "We're going to have another baby."

He looked at his hand. "Are you sure?"

"Dr. Conte's sure. I wanted to tell you yesterday, but you—"

"Were ranting." He shook his head. "Anna, I'm so sorry."

She stopped him with a finger on his lips.

He wrapped his arms around her and they leaned back on the couch, eyes closed and still.

"You know," he said after a minute, "I had more to do with this than God."

"Oh, Raffaele," she laughed. Then seriously said, "This baby is a gift from heaven."

He put his hands up in surrender. "Okay, okay." He pulled her back to him. "I did enjoy doing God's work."

Anna squirmed, "I'm glad you understand you're one of his special angels."

"Me? An angel? Only because of you, Anna. Do they know?"

Anna shook her head.

"Let's tell them the big news." He went to the stairs. "Children, come down here."

Amidst the sounds of feet tumbling down the stairs, Raffaele returned to the couch where instantly, Clara and Emma snuggled on his sides, Angelina, and Paulo on Anna's lap.

Raffaele cleared his throat. "Your mother has something important to tell you."

Expectant faces turned toward Anna.

"I'm going to have a baby."

"When Mama?" Clara, always the planner, peeked around Raffaele.

"The doctor thinks in December."

"What kind?" Emma asked quietly.

"Italian, of course," Raffaele answered.

"I think she means boy or girl," Anna chuckled.

"Oh." He squeezed his daughter.

"I won't know until the baby's born, Emma. What would you like, a boy or girl?"

"A girl," Clara declared, and Emma nodded.

Angelina sat up straight in Anna's lap. "Will she sleep with Paulo and me?"

Anna tousled her youngest daughter's hair. "No, at first the baby's crib will be in our room."

"I want another brother."

Anna put her head on Paulo's. "I know you do."

Her youngest tilted his head back and said, "Like Vincenzo…"

After a long silence, Clara broke the silence. "Can we name him Vincenzo?"

Raffaele glanced at Anna and shrugged.

Paulo looked up at his mother. "Please."

"If God decides to give us another son, it would be a very special gift."

"A Christmas gift," Clara added excitedly.

Emma looked at Raffaele. "Papa, would you like another Vincenzo from heaven."

He nodded, hugged the girls, and looked at Anna with tears in his eyes. He knew she would continue to pray and light candles.

Vincenzo was born December 4, 1916. For Raffaele he was an unexpected second son. For Anna, the baby was a redemptive gift from God. For the children he was the real-life replacement for the brother they'd loved and lost.

During the years at the Watkins house, Raffaele and Anna continued to work at Wanamaker's. They had three simple goals: to save for a bigger home back in Germantown, provide more for their children than the basics of food, clothing, and shelter, and teach them about the history of their country by taking them to the many historical sites from the American Revolution around them in Philadelphia. As the children got older, the house seemed to shrink, but the Colaluca family grew closer.

CHAPTER ELEVEN

BEAN SHOT 1921

Raffaele opened the front door as the grandfather clock in the hallway chimed six. "I'm home."

Suppertime at Raffaele's home was sacrosanct. He loved his wife's cooking that she learned at her mother's side. Anna didn't need recipes; she knew exactly how many pinches of rosemary or garlic would create the aromas and flavors of the traditional Abruzzo dishes he loved.

"How was your work this Saturday, my husband?" Anna called to him.

"I've almost finished carving the new leg." He hung his brown fedora and suit coat alongside the beveled mirror on the mahogany sideboard.

"The fancy lion's claw foot?" Anna asked.

With a quick look in the mirror, he smoothed his hair and went into the kitchen.

"Yes, it's beautiful."

As Anna was grating parmesan cheese, he moved behind her and wrapped his arms around her waist. "Just like you."

"Raffaele, the children."

He kissed her on the neck.

Anna scrunched her shoulders up but didn't resist. "Always with the kissing." She set down the grater and turned around into his arms. "You know where this leads."

"No. Where?"

"We have five beautiful children. That's more than enough, my Romeo."

"We'll see." He raised his eyebrow and winked.

She gave him a gentle push. "Go sit. I'll bring you a glass of wine.

You need to—"

"Be less romantic?" Raffaele shook head. "Never."

As Anna placed a tumbler on the end table by his armchair, he asked "Where are the children?"

"Upstairs. I told them not to come down until they were called to dinner." She leaned over and kissed him. "I thought you might like to relax before dinner."

Raffaele nodded and took a sip of wine.

"Dinner will be ready at seven," Anna said, returning to her cooking.

A short time later, Paulo heard his mother call and said, "Come on Vincenzo, let's beat the girls." His stomach growled as he hurried out their bedroom door and down the stairs, his brother a couple of steps behind, just in front of Clara and Emma.

Paulo glanced back to see Clara at the top of the stairs with her hands on her hips. "What?" he blurted. "I'm hungry."

"You exasperate me."

Paulo knew whatever that meant, it wasn't a compliment, but went past his father sitting in the armchair, and across to his seat.

Dinner was not a time for frivolity. The walnut wood under the blue tablecloth was always polished. The six place settings, with silverware on napkins, gleamed next to shiny white bowls on plates. Food was to be enjoyed quietly unless the children were answering parental questions about school or other events of the day. Each of his siblings took their places at the round dining room table.

His father rose, and when his mother came back out of the kitchen with a loaf of warm bread, he pulled out the chair for her.

Paulo's parents sat across from each other. His eldest sister, Clara, was to his mother's left. The next eldest, Emma, was on his mother's right. Paulo sat on his father's right, and his younger brother, Vincenzo, sat on his father's left. Angelina, the youngest sister was spending the summer with his father's sister, Erina, in Mahoning town.

The windows were open to the warm September weather, and a light breeze moved the curtains ever so softly.

Raffaele ladled out a steaming bowl of pasta fagioli, and passed it to Paulo, who passed it around to Clara for his mother. Anna handed the round loaf of crusty Italian bread to Emma, who took a piece and passed it to Vincenzo. When everyone had their soup and bread, Anna gave thanks, and they began to eat.

His father blew on a steaming spoonful, swallowed it, and looked across the table to Anna. "The soup is excellent."

Paulo, already on his second or third spoonful, paused with one in midair. "It's the best, Mama."

"Slow down, there's plenty more," Anna said gently.

"Do what your mother says. Good food is to be enjoyed, not gulped."

Paulo nodded, raising the next spoonful slowly.

Raffaele looked at Anna. "When is Angie coming home?"

"When I asked your sister a couple of days ago, Angie got on the phone and described a dress Erina bought her for school, the friends she's made, and then asked if she could stay longer. I didn't know what to say. I think she likes being an only child." Anna sounded sad.

Raffaele sat back and took a sip of wine.

All the children stopped eating, looking back and forth at their parents.

"She doesn't want to come home?" Raffaele asked.

"She likes getting all the attention," Anna replied.

"I could have the bed all to myself," Emma said quietly into her soup.

Raffaele frowned at Emma, then said to Anna, "She gets attention here."

"I know, but Erina always wanted to have children. She can't, and Angie's her favorite."

Raffaele tapped his finger on the table. "She should live here."

Anna pursed her lips and looked at the children around the table. "We've been given many blessings."

"But this is her family, Anna."

"And it always will be, Raffaele."

He put his elbows on the table, chin on clasped hands, and stared at his wife.

"Angie is a blessing for your sister," Anna continued, "let her stay a while longer."

Raffaele sat back. "Are you sure?"

Anna nodded.

"All right, but just a little while, and then back home."

Emma leaned forward and winked at Clara.

Anna looked at Emma. "Angelina's still part of our family, Emma. She'll be back. Okay, who wants to tell me about their day at school?"

Clara spoke first. "I got an 'A' on my famous writer's report in

English class."

Anna smiled at her eldest. "Excellent."

Paulo rolled his eyes.

"Emma, what about you?"

Emma paused. She was less enthusiastic about school than her big sister, "A boy in math class passed a note to me."

"What kind of note?"

"He wanted to know if I'd be his girlfriend."

"Did you tell the teacher?"

"No. I didn't want to get him in trouble."

"Emma—" Anna began.

"What's this boy's name?" Raffaele's asked, his voice low.

"Let's not worry about his name." Anna stared at her husband for a moment, and then looked at Emma. "You're too young to have a boyfriend. School is for learning, not romance. Do you understand?"

"But Mama—"

"Do you understand?"

Emma's shoulders sagged as she stared at her food. "Yes, no boyfriends."

Raffaele nodded to Anna. "I agree."

"Would you like some more wine?"

Raffaele shook his head and spooned another bite of soup.

Anna turned to Paulo. "And what about you? How was your day at school?"

Paulo wiped his mouth on his napkin, glanced at Clara, and said, "Mama, school was great today. I learned something in every class and got picked as a team captain in the dodge ball game at recess."

Clara murmured, "Oh, real impressive."

"Clara, any success in school is good."

His father reached over and tousled Paulo's hair. "That's my boy."

Paulo grinned at Clara.

"Well, good for you, Paulo. I can hardly wait to see your report card," Anna said.

"What about me, Mama?"

Anna turned to her youngest. "Vincenzo, what did you do at nursery school?"

"I painted a big picture."

"What kind of picture?"

"An elephant. He was gray with a long trunk."

"What else did you do?" Anna asked.

"Um…I played outside, ate my lunch, and teacher read a book to us."

"That's good." Raffaele reached over and patted his youngest son on the head.

Vincenzo beamed.

"We have smart children, Mama," Raffaele declared and reached for another piece of bread.

Between his slurps of soup, Paulo watched each of his siblings. He looked past his father to Vincenzo. As usual, his little brother was eating slowly, staring into the soup. Paulo looked down into his soup, eyes locked on a large cannellini bean at the edge of his bowl. Surveying the table and seeing everyone intent on eating, he picked up the single bean with his soupspoon and put it in his mouth.

He held it behind his front teeth with his tongue and peaked over at Vincenzo, still looking dreamy.

Anna asked Emma, "Besides the love note, weren't you learning to bake a pie in Home Economics class this week?"

Paulo glanced at his father, his face over his soup bowl, then back at Vincenzo. His little brother, off in his own world, was a tempting target.

"It was apple with a crisscross pattern on top. We got to eat it in class."

Paulo put his spoon back in his mouth, positioned it behind the bean, and checked around the table one more time.

"Maybe you could make one for us?"

Paulo sat up in his chair and held his breath.

Emma nodded. "I have the recipe, but could you help me?"

Paulo launched the bean at his daydreaming brother. It shot across the back of his father's lowered head and hit Vincenzo in the face.

Vincenzo dropped his spoon with a yelp. Soup splashed onto the table. He grabbed his eye. "Ow!"

His father's head jerked up and he looked across at his wife in confusion.

Vincenzo stood, took a breath, and yelled "Ow!" even louder.

Raffaele turned, put his hand on Vincenzo's chest, said "Sit down," and pushed him backwards into his seat. The push sent Vincenzo and his chair over backwards onto the floor.

Raffaele stared down at his youngest son. "No more yelling."

Vincenzo, lying on his back in the chair, hand over his eye, and mouth open, didn't move.

Clara glared at Paulo, who shrugged and looked at his soup.

Raffaele motioned for Vincenzo to get up. He rolled off his chair and stood, a hand still over his eye.

Anna got up, walked around, and took his face in her hands. "What happened? Why did you yell like that?"

Vincenzo pointed to a spot next to his right eye. "Something hit me, Mama."

"What? What hit you?"

Vincenzo shook his head.

Anna looked on his shirt and pants, surveyed the floor, and picked up a squashed cannellini bean.

She examined his eye. "Can you see me?"

He raised and lowered his head slowly.

Raffaele sighed. "Anna, please, he's okay."

Anna frowned at him. She took Vincenzo's napkin and wiped up the spilled soup by his bowl. "Go wash your face and hands and come back to the table. We have fruit and cheese for dessert." She pointed Vincenzo toward the bathroom and sat down.

Raffaele reached down and brought Vincenzo's chair back up to the table.

Clara cleared her throat. "Papa?"

Paulo stared at her wide-eyed.

Anna put her hand on Clara's and said, "Let's just eat." She looked at Paulo. "How did you like the cannellini beans in the soup tonight?"

Paulo looked down at his bowl. "They were good, Mama."

CHAPTER TWELVE

DECEMBER GIFTS 1922

On December 7, 1922, forty-four-year-old Raffaele stood before the Philadelphia County Court. His petition was read, in which he renounced Victor Emmanuel III, King of Italy "of whom I have heretofore been a subject; that I will support and defend the Constitution and the laws of the United States of America against all enemies, foreign and domestic; and that I will bear true faith and allegiance to the same."

At the conclusion of reading the Oath of Allegiance, the judge signed Raffaele's Certificate of Naturalization.

"Raffaele, you are now admitted as a citizen of the United States of America. Congratulations." When the judge reached to shake his hand, Raffaele, with tears in his eyes, hugged him.

"Grazie, grazie," he said excitedly, then froze. He clasped his hands together over his heart. "Per favore—thank you."

The judge smiled and pointed at Anna and the children. "Raffaele, I think you need to hug them, too."

After dinner on Christmas day, Raffaele and Anna had the children come sit with them in the front room. The scent of the Christmas tree mingled with the aroma of eggplant parmesan as the three older children sat on the floor in front of their parents, and Vincenzo snuggled in Anna's lap.

Raffaele cleared his throat. "There is one more gift too big to put under the tree."

The children glanced at each other with questioning faces.

"Is it new beds?" Emma asked.

Paulo's hand shot up. "A new car, Papa?"

"A new piano for Momma?" Clara added.

Raffaele raised his hands palms up. "Calm down. Your mother and I bought a bigger house for us in Germantown. It is a two-story rowhome with three big bedrooms, a real dining room, a full-length basement and garage below, a covered front porch, and a garden plot. Our new address will be 1216 E Price Street."

The children jumped up beside Raffaele and Anna, hugging and kissing them, asking a myriad of questions about the "big gift." It was seven and a half miles from Wanamaker's, an hour trolley ride, or a three-hour walk.

CHAPTER THIRTEEN

LEARNING SOMETHING NEW
1923

Raffaele was perfectly happy not driving, that is until one Sunday morning when he was in his basement workshop repairing dresser drawers from the boy's room.

Coming to his side at the workbench, Anna asked, "Have you ever thought about learning to drive, Raffaele?"

Puzzled, he said, "No. Why?"

"Oh, I just thought it would make it easier to get around."

"I don't need to drive, Anna. I have the trolley for work and walk everywhere in the neighborhood."

With admiration, she watched him continue his work with a small finishing nail. "I know, Raffaele, but what about in the winter? Remember last December when you slipped on the ice coming home from the delicatessen?"

Reaching for the hammer, he said, "Ah, that was nothing."

"That's not what Enrico said when he brought you home. Fortunately, he saw you fall from inside the store."

"I told him I was fine. He's a worrier." Raffaele said dismissively.

"You know, my love, you're not as young as you once were."

Raffaele looked at her. "What are you saying? I'm forty-five, not old."

Anna kissed him on the cheek. "I didn't say you were old. You will always be my strong and handsome husband. I just worry about you sometimes."

Raffaele returned to pushing the tip of the nail into the bottom runner of the drawer. Did she really think he was old? He drove the nail in with one blow.

Nothing was said for several days. After the children's bedtime, Anna sat at the piano playing softly. "Have you thought anymore about learning to drive?"

Hearing no response, she continued, "Some of our friends drive their children to the museums and parks downtown."

"Our children have been downtown, Anna…on the trolley."

"I know," she said, playing, "but with a car we could take them to the boardwalk."

"In Atlantic City?"

"It would be so much fun and educational, Raffaele."

He went to sit by Anna at the piano. "Cars are expensive."

She stopped playing and faced him. "Raffaele, you are a good man. You save and provide well for our family. Being so blessed, is a car such a big thing?" Cupping his cheeks, she kissed him. "I love you. Do what you think is best."

Anna turned and slid off the bench. "I'm going upstairs to bed, are you coming?" she asked, running her fingers lightly across his shoulders as she walked past.

That weekend, a mutual friend drove Enrico and Raffaele downtown, where he bought a brand-new Chevrolet. The shiny black four-door sedan was tall, boxy, and seated five comfortably, or six, if four kids squeezed in the back seat. It cost $800.

With permission, Paulo waited at the corner for his father. When Enrico made the turn and slowed, Paulo jumped on the passenger side running board and held on to the open window frame. His father, smiled proudly as they drove down the block, around to the alley behind their house and into the garage.

When the engine was off, Paulo ran upstairs to get his mother.

Anna came into the garage and gasped, "It's beautiful, Raffaele."

Proudly, he held out his hand. "Just like you."

"Come and sit in our new car," he said, assisting her to step on the running board and into the front passenger seat.

Every evening after dinner, Enrico rode with Raffaele as he drove cautiously to the end of the alley and back. Anna and the children watched every lesson, clapping and shouting encouragement each time he passed by. After two weeks, Raffaele ventured out onto Price Street. At the end of the month, he stood in line, passed the driving test, and got his license.

CHAPTER FOURTEEN

DREAM CAR 1923

A midday breeze moved leaves on Anna's geranium plants on the front porch. It was a cloudless July day. Paulo and younger brother, Vincenzo, sat on the shaded top step, watching Saturday activities up and down their street. Wives swept steps, tended flowers, shook out rugs, and of course, talked.

Paulo heard their neighbor Mrs. Vernati, exclaim "No, that's impossible," and wondered what the latest gossip was.

"Look Paulo." Vincenzo nudged and pointed at the horse-drawn wagon coming up the street. The shiny white wagon read Mannino Ice Company, painted neatly in bright red letters on the side. The horse's head bobbed in time with its hooves, clip-clopping on the pavement.

Signore Mannino smiled from under the wagon's overhanging roof as he went by. A wiry man, with thin gray hair combed straight back, was older than their father.

The wagon stopped two doors down the street, in front of the Peretta's house. Signore Mannino jumped down lightly to the sidewalk, went to the back of the wagon, lifted the dark leather flap, and grabbed a block of ice with a pair of metal tongs. Hefting the ice onto the padded shoulder of his thick black vest, he headed up the steps to the house, waved to the boys, and motioned for them to come.

Paulo jumped up with Vincenzo close behind and ran to the back of the wagon.

The ice man came out of the house saying, "It's pretty hot today, eh?"

Their eyes bright with hope, the boys watched water drip from the back of the wagon making a small puddle on the street.

Signore Mannino mopped his brow with a handkerchief. "I don't suppose you'd like some ice?" he asked, a smile spreading across his face.

"Yes please," they answered in unison.

Slipping his handkerchief into a back pocket, he reached under the leather flap, brought out two softball-size chunks, and dropped them into waiting hands.

Icy-cold water dripped through their fingers as Paulo and Vincenzo savored their treats.

"Please tell your mother and father I said hello." He ruffled each boy's hair and climbed back onto his wagon as the boys called out their thanks. The wheels creaked once as the horse pulled it forward and the clip-clopping music resumed.

Paulo and Vincenzo returned to their porch, sitting with knees apart, holding their pieces of ice, licking, and sucking until only wet spots remained on the steps.

When the boys went upstairs to their bedroom at the back of the house, Paulo pulled a cigar box from the low maple bookcase and stretched out on the floor.

Vincenzo laid on his stomach beside him. The short white curtains embroidered with red roses, fluttered in the open window above their heads.

Paulo opened the box and took out the top card. "My dream car, Vincenzo," he declared, beaming at a sleek convertible roadster. Golden yellow with gleaming black fenders, large yellow wire-wheels, bullet-shaped silver headlights, and a trunk rounded to a point. The convertible top was down, and the black-leather seats shined in the sunlight.

Vincenzo reached for the card. "Can I hold it?"

Paulo held it out of reach. "Uh-uh. You might bend it."

"Come on, it's just a car."

"Only the most beautiful car in the world." He turned the postcard over and read, "The Kissel Motor Car Company of Hartford, Connecticut, builder of custom, high-quality automobiles, hearses, fire trucks, and taxi cabs. But that's not the best thing. Do you know who has one of these cars? Do you?"

Vincenzo shook his head.

"Jack Dempsey, the heavyweight champion of the whole world."

Vincenzo's eyes widened.

"Do you know who else?"

Vincenzo shook his head again.

"Fatty Arbuckle, the movie star," he said to Vincenzo's blank face.

"Remember the fat guy on the poster outside the movie house?"

"Oh…yeah. Can he fit in it?"

Paulo laughed. "I'm sure his is extra big." Caressing the card, he continued, "You know who else famous has one of these? Amelia Earhart, the famous lady flyer."

Vincenzo looked at him blankly, "You know, the lady who flew higher than any woman ever—fourteen thousand feet! It was in the newspaper, and we talked about it in school."

To his brother's shrug, he said, "Well, she has one and calls it her 'Gold Bug.' I want my own Gold Bug when I grow up."

Paulo rolled on his back, holding the postcard above him, sighing, "It's a beauty."

"It is," Vincenzo repeated.

Shadows had crept up on the row homes across the alley. "Paulo, it's almost five o'clock," his mother called from downstairs.

"Jesus," Paulo muttered and hopped up. "I gotta meet Pop."

"Can I come today?"

"No, I'll be back," Paulo said as he took the stairs two at a time.

"Slow down," his mother admonished from the kitchen.

"Okay," he said as he landed on both feet at the bottom of the stairs.

His mother shook her head as he flew by and out the front door, closing it carefully, before leaping off the porch.

His mother's voice trailed after him. "Watch for cars. Be careful. Please."

As he went at a dead run, Paulo knew his mother was crossing herself. At the corner, he jumped up on the base of the streetlamp. With one arm around the pole, he scanned up and down the cross street. A minute later the black sedan came into view. Only his father's second week of driving to work, he took the corner slowly.

"Hey, Pop. You're doing great!" he yelled, like he had every day since his father started taking the car. As he jumped up to get on the passenger-side running board for his triumphant daily ride down Price Street, his feet came down on the pavement. Looking down, he saw the running board wasn't there and the passenger-side door was caved in. He jogged next to the car, tightly gripping the window frame.

"Pop, what happened?"

His father locked straight ahead, both hands on the wheel. "It wasn't my fault."

Paulo continued jogging next to the car. When they passed their house, his mother looked out the kitchen window. Clara, Emma, and Vincenzo were watching and waving from the girl's bedroom window above as they came into the alley behind their house.

Raffaele stopped on the incline in front of the basement garage and sat, looking straight ahead.

Paulo grabbed the metal handle and pulled the garage door up and out. He reached in and grabbed the hanging twine on the inside to slow its spring-loaded rise.

His mother stood in the doorway at the back of the garage, a hand on her chest.

Raffaele pulled into the garage and turned off the engine.

Anna walked to the driver's side door and asked, "Raffaele, are you hurt?"

"No. It wasn't my fault." His jaw muscles clenched.

She walked around, looked at the caved-in door and where the running board used to be. "Our brand-new car." Her hand went from her chest to her mouth.

Paulo came up next to his mother. "Pop, did somebody run into you?" His father turned and stared at him.

"Is that what happened? Did you get his name?"

"No."

"But if you didn't—"

"Enough. No more questions."

"Our beautiful car." Anna shook her head and walked into the house. His father got out, went around, and pulled on the passenger door, which opened with a popping sound. Shutting the door hard, he stared at the crumpled metal, crestfallen.

"Pop—"

"Close the garage door," Raffaele said, "and get my briefcase." He disappeared through the door into the basement.

Paulo retrieved his father's briefcase, pulled the garage door down, and followed him into the basement. Raffaele stood in front of the shelves holding rows of wine bottles.

"Put my tools on the workbench," he said, his back to Paulo, while he reached up and took down a bottle of wine.

Paulo laid the briefcase down carefully, opened it, and placed the wooden toolbox on the counter.

His father crossed to the stairs and started up. "Turn off the light when you come up." Raffaele walked past Anna without saying anything.

Paulo muttered, "You are one stubborn Italian." He saw his father's woodworking tools hanging on the wall behind the bench, everything neat as Raffaele liked it. The drawer that held big framing clamps was ajar, so he pushed it closed with his foot, before taking the stairs two-at-a-time. He flipped off the light switch, and opened the door with a jerk, startled by his mother standing there. "Paulo, please go to your room."

Up the stairs, the door to Clara and Emma's room was shut, but Vincenzo stood in their bedroom doorway. Paulo sat down on the top step and Vincenzo joined him.

"Is Pop, okay?"

Paulo looked at him. "What'd you think? Somebody hit his brand-new car."

"Can we still go on 'excursions' like Mama said?"

"Don't know…maybe."

Paulo heard his father's angry voice from the kitchen.

"Anna, it was not my fault. I came to a stop at the corner. I looked both ways. I put out my hand to signal. I turned left—"

"Was it your turn to go?"

"Anna, the other car didn't stop. It was not my fault."

"Was he supposed to stop too?"

"I don't know. When I got out of the car, he told me it was my fault. I said it wasn't. He told me the police would decide."

She gasped. "The police?"

"I said I was sorry and tried to give him money to fix his car, but he kept asking me my name. I put the money on the hood of his car, but he yelled at me, so I got in my car and left. It was not my fault. He ran into me."

"Raffaele, you must be more careful."

"I was careful. I told you, he ran into me."

It was quiet, then Paulo heard his mother.

"You'll need to ride the trolley to work again, until the car is repaired. It looks terrible." Her voice grew quiet, and he couldn't make out what she said next.

Later, when his mother called them for supper, he and his siblings came down silently, and sat with hands in their laps.

His mother announced that because someone had run into their car, they would not take any family excursions until it was repaired.

Paulo glanced at his father. "Shouldn't you have waited for the police?"

His mother stared at him "The accident was not your father's fault. She looked around the table. "We will not talk about this anymore. Do you understand?"

Everyone nodded.

"Good." She looked at her husband. "Would you please serve the pasta?"

As he reached for the serving spoons, Anna picked up her napkin, put it in her lap, and smiled. "Paulo, tell me what you learned in school today?"

CHAPTER FIFTEEN

UNPREDICTABLE SOVEREIGN
1923

Anna stirred the Friday night pasta fagioli, the aroma reminding her of cooking with her mother back in Bugnara. Memories of childhood friends, convent school, and her husband filled her mind. Back in their small village, his father was the Baron, and Raffaele his eldest son.

She recalled being annoyed when Raffaele watched her from the balcony of his parent's house as she walked to class with other novices, and then flustered when he waved and asked her name. Mother Superior glared at him, and Anna was mortified.

Baron Colaluca arranged formal introductions with her father, and over Anna's protestations, amorous Raffaele spent months courting her. Handsome and worldly, she grew fond of him, and finally fell in love. At seventeen she ended her dream of being a nun and became Raffaele's wife at the altar of her beloved church.

"Mama, I'm hungry. When's dinner?"

Her son's voice startled her. "Stop that," she said, swatting at Paulo who was trying to look in the pot.

He ducked. "It sure smells good. Can I have a piece of bread?"

She nodded, looking fondly at her eldest son. He was broad shouldered and brown eyed like his father and seemed to grow taller every day.

"Tell your sisters to come down and set the table."

Paulo held the treasured bread in his mouth, closed the breadbox, and scampered off.

Anna eyes drifted to the wall calendar…December 1923. They'd been married nineteen years.

Anna thought back to their shy first weeks of marriage, the arrival of baby Clara, Raffaele's growing dissatisfaction with the direction Italy was taking, and his eventual desire to go to America. Despite her objections, he went and here they are nineteen years later.

"I'm here, Mama," Emma announced, pulling Anna out of her revery.

"Where's your sister?"

Rolling her eyes, the fifteen-year-old said, "She'll be right down. She's reading of course."

"Please tell her it's time to set the table—now."

Emma left quickly, her footsteps echoing on the stairs.

Anna took two loaves of crusty Italian bread from the breadbox and put them in the oven to warm. Raffaele would be home shortly, and being a man of large appetites, liked his dinner on time. She'd been fending off one large appetite since their last child Vincenzo was born.

The girls came into the kitchen. Clara said, "Sorry, Mama, I was studying."

"It's good to study, but without plates and silverware, we can't eat."

As they opened the cupboards, Clara reached for the everyday plates.

"Not those," Anna said. "Tonight's special, the good china."

"Why is tonight special?" Clara asked.

"It's a surprise. No more questions."

The girls bustled in and out of the kitchen, and back upstairs without a word.

Anna thought of her childless friend, Rosetta. Children were a blessing—most of the time.

"I'm home," Raffaele called out.

"I'm glad. It's getting cold outside, and it might rain again tomorrow."

Raffaele breathed deeply. "I love that smell." He came up behind Anna, wrapped his arms around her, and kissed her cheek.

"What are you doing?" she asked with a hint of disapproval, but also a small smile. "Dinner's almost ready. Would you get the wine?"

"Not before I smell the soup. You make the best pasta fagioli." As he leaned over her shoulder and sniffed again, Paulo bounded into the room.

"Hey, there's my boy." Raffaele turned and spread his arms wide. His son, tried to sidestep around him, but Raffaele reached out, caught Paulo around the chest, lifted and hugged him. "How was school today?"

Paulo's feet dangled above the polished wooden floor. "It was ok, Pop."

He squirmed but could not avoid the kiss on the forehead that always accompanied Raffaele's hugs.

"Love before food." Raffaele set Paulo down and tousled his hair.

Anna ladled the steaming soup into a white ceramic tureen and carried it into the dining room, the aroma trailing behind her. "Paulo, get the bread from the oven, bring the salad from the icebox, and call your brother and sisters to dinner."

Raffaele got a pitcher of wine from the basement, put it on the table, and sat down. His family ate at home every night, except on those rare occasions when they visited friends. Like all Friday nights, the menu, especially in the winter, was pasta fagioli soup, salad, and warm, crusty Italian bread. It rained two days before, and the temperature was predicted to drop into the high thirties later that night.

His wife shopped for groceries Saturday afternoons, so by Friday night, she had the week's leftovers to make pasta fagioli. The soup was a combination of beans, pasta, and vegetables. Anna had a way with spices that always made it delicious.

Clara arrived last, reading a book, then laying it open across her lap.

Raffaele looked at his eldest daughter. "Clara, it's dinner time."

At the sound of her father's voice, she closed the book.

Anna ladled soup into a bowl. "Do you know what special day this is, Raffaele?"

"No, what?"

"Today is December 7. Exactly a year ago you were naturalized. Have you forgotten?" She passed the bowl to Emma, who handed it to Vincenzo, who gave it to his father.

"Ah, you're right," he said, nodding.

"It's the anniversary of that very important day. You deserve a toast." Clara, please get the wine glasses I set out on the counter. And no more reading."

Clara set her book on the floor next to her chair.

When she returned, she placed all the glasses by her father, who poured each half full and passed them out.

Anna raised her glass. "Here's to Raffaele Colaluca, the first naturalized American in our family."

Raffaele raised his glass and saw Vincenzo cradling his glass with both hands.

"Thank you, my family," he said, looking at each child and Anna, then drinking.

"Happy anniversary, Raffaele," Anna said softly.

He started to say something but picked up his napkin and dabbed at his eyes. Putting the napkin in his lap, he lifted his glass again. He nodded at Anna, took another swallow, and said, "Let's eat. Mangiamo!"

Everyone was quiet until each had a soup bowl and started to eat.

Raffaele looked at Clara who sat to her mother's left. At eighteen, she was their oldest child and a high school graduate with honors the previous June. Ever the overachiever, she was in her first semester of Normal School, studying to be a teacher. Clara stared into her bowl, slowly stirring the soup.

"Clara?"

Her head popped up. "Yes, Papa?"

"What are you thinking about?"

"Well, I have this lesson plan that's due soon, before Christmas break."

"When is this Christmas break?"

"In two weeks. It counts for a third of our grade."

"What is this plan you have to make?"

Clara set her spoon down and explained, "A lesson plan is what a teacher writes down, before she teaches something new to her students."

"Like a movie script?" Paulo asked.

"Sort of...but I have to write down the steps I'll use to present the concept."

Raffaele pursed his lips. "So, it's what you're going to say?"

"Like when you make wine, Papa. You do everything in a certain order. First you do this," she held her finger up, "and then this, and so on, until all the steps are done."

"Ah, so writing down the steps helps you teach?"

Clara smiled. "Yes, Papa."

Returning her smile, he said, "I know you will make a good plan, but right now please enjoy this special dinner your mother made and do the lesson plan after."

"Yes, Papa." She picked up her spoon and began to eat.

Raffaele sipped his wine and winked at Anna. Everybody resumed eating. A few moments later, he noticed a tiny ripple on the surface of his pasta fagioli. Puzzled, he held up his spoon and looked across at his wife. "The soup's moving."

Every child's head came up to look at him, except Clara's.

He looked around the table. "Who's shaking the table?"

Anna shrugged.

Raffaele nodded toward Clara and Anna reached over and touched Clara's shoulder.

Clara looked up and saw everyone staring at her. The table stopped moving.

"What's wrong?" she asked, looking confused.

Anna leaned back and looked down past Clara's lap, to where her daughter's knee rested against the table leg. "I think you're making the table shake with your knee."

"Oh, sorry."

"Still thinking about your plan?" asked Raffaele.

Clara nodded sheepishly.

"I like my soup to be still, okay?"

"Yes, Papa," she said quietly.

Anna asked Vincenzo what he'd done in school that day.

Raffaele loved listening to his wife ask the children questions.

"Anna, may I have another bowl please." Raffaele handed his empty bowl to Vincent, on to Emma, who held it for her mother to refill, and passed it back.

"Who would like some salad?" Anna motioned for their plates. They took them from under the soup bowls and passed them to be filled. Conversation about the events of the day and weekend plans continued.

Raffaele was halfway through his second bowl of soup when the table shook again. He looked across at Anna and nodded at Clara whose face was low over her soup, her spoon resting on the edge of the bowl.

He placed his spoon on the table, sat back, wiped his mouth on the napkin, and stared at Clara. He reached for the long loaf of bread in the middle of the table and rose.

"Raffaele, what are you doing?" Anna asked quietly. The others sat frozen.

Leaning across the table, the bread in his right hand, he tapped Clara hard on the back of her head.

Clara's face plopped into her soup. She jerked up, startled, mouth open. Thick soup ran down her face, onto her blouse, and into her lap.

"Jesus," Paulo muttered.

Vincent snorted a laugh and covered his mouth.

Emma just stared, wide-eyed.

Anna reached over with her napkin and began to wipe the soup off Clara's face. "Are you hurt?" She looked angrily across the table at her husband.

Raffaele straightened, replaced the bread, and sat down.

Paulo leaned a little further away from his father.

Anna dabbed at the soup on the front of her daughter's dress, and said softly, "Go change your clothes."

As Clara pushed back her chair and ran up the stairs, Anna glared at Raffaele, who simply took a swallow of wine, and picked up his spoon.

CHAPTER SIXTEEN

A PIE, PRIEST, AND PROVIDENCE
1924

After Mass and the Altar Society meeting, Anna walked to the church office, holding a small, wrapped box. She knocked softly on the ornate carved wooden door. Moments passed and she was about to leave when Father Donati opened the door, his broad-shouldered silhouette filling the doorway. His arrival at the parish, after Father Savona's retirement, reinvigorated the church with his youthful enthusiasm and infectious smile. He was popular, especially with the women in the Altar Society.

"I'm sorry to bother—"

"You're never a bother, Anna. Please, come in." He motioned to the two high-backed chairs across from his desk.

Anna entered and sat in the chair nearest the door.

Father Donati took the other chair.

Anna noticed other small gifts on the large mahogany desk, before placing her box on the marble top of the round parlor table between them.

"These are for you, Father. They're biscotti cookies."

"Why thank you, Anna. I'm sure they're delicious."

Anna held her purse on her lap and rested a hand on the arm of the chair, her fingertips moving lightly on the red velvet upholstery.

"How can I help you on this beautiful spring day?" Father Donati asked.

She saw concern in his deep-set hazel eyes. "Father, I was hoping you might know of someone who could give my son, Paulo, music lessons?"

"Oh…" He relaxed and ran his fingers through his wavy black hair. "I see. What instrument does he want to play?"

"I'm not sure. He sits with me when I play the piano, but he needs a real teacher."

The priest nodded. "Yes, of course."

"My husband, Raffaele, plays the clarinet, but sometimes he is too impatient."

"Yes, I know," he replied, eyes twinkling. "He does have definite opinions."

Anna looked down and felt her cheeks warm. "He's a good man, but his church experience in the old country was not good."

"Your faith led him to join us this past Christmas and Easter. Never underestimate the power of prayer. I'll make some inquiries and we will talk again."

Father Donati rose as did Anna, bowing her head. "Thank you, Father."

"Anna, it is I who should thank you for your faith and contributions to the parish."

Monday was a crisp spring day, finally warming after the cold winter. A light breeze moved the new leaves on the trees over the junior high school yard.

Paulo and his friend Eddie hurried down the hallway into the noisy cafeteria and sat down, side by side at their usual place, a pale green lunch table facing the wall of windows above the radiators. Paulo gazed at the cloudless blue sky and breathed deeply anticipating lunch recess on the roof playground and a game of dodge ball.

Eddie looked over at the little grease stains on the brown paper bag in front of Paulo. "What'd your mother fix today?"

Paulo pulled out an apple and an eight-inch roll wrapped in wax paper, laying them on his bag. "I think its mortadella and provolone, with peppers and sauce. Why?"

"You wanna trade?"

"Maybe. You always wanna trade." Paulo grinned and pushed Eddie's shoulder.

"Hey." He pushed back. "Your Mom's sandwiches are the best."

Paulo pointed at Eddie's bag. "What'd you got?"

"Roast beef on rye with mustard, a pickle, and a berry pie. So, want to trade?"

"A pie? Lemme see it."

Eddie put the contents of his paper bag onto the table. His inch-thick sandwich was square and wrapped in wax paper. The little pie was in a white cardboard box about five inches across, with Blackberry Pie in fancy dark blue letters across the top.

Though Paulo loved his mother's pies, he'd never had a store-bought one. "Okay." With great ceremony, they swapped bags as Eddie smacked his lips loudly, making them laugh.

Paulo's twelve-year-old-appetite made short work of the roast beef sandwich before carefully opening the little box and lifting out the pie. Paulo brought it to his mouth, closed his eyes, and breathed in the sweet scent of black berries. He took a bite. The light brown crust was chewier than his mother's, but wonderful.

"What are you doing?" Eddie asked, "You gotta take it out of the holder."

"What holder?" Paulo said, his mouth full.

"Look at the bottom." Eddie pointed his finger up under the pie.

Still chewing, Paulo held up the pie. "Jesus Christ, Eddie. Why didn't you say something?" The pie sat in a little cardboard pan.

"I thought you knew. Haven't you eaten one of these before?"

"No...I thought it was kind of chewy."

Eddie grinned and shoved Paulo's shoulder.

Paulo took the pie out and flipped the cardboard pan at his friend.

Eddie dodged and almost fell backwards off the bench. "Hey, dago boy! It's not my fault you never had a store-bought pie before."

Paulo took another bite, exaggerating his chewing motion, before swallowing. "It is better now," he said sheepishly.

Wednesday afternoon, after Anna's visit with Father Donati, she sang quietly as she fixed dinner. Eggplant parmigiana was one of her husband's favorites. Father Donati, called earlier and asked if he could come by that evening. He was not one of her husband's favorites.

When Raffaele came home, he went directly into the kitchen, hugging Anna from behind, and asking, "What smells so good?"

"Eggplant parmigiana."

"In the middle of the week? What's the special occasion?"

"Just because I love you."

"And I you, Anna." He squeezed her again, poured himself a glass of wine, and walked into the front room.

When everyone was seated around the dinner table, she took a deep breath and announced, "Father Donati is coming for a visit at seven o'clock."

Raffaele stared at her, tapped his index finger on the table, and asked, "The boy priest is coming here? Why?"

Anna dipped the spatula into the Pyrex baking dish, lifted out a piece of eggplant parmigiana, and placed it on the top plate in front of her. "I talked with him after Mass on Sunday and asked if he knew of anyone who could give Paulo music lessons," she said.

Raffaele frowned, opened his mouth to speak, then closed it.

"Pop, you're never going to believe what I did today, when Eddie gave me his berry pie," Paulo said.

Raffaele scowled at his son.

Paulo glanced down. "It was pretty funny."

"Raffaele, I know how much you've always liked playing your clarinet. Paulo loves music, just like you do. Don't you want him to know that joy too?"

He sighed, nodded, and reached for his wine glass.

"Emma, please pass this to your father." Meeting Raffaele's gaze, she added, "I made this especially for you tonight."

When everyone was served and eating, Anna, as she did every night, asked the children what they'd learned at school.

Emma shared and then Paulo told them about trading with Eddie for the store-bought pie, omitting the part about eating the cardboard.

"How was the pie? Did you like it?"

"It was all right, Mama, but yours are better."

"Thank you, but it's good to try new things."

Her husband listened to the children's accounts of what they'd learned but didn't say anything until dinner was over. "Thank you for the eggplant, Anna. It was delicious."

He pushed back his chair and walked into the front room.

"Children, please clear the table," Anna said, watching her husband's retreating back, then joined him in the front room. "Maybe Father Donati's found someone to give Paulo lessons?"

Raffaele stared straight ahead; his arms folded across his chest. "Maybe so." Turning to look at Anna, he said, "Why didn't you tell me about inviting him?"

"I didn't invite him, Raffaele. He called this afternoon and asked if he could come by. What was I supposed to say? He is our priest."

Her husband snorted.

Just then, Paulo, who was listening from the kitchen, came and stood by his mother. "Pop, if he did find someone to teach me, what instrument should I play?"

Anna put an arm around her son's shoulders and pulled him close. "Let's not get ahead of ourselves. Go upstairs and wash your face and hands." She motioned to the other children standing in the kitchen doorway. "You, too."

Raffaele put his hand out to stop Paulo as he walked by, looked up at his son, and said, "Music lessons, they are not free, son. We'll see."

Paulo nodded and went upstairs.

At exactly seven o'clock, the doorbell rang. Anna hurried to the front door to welcome Father Donati, his first time in their home. She escorted him into the living room where her husband was waiting in his high-backed green armchair.

Raffaele nodded to the priest.

Anna seated Father Donati in her chair across from her husband. She called for the children to come down, then sat on the ottoman next to her husband.

Clara and Emma sat on the couch, Paulo and Vincenzo sat cross-legged on the floor in front of their sisters.

Father Donati looked at Raffaele. "Thank you for seeing me this evening."

"Perhaps Father Donati would like some wine?" Raffaele said to Anna.

"Thank you. I understand you make very good wine."

Anna hurried to the kitchen and returned with red wine in stemmed glasses.

The priest held up his glass. "To you and your family, health and happiness."

Her husband held his glass out and both men sipped their wine.

Father Donati set his glass on the end table. "I understand you are an accomplished clarinet player."

"I played in a band, when I was younger."

"Your wife spoke with me on Sunday and asked if I could help find someone to give your son music lessons.

Raffaele looked at Anna. "Yes, I know."

Father Donati leaned forward in his chair. "I also understand Paulo likes to sit next to your wife when she plays the piano. You know watching and listening to music shows he has a definite interest."

Raffaele nodded his agreement.

Father Donati turned to Paulo. "I don't play the clarinet or the piano. I play the violin. Would you be willing to study violin with me, Paulo?"

"Yes," Paulo answered excitedly, and then looked at his father, who only went to church because his mother pleaded with him to go.

"May I, Pop?" he asked, hopefully.

"The lessons would be free of course, Mr. Colaluca. You're welcome to come and watch."

Moment passed before Raffaele nodded. "If Father Donati is willing to teach you. Yes."

Father Donati clasped his hands together. "Good. We can begin next Sunday after church. Paulo, I have the violin I used as a boy. You may use it until you require a better one."

"Thank you for your generosity, Father Donati," Anna said and crossed herself.

The young priest stood. "It's my pleasure to be of service. Thank you for the delicious wine."

Raffaele rose from his chair as Father Donati smiled at him and said, "I am pleased you encourage your children's talents, Mr. Colaluca. I look forward to seeing you and your family on Sunday."

Raffaele shook the priest's extended hand. "Thank you," he said and nodded.

Anna followed the priest into the foyer and bid him goodnight. When she turned around, she saw Paulo wrapping his arms around his father and squeezing him.

"Thanks Pop."

Raffaele hugged him back, then held his son at arm's length. "The violin is a good instrument. Practice will tell if you have talent, Paulo."

Anna came into the room and touched Raffaele's shoulders. "Thank you, Raffaele," she said, her eyes moist.

He looked at her and smiled. "Church next Sunday?" With raised eyebrows, he said, "We'll see." He tousled his son's hair. "We'll see."

CHAPTER SEVENTEEN

GREAT ESCAPE 1924

"*Do* I have to, Clara?" Emma whined, sitting on her bed. "I'm supposed to meet someone."

"Who?"

"You don't know him."

"A boy? What's his name? Did Mama say it was okay?"

Emma mumbled something under her breath.

"Well, if Mama said it was okay, Papa left the money for the three of you downstairs on the sideboard."

"What if my friends see me with them?"

"They know you have brothers. Think of it as an early birthday present."

Emma snorted. "Thanks."

"The movie starts at two. Paulo and Vincenzo won't want to be late."

Emma stood, hands on her hips, "Why can't you take them? You're the boss of us, aren't you?"

"I'm in charge when Mama and Papa aren't here, because I'm the oldest and the most responsible."

"I'm responsible, too."

"Well, here's your chance to prove it. You're almost sixteen."

"Okay, Miss Perfect."

"Emma, it's the start of my last year at Normal College. I need to study at the library."

"But a Tom Mix movie? At a Saturday matinee?"

"Hey, he's handsome, and Kathleen Keys is beautiful."

Emma rolled her eyes. "I don't think handsome and beautiful are why

Paulo and Vincenzo want to see North of Hudson Bay. It's gun fights and horses."

They left the house together. At the bottom of the front porch steps, Clara pointed a finger at the boys.

"You two mind Emma. I want a good report. Understood?"

When Paulo and Vincenzo nodded, Clara headed up the street, waving and saying over her shoulder, "They're all yours, Emma. See you later."

Going the opposite direction, Paulo said, "Can we hurry? We're going to be late."

Emma kept Paulo and Vincenzo in front of her. The walk was beautiful with September clouds across the sun, making flickering shadows on the sidewalk.

Emma stood in line for tickets, while her brothers studied posters of coming attractions. Inside, she tried to sit in the row behind them, but the boys moved back next to her. They squirmed, pushed each other, and waved to friends.

"Will you please settle down."

Paulo grinned. "Are we embarrassing you?"

Vincenzo yelled a name and waved at a boy several rows in front of them.

Emma slid down in her seat. "You are such brats."

Throughout the movie, Paulo and Vincenzo whispered excitedly in the dark. They did not notice the boy who sat down next to Emma until the house lights went on. When they looked, he and Emma were holding hands.

Paulo looked at him suspiciously. "Who are you?" he asked loudly.

"He's a friend," Emma said quickly.

"Is he a new friend," Vincenzo asked innocently.

"Does Mama know about him?" Paulo continued.

"Not yet, okay?" Emma stood. "Now let's go."

The boys walked to the end of the aisle, and when they looked back Emma was kissing her *friend*.

On the way home, Paulo and Vincenzo looked back at their sister, whispering, and laughing, then pretended to shoot each other.

"Did you see how fast he could shoot?" Paulo slapped his hip in a make-believe draw. "Bang, I got you!"

Vincenzo copied the movement, moaned, and fell to the ground. When he bounced back up, he galloped in place. "His horse, Tony, was the best."

"And where are you going keep a horse? In the garage?" Emma snorted.

"Come on, don't listen to her, she's a wet blanket." Paulo pulled his little brother ahead. "Did you see how he escaped from the hotel?"

"Yeah, it was slick."

At home, Emma went to her bedroom and shut the door.

Paulo and Vincenzo went to their room and continued acting out make-believe shootouts, dying dramatically, until they heard the front door shut downstairs.

"What ARE you doing?" Clara called out.

"Nothing," both boys replied in unison.

"Mama and Papa will be home in a few minutes."

"Okay," Paulo answered. He grinned at Vincenzo, put a finger to his lips, and motioned for him to close their bedroom door.

Vincenzo tiptoed and shut it silently.

Paulo pulled the knitted bedspread off the bed and piled it at the foot of the black wrought-iron bedframe.

Clara opened the door and demanded. "What are you doing? Why is the bedspread on the floor?"

"I'm going to escape," Paulo said.

"Escape from where?"

"Like Tom Mix did in the movie," he answered.

The metal frame squeaked when she sat down. "What are you talking about?"

"From there," he said, pointing at the bedroom window, "Tom Mix escaped from the hotel, by tying sheets together. I bet I can do the same thing."

Vincenzo stood by the window grinning back at Paulo.

"Where's your sister?" Clara asked. "Emma Colaluca, come in here right now!"

"I'm coming," came the put-upon reply from across the hall.

"You're supposed to be watching them."

"I did. I took them to the movie and brought them home. They were so excited, I told them to go play in their room. I didn't think—"

"No, you didn't." Clara glared at her.

The room was silent as she looked at each of her siblings in turn. "It's two stories down to the driveway. What do you think Mama and Papa would say? No escaping, do you understand? I've got to start dinner."

To Emma, she said, "You're unbelievable," on her way out the door.

"So are you," Emma whispered.

Paulo gave Emma a thumbs-up.

She shrugged and returned to her room.

Paulo motioned for Vincenzo to close the door, crossed to the window, pushed it up with a grunt, and stared down at the driveway that led into the garage under the house.

"It's a long way down. Can you really do it?"

"Yeah, I can do it. Help me get the sheets off the bed."

Vincenzo watched Paulo tie the two sheets together, then to one end of the bedspread, then the other end of the bedspread to the middle of the bedframe. He tugged on each piece to make sure the knots were tight before lowering the "rope" out the window and down the back of the house. It barely reached the top of the garage door, and swung from side to side, right in front of their parent's bedroom window.

"They have to hang lower. Vincenzo, help me pull the bed."

One on each side and on the count of three, they grabbed the frame of the bed and pulled. The bed squeaked, but only moved a couple inches.

Emma heard the squeak and yelled from across the hall, "Don't jump on the bed. You heard what Miss Perfect said."

"We're not," Paulo answered. "Vincenzo, pull really hard this time."

The boys planted their feet, and with one continuous scraping, squeaking sound, dragged the bed across the floor; it stopped a foot from the window.

Paulo sat on the windowsill and swung one leg outside.

Emma opened the door and screamed. "What are you—Clara, Paulo's going out the window."

Paulo didn't wait. He clutched the sheet with both hands and put the other leg out the window.

Emma bolted and grabbed Paulo's shirt, as he tried to wrap his dangling feet around the sheet.

Clara burst into the room to see Paulo trying to wriggle free from Emma's grasp.

"Oh my God!" Clara yelled and rushed to the window, knocking into Emma, who lost her grip on Paulo's shirt.

Vincenzo started to cry.

With Paulo's full weight on the sheets, the squeaking bed lurched toward the window, pinning his sisters against the windowsill.

The girls screamed. Vincenzo's crying became a wail.

When the downward movement stopped with a jerk, Paulo, never able to get his feet around the sheets, slid to the end of his so-called rope, and into thin air from six feet above the driveway. With a loud thud, he landed on his back. He didn't move. His hands throbbed, he couldn't breathe, and heard screaming somewhere. Panicking when he tried to speak and nothing came out, he gasped, sucking in one small gulp of air, then another. Suddenly, he felt a vibration in his back, and turned his head to see the family car at the top of the driveway.

"Oh my God," Anna exclaimed. The engine was running when his mother pushed open the passenger door to rush down the driveway. She knelt beside him and cupped his face in her hands. "Are you hurt?"

He moved his head slightly and smiled weakly.

His father stopped the engine, got out, looked up at the sheet hanging out the window, and walked down the driveway.

Paulo looked up to see Clara and Emma staring down at him. At least they'd stopped screaming, although he could hear Vincenzo crying.

Finally, he was able to take a deep breath.

His father knelt and gently felt along his arms, legs, and behind his head.

Paulo was afraid to move.

"I don't think any bones are broken."

"Thank God," she said quietly, crossing herself.

Raffaele looked at the sheets, back at Paulo, and exploded, "Jeeza ma Christ. Why did you do this?"

"I wanted...to be like...Tom Mix...in the movie."

"Movies are not real. This was a stupid thing to do."

Paulo tried not to cry. "I'm sorry, Pop."

His father slid his hands under his knees and back and lifted Paulo up into his chest. With his son cradled in his arms, Raffaele walked into the garage.

Paulo felt his father's grip tighten as they climbed the stairs. His mother opened the door into the front room, so Raffaele could lay him on the couch.

Anna sat on the edge, held her rosary beads, and prayed.

Clara, Emma, and Vincenzo stood silently staring at him.

Vincenzo snuffled and wiped his nose on his sleeve. "Is he going to die?"

Raffaele looked at them. "No, our hero is not going to die. Not today, anyway."

That evening, the doctor came and examined Paulo, and said that although his back was bruised, and he had a throbbing headache, no bones were broken.

Paulo was stoic but flinched when the doctor touched his red and swollen hands.

He knew that was his last movie for a long time.

Raffaele carried him up to his bed. After his parents went downstairs, Clara came to Paulo's bedside, leaned down close to his face, and in a low voice growled, "Don't you ever do anything like that again. You scared me to death."

Paulo nodded weakly.

She shook her head and smiled. "The movie was good, huh?"

He nodded again.

"Did you and Vincenzo give Emma a hard time?"

He moved his head back and forth.

"Well…I'm glad you had a good time." She kissed him on the forehead and stood.

"Emma kissed a boy," Paulo whispered.

Clara turned back to him. "What did you say?"

"At the end of the movie, when I turned around, she was holding hands with a boy. She said he was a friend and we had to leave. She kissed him before we left."

Clara looked at him skeptically.

"It's the truth," he said, crossing himself.

Clara looked across the hall. The door of the bedroom she shared with Emma was closed. "Thank you for telling me."

Shortly, Paulo heard his sisters muffled voices arguing as he drifted off to sleep.

The next day, after church, Clara made Emma tell her parents about the boy.

"His name is Joseph. He's a senior at our high school," Emma said, sitting by her mother on the couch. We met last year." Her eyes welled with tears. "I love him, and we want to get married," she said, the tears now on her cheeks.

"Emma, you are too young to get married," Raffaele said. "I will not permit it."

"Your father's right, you need to finish school," Anna said, her voice soft.

Emma wiped her tears. "You were young, Mama, when you married Papa."

"That was different and a long time ago."

"No, it's not. You loved Papa and got married when you were only a year older than me. What's so different?"

"That was in Italy, and this is America," Raffaele said sternly. "We know nothing about this boy or his family. What does his father do?"

"I don't care what his father does, Papa, I not marrying his father. I know all I need to know about Joseph. He's a good boy!"

Raffaele looked at Anna, who took her daughter's hand. "Emma, when I married your father, he was a man. He'd been in the Army and traveled.

"I love Joseph and we want to get married," Emma repeated coldly.

"You must finish school before thinking about getting married," Anna insisted.

"And I," Raffaele said, jabbing his chest, "want to meet this boy who wants to marry my daughter, capisci?"

Joseph was invited for dinner, came dressed in his Sunday clothes, was polite and respectful. He was an only child whose mother died when he was young; his father remained a widower. He spoke with passion about his love of Emma and desire to marry.

Raffaele and Anna reiterated that Emma had to finish school before getting married but gave Joseph permission to see Emma at school-sponsored activities. All was going well, until a week after her birthday. Emma came home from a supposed school outing to announce that she and Joseph were married. They had gone downtown to the courthouse and a Justice of the Peace performed the ceremony.

Raffaele was angry at being deceived. Anna was heartbroken but more understanding. Emma was always in her older sister's shadow, more interested in her social life than school. A different kind of child, she preferred the fanciful over the practical. She moved in with Joseph and his father and dropped out of school. As the weeks went by, they saw her less and less. At just eighteen years old, she died of tuberculosis in 1926.

CHAPTER EIGHTEEN

ATLANTIC CITY GYPSIES 1926

"Anna let's go—please! It's almost eight o'clock."

Fussing with her hat, she said, "The boys are in the car. I'm coming."

"I'm going to the car. I'd like to have my lunch at lunchtime." Since he got his driver's license at age forty-five, he was proud of himself for learning all the rules.

He couldn't resist asking again. "Anna, are you coming?"

Despite two minor accidents, he'd managed to avoid any contact with the police. Both times he was sure he had the right-of-way.

Thinking about his studious daughter with her non-stop comments, he was glad she wasn't coming, which would have made the three-hour drive seem longer.

Coming into the garage, he heard the boys laughing, and saw them bouncing up and down in the back seat.

"Hey!" The bouncing stopped. He looked in the window to see Paulo and Vincenzo sitting perfectly still with their hands in their laps. Opening the rear door, he placed the square wicker basket on the seat between them. "No more bouncing."

"Yes, sir," the boys said in unison.

"I know you're excited about going to the ocean." He patted the basket. "I'd like my sandwich in one piece when we get there, capisci?"

This would be their longest family trip. They planned to spread their blanket under the famous boardwalk and have lunch by the sea. He'd salute the day with a bottle of his homemade red wine and drive home before dark.

Anna got in the car, laid her purse on the seat, smoothed her dress, and turned to Raffaele. "Clara is going to spend the day studying at the library."

"Of course. It's her second home."

Anna sighed and dabbed her eyes. "I wish Emma was still here, she would have liked today."

Raffaele reached over and patted her arm. "I wish she was here too, but it's been six months. Per favore, can we just enjoy the day?"

"Yes, let's not worry about anything. This will be our special day."

He backed out of the garage and stopped so Paulo could jump out, pull the garage door down, and get back in the car.

Raffaele backed up the driveway and drove slowly down the alley. He wended his way through the neighborhood, around downtown Philadelphia, then turned southeast, down Highway 30.

He pulled his fedora lower on his forehead as the highway faced the early morning sun. After passing through Gloucester Township the landscape flattened out.

When he glanced over, Anna was smiling.

"It's so nice to be out in the country, Raffaele."

"Yes, it is, Anna."

Houses with barns and outbuildings behind them stood along the intersecting roads, growing farther apart as the countryside became more rural.

"Look at the fields, Raffaele. They remind me of the old country, so open and green. Aren't they beautiful?"

Raffaele glanced out her side of the windshield at a farmhouse and a large red barn off in the distance, surrounded by fields of yellow and green.

"Look boys. Look at all those corn stalks."

"What's the green stuff, Mama?" Paulo asked,

"This time of year, it looks like cabbage." Further down the road, she pointed out fields of squash, onions, and tomatoes.

"Look! My favorite eggplant on this side," Raffaele announced.

Anna chuckled. "Yes, we know. Especially in eggplant parmigiana."

"Remember when we used to walk in the countryside around Bugnara."

"Yes. What made you think of that?"

"You delighted telling me the name of all the plants in the fields."

Anna patted his thigh. "I remember."

Along the way, a few cars went by going back toward Philadelphia. Raffaele drove well below the speed limit. Drivers behind him honked, went around his shiny black 1923 Chevrolet, and were soon out of sight.

At five-foot six inches, Raffaele sat up proudly in the driver's seat, both hands on the wheel, eyes straight ahead. He pulled the brim of his brown fedora down to keep from squinting into the mid-morning sun.

"You look very handsome today in your Sunday suit and tie," Anna remarked.

Before he could thank her, Vincenzo asked, "How much longer until we get there?"

Anna glanced back at her youngest. "Be patient. The ocean is worth the wait."

The boys talked in low voices about the animals, people, and farm equipment they saw along the way. Raffaele turned on the radio, set on his favorite station. John Phillips Sousa's The Gallant Seventh march played, and he tapped the steering wheel in time to the music. At the end of the song, Raffaele lowered volume and asked Anna, "How do you like our excursion so far?"

"I like our excursion very much." Anna smiled at him. It was one of her fancy vocabulary words from English class. "This will be a fun trip."

He turned the volume up again and hummed to himself.

Halfway to their destination, Raffaele noticed a car off to his right, travelling on a road that looked like it would intersect and join the highway up ahead. He watched a few moments then said, "They're not going to stop."

"What'd you say, Pop?" Paulo asked from the back seat.

Anna looked over at Raffaele. "Who's not going to stop?"

He turned the radio off and pointed at the car that was kicking up dust as it came toward the highway.

They all looked out and saw the car on a dirt road that would join theirs.

"How do you know they won't stop?"

He glanced at the other car and scoffed, "They look like Gypsies."

Both boys rested their chins on top of the front seat.

"Are they really Gypsies, Pop?" Paulo asked.

Raffaele pointed again. "Look at them, packed in the car like animals."

"This is not the old country, Raffaele. I know your father thought they were thieves and cheats, but this is America."

"Just watch. They're not going to stop."

The old four-door Model T was an open-air touring car, packed to overflowing with adults and children. Boxes and baskets were tied onto the running board.

"Raffaele, slow down."

"They should stop," Raffaele answered. His hands gripped the steering wheel, he took his foot off the gas.

The touring car was on a road lower than the highway and rose sharply where they intersected. The other driver never looked over and drove right onto the road.

"Raffaele, stop!" Anna cried out, her hands on the dashboard.

He braked but rear-ended the accelerating touring car. The low-speed impact sounded like metal trashcans being thrown together.

The touring car slowed, came to a stop, with the passenger side wheels just off the asphalt.

"I told you they wouldn't stop." He looked at Anna, whose hat had slipped forward on her head. "Are you alright?"

She sat up straight, pushed her hat back, and took a deep breath. "I think so."

As Raffaele watched the driver get out of the car, he asked, "You boys, okay?"

"Yes, Pop," Paulo answered, rubbing his knee.

"Vincenzo?"

Silence.

"He has his hand over his mouth," Paulo replied.

Anna looked back at Vincenzo. "What's wrong?"

"I bit my tongue." He started to cry.

"Let me see. Stick out your tongue." Frowning, she reached in her purse and handed Vincenzo a folded handkerchief. "Here, suck on this. It'll stop the bleeding."

Raffaele opened his door and got out of the car.

"Be nice, Raffaele," Anna admonished. "You ran into him."

Raffaele glared back at her through the windshield, walked to the front of their car, and stared at the bent bumper and crumpled fenders.

A blue roadster with the top down went by slowly. The man and woman stared at Raffaele, then at the other car, and continued down the road.

The driver of the touring car yelled and motioned for Raffaele to come.

Raffaele walked slowly up to the rear of the other car.

The other driver was a big man, taller than Raffaele, with curly brown hair and a bushy mustache. His bib overalls were well-worn and shirt cuffs frayed.

He took a step toward Raffaele. "Where'd you learn to drive?"

Two children leaned out of the car watching and a woman stuck her head out. "Don't do anything stupid. No one's hurt here and he's dressed all fancy."

Raffaele doffed his hat to the woman and looked back at the man in front of him. "You should have stopped."

"What are you talking about? I got here first."

Raffaele pointed at the white markings in the middle of the road. "See those? This is a main road."

"So?"

"I have the right-of-way. That's the law."

"What are you, some kind of lawyer?"

A delivery truck pulled up next to them. "You need any help?" an older, gray-haired man yelled out the passenger-side window.

"No," the other driver replied.

Raffaele waved the delivery driver to continue, and the truck pulled away.

The big man put his hands on the top of the spare tire. "Look what you did to my car." He kicked the bumper that was pushed into both rear fenders. "This is your fault. What's your name?"

"Raffaele Colaluca, and it's not my fault."

"You a dago?"

Raffaele glared at him and took out his wallet.

"What are you doing?"

He held out two twenty-dollar bills.

The man crossed his arms. "It'll cost more than that to fix what you did."

"You're the one who didn't stop, and your car is old." Raffaele thrust the bills at him, hearing the woman say, "Take the money. Don't be stupid."

"This wop thinks he's all high and mighty."

Raffaele took another twenty out of his wallet, dropped the bills at the man's feet, grabbed his own bicep, raised his forearm straight up, and headed to his car.

"Where you are going?" the man said, hands on his hips.

"Pick up the money, stupid," the woman said.

Anna and the boys watched Raffaele walk back to their car and get in.

"Jeeza ma Christ," he said under his breath. He gripped the steering wheel with both hands, took a deep breath, and let out a long sigh.

The other driver gestured for Raffaele to come back, and then he and the woman yelled at each other. Finally, the man bent down to pick up the money.

"Pop?"

"What, Paulo?"

"That man is really mad. What'd you say?"

Anna turned and looked at Paulo. "No more questions."

Paulo nodded and sat back.

The other driver pointed at the back of his car one last time, got in, and drove away.

"My father was right. They weren't from the old country, but they are like gypsies." He started the Chevrolet, looked behind him and turned across the road.

"Where are we going?" Anna asked.

"Home."

"What about our excursion?"

Raffaele stared straight ahead.

"What about the boardwalk and our picnic for the boys?"

"Maybe another day, Anna." He gestured to the front of the car. "The car needs to be fixed."

"We're not going to the ocean, Pop?"

Anna turned and shook her head at Paulo.

As the landscape passed in reverse, no one spoke.

An hour and a half later, when Raffaele stopped the car, Paulo hopped out.

"I'll get the garage door, Pop."

"Vincenzo, take your mother's basket upstairs," Raffaele ordered.

Anna sighed and got out of the car, Paulo and Vincenzo following.

Raffaele rested his hands on the top of the steering wheel, and shook his head, "Jeeza ma Christ." He put the car in gear, drove slowly into the garage, turned off the engine and just sat. His wife was upset. His sons were disappointed. The muscles in his jaw tightened and he hit the steering wheel.

Raffaele got out and slammed the car door, pulled the garage door down with a bang, and stomped into the basement. As he passed the workbench, he saw the wooden sailboat he was carving for Vincenzo. He stopped and raised his arm to bat it off the workbench, but froze, his hand above his head. His youngest loved boats.

He picked up the foot-long hull that Vincenzo sanded smooth. He turned it around in his hands and ran his fingers along the hull. It was ready for painting. He laid it down gently. "My little sailor."

When he opened the door into the house, Anna had their 'picnic' on the dining room table. The boys sat in their seats waiting. They watched him walk into the kitchen and shut the door.

"Anna—"

"What?" she snapped and turned to face him.

"I want—"

"To apologize?" she said, glaring at him.

"It wasn't my fault," he said, hands extended.

"You didn't stop Raffaele." Anna said through tight lips. "You hit them."

He shook a finger at her. "I told you they wouldn't stop."

She took a deep breath, dipped her head slightly, and stared at him.

"If you knew that, why didn't you stop?"

"But Anna—"

"No, Raffaele. We could have been hurt. Our beautiful car is smashed, the boys missed seeing the ocean, and we're having my picnic lunch in the dining room."

She pushed on his chest, then poked him. "You should have stopped. You are your father's son, always right in everything. Today, you were wrong. You are not a Baron here in America."

"But—" His shoulders sagged.

"No excuses." Anna glared at him, again. "You get our car repaired so our sons can see the ocean. Do you understand?"

She was furious. He knew he'd crossed the line, so he just nodded.

"Now we are going in there to have our picnic lunch." She took a deep breath and said, "You are going to tell the boys you're sorry for what happened, and that as soon is the car is repaired you will take them to the beach. Any questions?"

He swallowed tight-lipped and shook his head.

She brushed by him into the dining room.

He turned and followed her.

She sat and smiled at the boys. "Your father wants to talk with you about what happed today. Don't you, Raffaele?"

CHAPTER NINETEEN

SNOW CONES 1927

"Come here, Paulo," his father called up the stairs.

Paulo turned the English book face down on his homework and bounced down the stairs, his second trip down in the past half hour.

His father and some friends sat around the dining room table. They greeted him with even more enthusiasm than when he brought up the first pitcher of wine.

His father held out the big ceramic pitcher. "Bring more wine for our guests."

Paulo went to the basement, filled the pitcher from a small barrel, and carried it up to the circle of men. The lively discussion quieted as he reappeared.

"Here's my boy," Raffaele said proudly. "Thank you, son."

"Anything for you, Pop." Paulo bowed theatrically from the waist, causing the group to break into laughter and applause.

His father lifted his glass. "Salute, my friends."

"Salute," chorused the group.

Paulo turned and took the stairs two at a time back to his room.

This Saturday afternoon gathering was a ritual at the Price Street home. His father and friends discussed current events, family achievements, and always the old country.

Enrico, who owned the delicatessen was a regular. Mr. Mannino, the iceman came most Saturdays. Musician friends, from his father's time playing in the band, often dropped by, along with co-workers from Wanamaker's. Depending on how many pitchers Paulo brought them, there could be music and singing before dinner.

In his bedroom, Paulo glanced at the homework on the small table against the wall. He couldn't face diagramming sentences so closed the schoolbook.

Instead, he walked to the window and stared at the clouds above the row home roofs on the street behind his house.

"Who cares about the difference between a subject and verb?" he muttered. Stretching his arms over his head he yawned and flopped down on the bed with his hands behind his head, listening to the conversation downstairs.

"The grapes were good this year," he heard his father say. "Already I have barrels fermenting."

"How do you crush so fast?" Enrico asked.

"Planning, my friend—and responsibility."

"Responsibility?" asked Mr. Mannino.

"Every day, when Paulo comes home from school, he turns the handle on my press. Everyday. That's his responsibility."

Paulo grinned. "You got that right. I'm the royal grape squeezer."

"Paulo's a good boy," Enrico added.

Paulo made a thumbs up sign and mouthed, "Thank you,"

"On the weekends, he and Vincenzo help me put the juice into barrels. Both my sons are good boys," Raffaele said.

"It's good to have Italian sons, eh?" Paulo heard Mr. Mannino say.

"Salute!" said the group and the conversation continued.

Paulo lost interest until he heard his father say something about prohibition. He got up, stood by the bedroom door, and peeked downstairs.

"It makes no sense. People drink, right?" his father said louder.

There was boisterous agreement from the entire table.

"Now people sneaking to speakeasies make gangsters rich."

"Like Mafioso in the old country."

"Well, it's good to be an Italian in America," his father declared. "We can make good wine, give some to our policeman, and nobody bothers us."

His father raised his glass. "Salute, America."

Another chorus of "Salute" was accompanied by the sound of clinking glasses.

Paulo shut the bedroom door and sat down to his homework. He counted the mimeographed pages and mumbled, "Only three more to go. Yeah, for me."

The following Tuesday was a hot and humid September day. Paulo, Eddie, and Alonso stopped in the shade of a tree on the way home from high school.

Paulo wiped the sweat off his forehead with the back of his hand. "You guys want to stop by my house for something cold to drink?"

"Okay by me," Eddie said. Alonso added, "Sure."

Paulo unlocked the front door and went into the kitchen. On the counter up against the backsplash sat an empty wine bottle. Thinking of his daily chore in the basement, he asked, "How'd you like a snow cone instead of just water?"

"Yeah, that'd be great," Alonso said with Eddie nodding in agreement.

"Come downstairs and, help me find something sweet to put on them."

In the basement, he turned the press handle the required turns, before the three boys took sips from the different small barrels of fermenting wine. Nothing was sweet.

"What about those?" Alonso said, pointing to racks of bottled wines on shelves above the small barrels.

Paulo thought his father wouldn't miss a little from a barrel. But a bottle?

Eddie came up next to him. "What's wrong?"

"My father corked every one of those himself. He knows when each will be ready to drink."

"Okay…" Alonso swept his hand around the room, "Any he won't drink right away?"

His father hung special white grapes on drying racks before pressing them to make his Vino Santo, a dessert wine he only served on special "occasions."

"Yeah, I know one, and it's sweet." Why not take a chance? Maybe he wouldn't miss one. He pulled a dusty bottle from the top rack.

Back upstairs, Paulo took one of the metal ice trays from his mother's new, white Kelvinator, ran water on the bottom, and banged it on the cutting board to dislodge the ice cubes. He put a dishtowel over them, and with the tenderizing mallet, pounded them. "Get some glasses," he said, pointing to the cupboard in front of Eddie.

Paulo lifted the towel and put it back down. After a few more hits he laid the mallet down, uncovered the chips, and scooped them into their glasses.

He wiped the bottle off with a damp dishtowel, opened it, and poured a little of the wine over their snow cones.

All three took a sip, looked at one another, and pronounced it good—very good!

Paulo led them to the dining room. They sat, treasuring the unexpected treat.

When they finished, Paulo crushed a second tray of ice cubes and Alonso scooped chips into his empty glass.

"What a great idea, Paulo." Eddie grinned, refilling his glass with pieces of ice.

Back at the table, Alonso, and Eddie toasted their host and consumed the snow cones with relish.

Crushing the third tray of ice cubes took Paulo longer, his pounding less accurate.

"Come on, you're missing them," Eddie teased.

Alonso, leaned on the counter, giggling. "Maybe they're moving."

Paulo tried to bop him on the head with the mallet but missed.

The final round of snow cones was more wine than ice chips.

Around four-thirty, Eddie, his words slurred, announced, "I gotta go home now."

"Yeah, me too." Alonzo pointed at Eddie, "With him."

Paulo opened the front door and watched the two of them carefully navigate the front porch steps one at a time. "See you guys tomorrow."

"Okay, tomorrow," Eddie answered, bumping into Alonso.

Paulo grinned as he watched his unsteady friends go down the sidewalk. He shut the front door, and concentrated as he put the glasses, ice cube trays, and mallet in the sink and the Vino Santo bottle in the trashcan. As he climbed the stairs slowly, he stopped to lean against the wall, held onto the jam of his bedroom door for a moment, before falling face down on his bed.

On her walk home, Anna stopped for Vincenzo, who played after school at a neighbor's house. They arrived home a little after five o'clock. Not hearing any noise from upstairs, called out, "Paulo?"

No answer.

"Vincenzo, see if your brother's home and wash up."

He went up and immediately and came back down, saying Paulo was sprawled across his bed.

"I touched him, Mama, but he didn't move."

Her energetic eldest son never took naps, so she went to check on him.

The bedroom door was open, but Anna called his name as she entered. Paulo was lying on his stomach. Anna went to the bed, sat down, and touched his shoulder with no response. She pushed harder. "Paulo." He mumbled something she didn't understand.

Just then, Anna heard Raffaele's car on the driveway behind the house. She told Vincenzo to get his father. When she heard her husband come in the house, she called to him in an anxious voice. "Raffaele come upstairs. Paulo's sick."

By the time her husband came through the bedroom door, Vincenzo was on the other side of the bed staring at his brother with worry.

Anna sat on the bed, rubbing Paulo's back, her anxiety growing. "What's wrong with him, Raffaele? Do we need to call the doctor?"

With his hand on her shoulder, he said sternly, "Paulo, wake up."

Anna stood. Raffaele sat on the bed and turned Paulo onto his back.

Paulo's eyes fluttered open and he looked at his father with a glassy stare.

Raffaele leaned over for a closer look, just as Paulo belched.

"Jeeza ma Christ," he said, waving his hand in front of his face. "He smells of wine. I think he's drunk."

"What?" her voice rose.

Raffaele looked across the bed at Vincenzo. "Did you drink, too?"

Vincenzo shook his head vigorously. "I came home with, Mama."

"He's just boy." Anna's voice trembled. "Should we call the doctor?"

"No. He'll have a headache tomorrow. That's all."

"Are you sure?"

"Let him asleep. He'll be fine." He looked at Paulo and smiled.

Anna saw the smile. "Why are you smiling? Our son is lying there—"

"He had a little too much wine, that's all."

"But—"

"He's a good boy," Raffaele said. "I was about his age the first time I got drunk."

Anna took a deep breath, frowned at her husband, crossed herself, and shook her head. "Our son's drunk, Raffaele." She glared at him, turned, and went downstairs.

Raffaele followed her downstairs into the kitchen. "He'll be all right, Anna."

She put on her apron then spotted the glasses, ice cube trays, and mallet in the sink, she said, "Raffaele, Paulo didn't drink alone."

"What? How do you know?"

"Come and see for yourself," she said, standing with her back to the counter and arms crossed. She glanced into the sink and back at him.

He peered in the sink. "I wonder what they drank?"

She snorted. "I want to know who else was here."

"Probably his friends."

"Those parents are going to be upset!"

Raffaele opened the cupboard door under the sink and pulled out the trashcan. "Ah, Vino Santo and smashed ice. They made snow cones."

"And got drunk, Raffaele."

Anna's hand went to her mouth when the phone rang.

Her husband picked up the receiver. "Hello?"

Alonso's father was on the other end of the line.

Raffaele listened for a few moments. "He probably was here. Paulo's asleep too. We found glasses in the sink and an empty wine bottle."

He was silent again. "Hey, Paulo's a good boy, too. It was hot today. They poured some Vino Santo over ice chips. How old were you the first time you had too much wine?"

After listening some more, he said, "I will talk to Paulo," and hung up. Eddie's father called fifteen minutes later; Anna heard a similar conversation.

When Raffaele got off the phone, he looked at Anna, and shrugged. "Some people don't want to remember their youth."

She followed him into the front room, wiping her hands on her apron, and sat down on the end of couch closest to his armchair. "Were they very angry?"

"A little. Don't worry."

"Eddie and Alonso are Paulo's best friends. I hope this doesn't—"

"Anna, their father's will tell them not to drink, that's all. They're still going to be friends." With a sympathetic look, he added, "It'll probably be talked about at church."

"I know," she said, crossing herself again.

"Anna, you're a good mother, and Paulo's a good boy. They didn't do anything bad. They're boys, and boys sometimes break rules."

Before the dinner was served, Raffaele smiled at Anna and Vincenzo.

"I'm a lucky man to have a beautiful wife, and good sons." He raised his glass. "To my family." Looking at the stairs, he added, "And to our sleeping wine taster."

The next morning, Anna took Vincenzo to Mass with her.

Paulo came downstairs an hour after they left and found his father in the basement. "Pop—"

"Well, good morning snow cone boy."

Paulo's eyes dropped. "I'm sorry about the wine."

"Never be sorry about good wine." Raffaele motioned for his son to come closer and hugged him. "How does your head feel?"

Paulo rubbed his temple. "It hurts a little."

Raffaele held him at arm's length. "You can't drink Vino Santo like Chianti." He lifted his son's chin. "It's also not good to get your friends drunk."

"Yes, Pop."

Raffaele kissed him gently on the forehead. "Your mother is at church praying for your soul. If I, were you, I'd look my best and be ready for an inquisition when she's home."

He watched Paulo go up the basement stairs slowly and smiled, thinking how much the Saturday group was going to enjoy hearing the snow cone story.

CHAPTER TWENTY

GYMNASTICS 9TH GRADE SPRING SEMESTER 1927

In middle school, Paulo's primary extracurricular activity was the violin. He'd enjoyed dodge ball on the playground, indoor bombardment dodge ball, and ping pong at the YMCA. When he enrolled at Germantown High School, he was five-foot-seven, weighed a hundred and five pounds, and wisely chose not to play football. After the Christmas holidays, when tryouts for spring sports were announced, he discovered gymnastics. A competitive sport, it was based on individual effort, and considered cool. His counselor switched him into sixth period gym, and the coach assigned him to the Junior Varsity squad.

The first day of class, Coach Gallo tested everyone's physical fitness, then had them watch the Varsity Squad workout. The older boys were muscular and graceful, controlled and explosive at the same time. The fluid movements entranced Paulo. He never missed a day of school after that, was never tardy for sixth period, and frequently stayed after school to practice. His favorite apparatuses were the horizontal bar and still rings.

At the end of the semester, Coach Gallo talked to his students individually, about their effort, skill development, performance, and intentions for the next year. At the end of meeting, he gave them their grade. He met with varsity students first, and then junior varsity students. Paulo was the last student he called into his office.

"Come in, Paulo," Coach Gallo said, motioning to a chair in front of his desk. "How are you, today?"

Paulo swallowed. "A little nervous, Coach."

"Why?"

"Cause I'm the last one."

Coach smiled and leaned back in his swivel chair. "Tell me…what kind of grade do think you've earned in gymnastics?"

He thought for a moment before saying, "I think…maybe a 'B'."

"Really?" Coach Gallo put his elbows on the desk, rested his chin on his hands. "Why is that?"

"I've worked hard, never missed practice, and I've improved on the apparatuses."

"I agree with the first two, but not the last one. You haven't just improved you've shown remarkable skill development. You can almost do a 'Baby Giant' swing on the high bar."

Paulo grinned.

"None of the other freshman worked as hard as you in the weight room."

"Thanks Coach."

"What about next year. Are you coming back?"

"Absolutely."

"Excellent." Coach Gallo came around the desk and shook Paulo's hand. "I'm giving you an 'A' in gymnastics…and promoting you to next year's varsity squad. Have a great summer, Paulo."

Paulo jogged most of the way home, bounded up the front steps, and burst into the house.

"Guess what, Mama?"

Anna startled, turned, with her hand on her chest.

"I got an 'A' in gymnastics," Paulo said, picking her up and giving her a big hug.

When he let her down, she looked up at him and patted his cheeks. "That's my bambino. What about music?"

Paulo smiled, "An 'A' of course, Mama."

"And your other classes, English, history—"

"A's" he said quickly.

"And—"

Paulo glanced down. "A 'B' in geometry, but a 'B plus' in science," he said meeting her eyes.

"That's good, Paulo." She wagged a finger at him. "Never forget, school is the door to your life."

"Yes, Mama."

On Saturday morning, Paulo went for his weekly violin lesson with

Signore Lombardi. Three years had passed since Father Donati gave him his first violin. After a few months of lessons from the parish priest, Paulo's musical talent was obvious, so Father Donati arranged for Signore Lombardi, a professional teacher, to work with Paulo, as his contribution to the church.

Paulo knocked on Signore Lombardi's door.

"Avanti, Signore Colaluca," came the welcoming voice.

"Good morning, Signore Lombardi," Paulo said, bowing his head slightly as they shook hands.

"And how are you this fine day, Paulo?" asked the elderly man. He was shorter than his student, with wispy gray hair, bushy eyebrows, and smile crinkles framing his clear blue eyes.

"Good, thank you."

"And your family?"

"Everyone is well, thank you."

And your practice, it has gone well?"

Paulo nodded. "Yes."

"Let me hear, per favore."

Paulo set his sheet music on the stand, took his bow out of the case, tightened it, rubbed rosin on the hair, and carefully lifted the violin out of its case. He plucked the strings to check the tuning and quickly played a series of scales. He glanced at Signore Lombardi, who nodded, and the lesson began.

Signore Lombardi listened intently, swaying his head, and occasionally closing his eyes.

When Paulo finished the piece, his teacher said, "Play it again, piu lento, slower."

Each time Paulo finished playing the piece, Signore Lombardi talked to him about technique and musicality, sometimes playing his own violin to demonstrate.

"You did well today, Signore Colaluca," his teacher said, as at the lesson ended. He shook Paulo's hand, then turned it over and gently rubbed the callouses. "These are from your swinging class?" he asked.

"Gymnastics, yes," Paulo answered.

"They could be why you struggled a little with fingering today. Will you continue with the swinging class?"

"Not until next year...in the spring."

"Good." Signore Lombardi smiled. "Ask your mother for some lotion to soften your hands. It will help your playing. You are a talented young man, Paulo. With your gift, and serious practice, you can realize your dream of being a concert violinist.

As Paulo reached the door, Signore Lombardi said, "I almost forgot, how are your students doing?"

"I think well," Paulo replied. Father Donati had asked him to work with two young students at church who wanted to learn the violin. Paulo had said he wasn't good enough to teach yet, but both Father Donati and his teacher encouraged him to try. His mother simply said he should.

"We're practicing the basics…you know, care of the bow, tuning. It's only been a month. They've learned how to grip the bow and hold the violin but are still working on hand position. We play the strings each time," Paulo grimaced. "Such sounds. Was I like that?"

Signore Lombardi chuckled. "Only for a short time."

"This week I'll start them playing the open strings—"

Winking at Paulo, Signore Lombardi said, "Go slow, Paulo, let them have small victories at first, and enjoy their time with you."

After Sunday church, Paulo relaxed with his students, complimenting them often, and played simple tunes for them using only open strings.

Father Donati was at the classroom door and praised the children as they left. "Things seem to be going well, Paulo."

"Thank you, Father."

Father Donati handed him an envelope.

"What's this?"

"Your student's parents wanted to give you something for teaching their children. I told them it was not necessary because you were volunteering your time, but they insisted. My parishioners are proud people, Paulo, so I said you would except their gift this one time."

Paulo was quiet, then in a soft voice said, "Thank you, Father Donati."

Outside the church, he looked in the envelope and found four one-dollar bills. It was the first money he'd earned playing the violin.

On his walk home, he passed the neighborhood diner with its familiar, red-bordered sign in the window, advertising "Salisbury Steak Dinner $1.50."

Paulo walked a few more steps. Hearing his stomach growl, he thought, "Sunday dinner won't be until four o'clock." His stomach growled again.

He'd never had a Salisbury Steak—or four dollars. Inside he sat down by the window and a motherly looking waitress brought him a menu.

"What would you like to drink, young man?" she asked, looking at his violin case.

"Uh, nothing, thank you."

"You play?"

"Yes, in the school orchestra."

"What grade are you in?"

"Ninth…well, tenth grade in the fall."

"I see. Have you decided what you'd like?"

Paulo pointed on the menu.

"Excellent choice…are you sure you can afford it?"

Paulo pulled out the envelope and held it open, "I just got paid for teaching violin."

"How about some water? It's free," she said with a smile.

The water glass came quickly, but it seemed like forever until she brought his meal.

"Be careful, sweetheart, the plate's hot."

Mashed potatoes nestled on one end of the sizzling steak, and peas and carrots on the other end. Paulo put his napkin in his lap, carefully cut a piece of the "steak", and began to chew. He stopped and stared at his plate. The "steak" was hamburger. "Like Mama's meatballs," he thought, "but not as good." Paulo stared at the plate for a moment, and after his stomach growled, he finished every bite. He never told his parents.

CHAPTER TWENTY ONE

DIFFICULT CHOICES 10TH GRADE SPRING SEMESTER 1928

His second year on the gymnastics team was even better than the first. Working out with the Varsity Squad was tougher and pushed him to improve his skills. Paulo's daily workout in the weight room showed in his upper body and core strength. The high bar was his favorite apparatus. By June, he could Kip up on the bar, do a Cast Handstand into Baby Giant Swing, and land a Flyaway dismount.

One day, after dismounting, Paulo felt Coach Gallo's muscled hand squeeze the back of his neck. "That was a good routine. Your strength training is paying off."

Coach Gallo turned him around. "I'm really pleased with your progress. Keep this up and I'll have to make you a team alternate on the high bar next year."

"Wow! Thanks, Coach."

At his Saturday violin lesson, Signore Lombardi was not as pleased as Coach Gallo. The teacher asked him to replay "Gaviote from Mignon." He listened, eyes closed, then asked, "Are you practicing your scales?"

"Yes. Everyday."

Signore Lombardi rose from his wine-colored, wingback chair, walked to Paulo, took the violin, and played the beginning of the piece. Handing the violin back, he said, "Again, favore."

Signore Lombardi intently watched his fingering and bowing. "Stop. Let me see your hand." He touched the callouses on Paulo's left hand and shook his head. With sad eyes, he cradled Paulo's face in his hands. "You have such talent, bambino."

He returned to his chair and motioned for Paulo to sit on the ottoman.

"You told me you dream of being a concert violinist. Do you want to reach your dream?"

Paulo looked down, then nodded.

Signore Lombardi lifted his chin and looked into Paulo's eyes. "You cannot advance with those hands, so you must choose violin over your swinging class. In two years, you will be ready to apply and, I believe, win a scholarship to the Philadelphia Conservatory of Music, where you will find your dream."

As he walked home, Paulo thought about Mr. Lombardi's words, and then what Coach Gallo said about next year, replaying each conversation in his mind. He was quiet when he came through the front door at home and went to his room.

Anna looked quizzically at Raffaele sitting in his armchair, who shrugged his shoulders and shook his head.

"Go talk to him...something's wrong."

When Raffaele looked in the room, Paulo was face down on his bed, looking away from the door. He sat on the edge of the bed. "What's wrong, Paulo?"

"Nothing..."

"Turn over, let me see your face."

"No!"

"Paulo, favore."

As he rolled over, he wiped his wet cheeks with the backs of his hands.

"Bambino, why are you crying?"

"Because I don't know what to do?"

"About what?"

Paulo shared what Coach Gallo told him, and then what Signore Lombardi said. "I want to please them both. How can I choose?"

Raffaele considered his words before saying, "It's not about pleasing them, Paulo, it's about pleasing yourself. Choose what you love—and it will be with you always." He stood, bent down, and kissed Paulo on the forehead.

Later in the afternoon, Raffaele and Anna heard violin music wafting up from the basement, as Paulo played a lively minuet.

Monday, at sixth period, Paulo asked to talk with Coach Gallo privately.

"Sure, Paulo. Can it wait until after class? I'm busy spotting beginners."

Paulo nodded and went to the weight room to stretch and work out.

After class, Paulo stood outside the office door when Coach Gallo walked up.

"Okay, what's up?" He motioned Paulo inside and sat on the corner of his desk.

"I need to…I want to tell you…I won't be coming back next year."

"I'm sorry to hear that, Paulo. I will miss you. Where are you moving to?"

"Uh, I'm not moving, Coach. I just won't be in gymnastics."

"May I ask why? You're doing so well."

Paulo sighed. "You know I play the violin?"

"Yes, I've heard you play with the school orchestra. You're very good."

"Thank you, but my violin teacher, Signore Lombardi, says I won't be able to play more advanced music with these callouses." He held out his palms. "It makes fingering difficult." He pretended to play, moving the fingers on his left hand.

"I see."

"I'm sorry, Coach."

"No, Paulo, I understand. When you played your solo at the school recital, I could see you love playing the violin."

Coach extended his hand and the two shook before Paulo hugged his coach, who hugged him back and held him at arms-length. "Finding what you love to do, Paulo, is what life is all about. The violin will always bring you joy."

"Thanks, Coach." Paulo waited until he was outside to wipe away his tears.

Over summer, Paulo concentrated on his violin lessons, using lotion each morning to soften and remove the callouses. As his renewed focus showed, Signore Lombardi assigned him intermediate level concertos to memorize. Paulo found his "after Mass" students more fun to teach.

With no organized outlet for his energy, Paulo decided to go back to the Germantown YMCA, his afterschool hangout during middle school, where he learned to play ping pong. When he walked into the familiar room a young boy at one of the tables motioned to him.

"Wanna play?"

Paulo shook his head.

"Please."

Paulo looked around, saw nobody else interested and said, "Well…okay."

"Thanks. No one wants to play me. I'm not very good."

When the boy hit his serve into the net, Paulo said, "How about we work on getting the ball over the net, okay?"

"Okay," he answered sheepishly.

Paulo picked up the ball. "What grade are you in?"

The boy looked up. "Eighth,"

"What's your name?"

"Luca."

"Nice to meet you, Luca. I'm Paulo. Hold the ball in your hand like this, and hit it a little downward, not at the net." He served. "Now you try."

For the next fifteen minutes, Paulo rallied gently with the boy, explaining how to play, until they could keep the ball in play for several hits back and forth.

Fred, the YMCA Counselor walked up. "Luca, your mom said you could stay only until lunchtime...remember?"

"Will you play with me again?" Luca asked.

Paulo grinned. "Maybe."

"I hope so," he said as he ran toward the door.

"You made quite an impression on him." He extended his hand. "My name's Fred, I'm a part-time Counselor here."

"Paulo," he said as they shook hands. "You go to Temple?"

Fred looked down at the logo on his shirt. "Yep, a junior this fall."

Paulo gave an appreciative nod.

"What about you?"

"Germantown High School, also a junior this fall."

"Well, I hope you come back." He pointed to the lacquered board on the wall by the door. "Maybe get on our ladder? See how high you could get?"

"I know Luca will appreciate any time you could give him. Nice meeting you."

Paulo found time to play and coach Luca a couple of times a week. By the end of summer, his protégé was no longer at the bottom of the ladder.

CHAPTER TWENTY TWO

PING PONG BOY 11ᵀᴴ GRADE
END OF SPRING SEMESTER 1929

The dismissal bell started ringing; Paulo was at the door before it stopped. Students jostled behind him, waiting for the magic words.

"Class dismissed," the teacher intoned, adding, "have a nice weekend."

Paulo quick-stepped along the fast-filling hallway, taking the stairs two steps at a time. *Only two more weeks until I'm a twelfth grader*, he thought. Outside, he headed to the "Y".

Since quitting the school's gymnastics team, ping pong at the Germantown YMCA, was his afterschool sport. The frosted-transom windows high on the outside wall of the gym were open but couldn't disperse the smell of sweat from basketball drills.

"Pretty steamy in here," he said, coming through the open double doors.

"Always on Fridays—and it's June," replied Fred, in a Temple University T-Shirt. He directed boys, wheeling folded ping pong tables across the floor.

Paulo dropped his binder and books by the wall and pulled the last table out of the equipment room.

Fred straightened the polished oak board on the wall behind his card table and sat down. LADDER BOARD was printed across the top in one-inch, black letters. "Come sign in, guys, and tell me who you're challenging."

Paulo lowered the table, tightened the stiff green net, and stood in line to study the board. Ten brass cup-hooks in each of the five vertical rows had a small, metal-rimmed, paper disc with a boy's name. To the left of the discs were numbers in descending order. His disc was number three in column one.

Paulo signed in, checked the line, and said to Fred, "Jackson's not here...again."

"I think he's afraid of you." Fred grinned.

"He should be," Paulo said. "Who's challenging me?"

"Number 4, Alonzo." The rule was that you had to challenge and beat the number above you to advance up the ladder board.

"Again? He's persistent, I'll give him that. Fred, I've been number three for the past month because Jackson and his buddy, Cornelius, are avoiding me. It's not fair. Isn't there some rule about not showing up?"

"Yes, for team sports. I'll talk to the Director, okay?" He lowered his voice. "Think of Alonzo as a warm-up for the big tournament in couple of weeks."

"Jackson would be better." Paulo walked to the first of the six tables in the middle of the gym, where Alonzo waited. He picked up the red, dimpled paddle and ball and bounced the ball to him. "Challengers serve first."

The game took twenty minutes, with a few closely contested points. The final score was 21-14.

"Thanks for the game," Paulo said, as they shook hands, "you had me going a couple of times. Want to practice and work on your backhand?"

"Thanks, Paulo, but I see number five is waiting to challenge. Maybe after that?"

"Sure, any time," he said, walking back to the sign-up table, just as Fred came through the double doors.

"Paulo, the Director's in a meeting but I left him a note about your question."

Paulo hung around for another hour, playing practice games. When Jackson didn't show, he went home.

At the gym Monday after school, Fred called Paulo over.

"The Director called me to his office when I arrived today and handed me this." He read from the mimeographed sheet. "Ping Pong Rules Addendum: Players who are challenged have a week to play the challenger, or will forfeit the match, and the challenger will be declared the winner."

He gave Paulo the paper. "It's being added to the section on sports rules."

With raised eyebrows, Paulo said, "That was fast...when does it start?'

"Today." Fred picked up the sign-in book, and in a voice loud enough for everyone in the gym to hear, he asked, "You, Paulo, are officially challenging Jackson to a match, is that correct?"

"Yes, I am."

Fred entered it with a flourish.

"How will he know he's been challenged?"

"I've called and left a message with his mother about the new rule, and your challenge."

"What happens if I'm not here when he finally decides to show up?"

"He has to play you within a week, or he forfeits, period."

There was a hint of a smile on Paulo's face. "So, say I don't come in tomorrow, and he does, does my challenge still stand?"

"Until Monday, whether you're here or not."

Paulo grinned. "Okay then, I'll see you later."

"Where are you going?"

Paulo shrugged. "Not sure…I've got things to do."

The next Monday, Paulo strolled into the Y and saw an unhappy Jackson.

"I've been here all week! Where the hell have you been?" he said so everyone in the gym could hear.

"Around," Paulo said calmly, "How does it feel to be kept waiting?"

"You damn wop!"

"This damn wop is going to beat your ass."

Fred stepped between them. "Gentlemen! Do not forget this is the Young Men's Christian Association. Watch your language."

All activity in the gym stopped as Paulo and Jackson took their places at opposite ends of the table. Paulo, the challenger, served first and scored the first point on a flip of the wrist backhand, down the center of the table, that Jackson wasn't quick enough to block. Paulo scored five points in a row and Jackson's frustration was obvious. He pushed too hard, smashing errant balls off the table.

The angrier he became, the calmer Paulo played. His opponent's preferred offensive shot was a forehand topspin smash that Paulo defended with backspin returns, too low for Jackson to smash. It forced him to block Paulo's returns, which lifted the ball high enough for Paulo to counterattack. Jackson won a point here and there, while Paulo continued to score two- or three-point runs. The final score was 21-12.

Embarrassed at the lopsided defeat, Jackson slammed his paddle down on the table and left in a huff.

Paulo walked over to Fred, who was switching the number three and number two discs on the Ladder Board. "Quite a game, Paulo."

"Thanks. I liked it."

"You know, Seniors don't like to be embarrassed by lowly eleventh graders."

"They better get used to it…I challenge Cornelius."

Fred rubbed his forehead. 'You don't want to wait until after the city tournament on Saturday?"

Paulo shook his head. "Nope. He'll be a warm-up game—if he shows."

"Don't get cocky. He's better than Jackson."

"We'll see," Paulo said with a tight-lipped smirk.

Leaving the Y, he bounced down the front steps. Walking home, he thought about how much he'd missed being on the school gymnastic team he'd dropped to focus on his dream of becoming a concert violinist. Ping pong at the YMCA, had given him a way to be athletic and compete without damaging his hands. He'd played almost every day after school, challenging whoever had beaten him, learning about the other player's preferred side, forehand or backhand, how to maneuver him to set up a smash, when to use backspin, topspin, or angle the ball with a slice. Doing it with the flick of his wrist felt even better than giant swings on the high bar. He'd moved up the ladder steadily, each win boosting his confidence and, each loss fueling his drive to be better.

At home, he set his binder and books on the mahogany sideboard.

"I'm home, Mama."

"How's my ping pong boy?" Anna said from the kitchen. "Did you win?"

"Yes, Mama," he said, walking into the kitchen. "What are you making?"

"Rigatoni."

"Sure smells good." He reached in the breadbox and dipped a piece into the simmering saucepan.

"Are you ever full?" she said with a hint of a smile.

He blew on the bread. "You're just too good a cook, Mama."

"Oh, my—what a smooth talker."

"Did Vincenzo remember to turn the wine press?"

"He got home before me, you better check."

Paulo opened the basement door, switched on the light, and went downstairs. His father's wine press stood in the corner. The slatted wooden basket was eighteen inches high, fifteen inches in diameter, and set in a sturdy frame. A three-foot metal screw with a handle at the top ran through the crossbar, down into the basket, and attached to a pressure plate.

Vincenzo was now responsible for turning the handle half a turn every day after school, to gently crush the grapes for his father. Paulo looked to see if the tight slats were moist from juice being squeezed through. They weren't and nothing was dripping into the bucket underneath.

On his way up to their bedroom, Paulo grabbed his books and binder off the sideboard. Vincenzo was lying on his bed engrossed in a book.

"Did you turn the press?"

"Not yet."

"You're supposed to do it right after you get home from school."

They both heard the garage door going up

"Good luck explaining that Dr. Dolittle is more important than his wine."

Vincenzo was out the door before Paulo finished. "No snitching," he said.

"Dinner's ready," Anna called. "Paulo, would you go tell Vincenzo?"

"I know, Mama," Vincenzo yelled, going down the basement stairs.

By the time, Raffaele lowered the garage door, got his briefcase out of the car, and walked through into the basement, Vincenzo was at the wine press watching juice starting to drip into the bucket.

"Everything okay, Vincenzo?" Raffaele asked.

"Yeah, Pop, I'm just checking to make sure it's draining."

Raffaele ruffled his son's hair. "Good boy."

Upstairs, Paulo set the table and helped his mother bring in the rigatoni, salad, and warm bread.

When the four of them were seated, Anna said grace, and passed the salad and bread, while Raffaele served the pasta and meatballs.

"Where's Clara, tonight," he asked Anna.

"She's out with some teacher friends."

"Our family's shrinking," Raffaele said wistfully,

"I miss her too," Anna said, hand on her heart, "but we still have our boys."

"Boys are the best anyway," Vincenzo declared, earning a long disapproving look from his mother.

"Paulo, any nervousness about the big Saturday tournament?" Anna asked.

"Why would he be nervous?" Raffaele said, fork in midair. "He's the best ping pong boy at the YMCA."

"A lot of good players will be there, Pop, from the YMCA, Boy's Clubs, and high schools. It's a city-wide tournament."

"I think you're going to win, Paulo," Vincenzo chimed in.

"I'm going to do my best."

"That's all that's important," Anna said, smiling at her eldest son.

The YMCA was hosting the city-wide tournament at their newly opened Armed Forces Branch, a towering, redbrick high-rise, on Fifteenth Street, near the Navy Yard. Raffaele parked, and the family walked through the gymnasium's double doors a half-hour before the official nine o'clock registration. Inside a wide hallway were tables running down the right side. A few other families also arrived early and were signing in.

Paulo led his parents and brother down the row to where Fred sat behind a table and introduced his parents and Vincenzo.

"Mr. and Mrs. Colaluca, I want you to know it's been a pleasure to work with Paulo this past year," Fred said, as he shook Raffaele's hand. "He's worked hard to improve his game and is always willing to coach other boys. He is one of the best ping pong players here today."

"Paulo," Fred pointed behind them, "the first row of bleachers inside, on both sides of the gymnasium, are reserved for contestants. If your family sits a few rows up behind you, they can watch all the action. Best of luck today."

The YMCA's gymnasium was bigger than the gym at the Germantown Branch. When the bleachers were pulled back, three basketball games could be played at the same time. Under the big clock, high on the back wall, was a long banner in large block letters: "Philadelphia City-Wide Ping Pong Tournament."

With the bleachers pulled out, a row of ten, shiny-green, ping pong tables filled the center court, with red paddles in place. The ends of the tables faced the bleachers. Paulo helped his parents get seated on the left side of the gym. He told Vincenzo he couldn't sit with him on the contestant's bench, then went down to the floor, sitting at the end of the growing line of boys.

The boy next to him stuck out his right hand. "My name's Dominic."

Paulo shook his hand. "Paulo. Where do you play?"

"Boy's Club. You?"

"Germantown YMCA."

"What grade you in?"

"Eleventh for a few more days."

"I graduated on Thursday. No more school for me," Dominic said smiling.

Paulo leaned forward and counted. There were seven boys ahead of him in line. "*I'm eighth, he thought. I'll play in the first round.*"

The contestant lines on both sides of the gym kept growing. Paulo watched Jackson and Cornelius walk in on the opposite side of the gym, just before ten o'clock and sit at the end of the line. There were over a hundred contestants.

The mayor welcomed all the families and contestants, thanked the YMCA for hosting the tournament, recognized the school district, Boy's Clubs, other organizations with contestants at the tournament, and officially opened the competition. The first ten boys from both sides of the gym went to a table, balls were distributed, and play began.

Paulo's first opponent would not have made his club's top ten, losing 21-10. After the game, they shook hands, left the paddles on the table, and handed the ball to the referee. Winners went to the end of their contestant line and losers joined their parents in the bleachers.

Paulo watched each match, intently checking out which boys were winning on the other side. His second match was against a tall rangy kid whose offense was good, but who lacked quickness on defense. The boy lost 21-13 because he couldn't return sharply angled shots to the sides of the table.

The contestant line started moving more quickly, so Paulo didn't wait long to play again. His third match was harder. The boy was a head shorter, thin, wiry, and quick as a cat. They traded points as Paulo probed for weaknesses in the other boy's game. Finally, at 10-10, he noticed his opponent liked to run around smashes to his backhand side, so he could return it with his stronger forehand. Paulo repeatedly hit to the boy's backhand and won 21-14.

On it went for rounds four and five. Although the scores got closer, Paulo was never behind. He always figured out and exploited their weaknesses.

Then came round six with only four contestants left. Cornelius glared at him from another table. Paulo was overly confident and made two sloppy errors at the start. His opponent held the lead until the score was 17-19. It was hot in the gym and both boys were sweating. As the other boy started to serve, the paddle slipped in his hand, netting the serve, which gave Paulo the serve. He won the next four points, making the final score 21-19.

Many families of losing contestants stayed to see the end of the competition and moved down the bleachers to watch the championship match.

When their names were announced, Cornelius looked over at Paulo and said, "This will be my warm-up for Monday, wop."

"In your dreams, Corny."

Cornelius sneered at him, won the coin toss, served, and smashed Paulo's return for the first point. Score 0-1.

Paulo knew he'd have to play his best to beat the blonde-haired boy across from him. He backed up two steps and crouched, bent his knees, and leaned forward, for the next serve. Again, it was low, fast, and down the middle of the table. He blocked it back low to Cornelius' backhand, who lifted his return enough for Paulo to rip a forehand to the other side of the table, just past his opponent's outstretched paddle.

Paulo's back spin serves surprised Cornelius who netted his return. Score 1-1. For the rest of the match, both used every shot they knew, trying to gain an advantage. From either their forehands or backhands, they used top-spin and back-spin, sliced shots off the sides of the table, hit whistling smashes to the corners, or right down the middle, sometimes forcing the defenders back ten feet from the end of the table to return a shot.

At 11-11, Cornelius' high arching return of a smash bounced just on Paulo's side of the net. Paulo ran around the side of the table and hit the ball down on the other side so hard, it sailed high over Cornelius' head and out of play. Score 12-11. That was the turning point in the match.

Paulo scored two straight points, before Cornelius recovered his composure. Score 14-12. They traded points back and forth until the end. Final score 21-19.

The audience erupted in applause. Both boys were exhausted. Paulo walked around the table toward Cornelius and stuck out his hand.

"Lucky game, wop," and shook Paulo's hand.

"See you on Monday, Corny. You owe me a challenge."

After the trophy presentations for third, second, and first place, other contestants and their parents came to congratulate them and shake their hands.

Paulo's mother, eyes moist, kissed him. He was too tired to be embarrassed.

His father bear-hugged him. "Didn't I say you were the best ping pong boy?"

Vincenzo cradled the trophy all the way home in the car.

That afternoon, Anna placed the two-foot, marbled-based, red and gold trophy on the sideboard by the front door—so everyone who came in would see it first thing.

CHAPTER TWENTY THREE

THE CRASH AND A NEW FRIEND
12TH GRADE FALL SEMESTER 1929

The Stock Market's over-valued climb ended on August 1, 1929. Reckless speculation, coupled with a struggling economy hamstrung by drought, falling food prices, and an excess of large bank loans that couldn't be liquidated, ended the "Roaring Twenties."

A new transfer student, David, showed up in music class the first day of school in Paulo's senior year. David, who was also a senior, played the violin and auditioned for the orchestra with the others. The results would be posted the next day.

After class, Paulo introduced himself. "Hi, I'm Paulo. You play very well, David."

"Thanks, you do too. Friends call me Dave," he said, extending his hand. "Italiano?"

"Si." Paulo grinned. "You?"

"Of course!"

"Where are you—"

"South Philly." Dave said proudly.

"Me too." They walked together down the hallway to the stairs to the cafeteria. "I used to live on Sears and Watkins Streets before moving here in the sixth grade."

"Cool. Those streets aren't far from where I lived," Dave said.

"How's my old neighborhood?" Paulo asked.

"Probably hasn't changed much since you were there."

As they ate lunch, Dave asked, "Who was first chair last year?"

"I was."

"So was I at my last school."

Paulo grinned. "Looks like we both want the same thing."

"Best of luck, Paulo."

"And to you, friend."

The next day, audition results were posted outside of class. Paulo was first chair violin, Dave second chair.

After work that evening, Raffaele went silently to the kitchen, poured a glass of wine, and went to his armchair in the front room.

Anna turned the fire down under the bubbling soup and sat down across from him. "What's wrong?"

"Two men in my department were laid off today."

"Why?" Anna asked, concerned.

"My manager said that furniture sales had dried up."

"What does that mean, Raffaele?"

"It means customers are not buying furniture at Wanamaker's."

"What about your job?"

"He told me furniture always needs to be repaired and after fifteen years with Wanamaker's, I don't need to worry. I'm sad for my friends, Anna."

She saw his moist eyes. "I know, amore mio. I know." She kissed his forehead, squeezed his hand, and went back to the kitchen to finish dinner.

Raffaele took a sip of wine.

Paulo came in the front door from afterschool violin practice and announced, "Mama, you're looking at the new first chair violinist in the Germantown High School Orchestra." He lifted the kettle lid, then dropped it. "Hot!" he said, blowing on his fingers. "What's for dinner?"

"Zuppa Pancetta, Mr. First Chair. Out of the kitchen. It'll be ready in a few minutes. Go wash and make sure Vincenzo does, too."

At dinner, Paulo told his mother, father, and brother about his selection as first chair, and practicing after school with the violin section.

"How good is the new kid?" Vincenzo asked.

"Dave is a very good violinist."

"Just not as good as you, right?" Vincenzo added.

Anna gave her youngest a reproving stare, as Raffaele cleared his throat.

"First chair is an honor. You must know the music better than anyone else. Practice and love of the music is what makes a good First Chair."

Paulo nodded. "I know, Papa."

Slow rolling-layoffs continued at Wanamaker's in all departments throughout September and October, mainly those most recently hired. With Halloween looming, the Stock Market started downward. On October 24, 12.9 million shares were sold at a loss, on what became known as "Black Thursday." Five days later, on October 29, another 16 million shares were traded, and the Stock Market crashed.

In Paulo's Economics class, "The Crash" was the only topic for the rest of the semester. In the evenings, he tried to explain the news his parents heard on the radio.

One night at dinner, a frustrated Raffaele, said, "I don't understand. None of my friends had these crashed stocks and still they lose their jobs."

"Pop, when the Stock Market crashed, the people who bought shares in it, lost all their money."

"What are these shares?"

"They are pieces of paper with a company's name on them. The company says they are worth a certain amount of money, you buy them and hope the company does well and the value of your shares goes up."

When Raffaele still looked confused, he went on, "The reason the Stock Market crashed is complicated, Pop. The main reason is people stop buying items, so companies stop making them, causing the value of their shares to drop to nothing so people who owned shares lost all their money. Capisci?"

"Un po', a little."

Paulo liked helping his father understand. "My teacher says people who saved their money, like you, will be able to buy things for pennies on the dollar. It means, if something cost a dollar before the crash, now you might be able to buy it for a lot less, maybe even for pennies. Companies are desperate to sell whatever they make, Pop."

"According to the newspaper ads," Anna added, "Wanamaker's is already lowering the prices on your beautiful chairs and tables, Raffaele."

"But without jobs, my friends at work cannot buy anything."

"That's right," Paulo said, pleased that his father was understanding.

Anna let out a long sigh. "No food for their families."

"Worse than that," Paulo said, shaking his head, "they won't be able to make their mortgage payments, and banks will be forced to foreclose on their loans to stay solvent."

"What is this 'foreclose?'" Raffaele asked, his face serious.

"Foreclosure means if people can't make their monthly payments, the bank takes back their house."

"The people can't live in their house anymore?"

"No," Paulo said quietly. "They have to move."

Raffaele looked at Anna, who nodded. "Some people at church have had to move. It's very sad, Raffaele."

During the holidays, as more people lost their jobs, Father Donati's church became a vital place of support for his parishioners. Anna, ever the seamstress, volunteered in the church's thrift shop repairing donated clothes. Raffaele, the master craftsman, began helping neighbors with household woodworking repairs.

"When will we get our Christmas tree?" Vincenzo asked, a week before Christmas

"Your father and I have decided not to have one this year," Anna said.

"Why?" Vincenzo asked plaintively.

"Out of respect for our neighbors who have lost their jobs."

"But you haven't lost your job, Papa," Vincenzo said, confused.

"Vincenzo, if we have a tree, it will look like we don't care about what's happening to them," Anna added.

"I care, but Christmas trees make people happy."

"I think Vincenzo is right," Paulo said, looking at his younger brother, then at his parents. "Celebrating Christmas does make people happy. It always has for our family. Why not invite our friends and neighbors to join us, say on Christmas Day, and instead of presents ask them to bring food to share?"

Anna looked at Raffaele who pursed his lips and nodded slowly.

"We could do it after Christmas Mass," Anna said, excitement in her voice. "Maybe we could invite Father Donati?"

"Can we Papa, can we?" Vincenzo said, pleading, "and get a tree? Please."

Raffaele raised both hands to stop the talking, and looked at Anna, "Mama?"

"Yes, amore mio."

The next few days were hectic, with phone calls to friends and neighbors, cleaning the house, getting groceries, and of course buying a tree. On Christmas Eve, Raffaele brought out the doll house he made for the girls, back when they'd moved to 2334 Watkins Street after Vincenzo died.

Clara put it by the tree that Christmas, starting a family tradition.

Vincenzo lay down in front of the house and peered inside. The white, two-story doll house was 14" high, 18" wide, and 10" deep. The brown peaked roof had two dormers. Windows with blue shutters were on each side of the front door, and on the front and sides of the second story. A shaded porch, enclosed with a miniature railing, ran across the front of the house. Inside, the walls were papered, and hand-carved furniture filled the rooms.

Anna dabbed her eyes. "So many wonderful years to remember…"

Standing back to admire the decorated tree, Raffaele said, "Do you remember the party we had at Enrico's delicatessen?"

Anna closed her eyes, smiling with sweet memories. "I remember men making music, everyone singing, and Rosetta's wonderful food. It was good to be alive then."

"It's good to be alive now, amore mio," Raffaele said gently, and pretended to play the violin. "Tomorrow we'll have beautiful music and celebrate again with our friends and neighbors."

When they left for church, the morning was bright and chilly. The snow had melted and there were thin cirrus clouds high overhead.

Paulo played Bach's "Ave Maria" before the early and late morning masses, then hurried home to help his parents.

Enrico and Rosetta were the first to arrive, a little after one o'clock.

"Benvenuto, welcome," Raffaele said as he hugged them at the door.

Anna said, "Molti grazie, thank you very much," as she took Rosetta's covered platter of food into the kitchen and motioned for her to follow.

Vincenzo took their coats into his parent's bedroom and laid them carefully on the bed, exactly as his mother had instructed.

As their friends and neighbors began arriving, Paulo poured wine and punch from the sideboard.

Anna and Rosetta oversaw the serpentine serving line that snaked through the kitchen and around the heavily-ladened dining room table.

People sat on the sofa, in armchairs and dining room chairs, and on the piano bench, the stairs, and the floor, enjoying the food, and talking and laughing.

When most had finished eating, Raffaele cleared his throat and raised his wine glass. "Thank you all for coming to share Christmas with us. Saluto!"

A loud chorus of "Saluto" and "Thank you" rang out.

"As a special treat, my son, Paulo would like to play for you."

Paulo stepped forward. "I've selected three Christmas songs I think we all know. Please sing along."

They did, quietly at first and then with more emotion, as he played "It Came Upon a Midnight Clear", "O Little Town of Bethlehem", and "We Three Kings".

All the guests left by four o'clock, and after cleaning up the four of them sat in the now quiet front room—Raffaele in his armchair, Anna on the couch with her arm around Vincenzo, and Paulo in the other armchair.

Anna squeezed Vincenzo. "Thank you for wanting a Christmas tree." She looked at Paulo, "And thank you for the beautiful music." She gazed at Raffaele. "Thank you, amore mio, for knowing how to celebrate life." She blew him a kiss.

CHAPTER TWENTY FOUR

HONOR AND SOUL
SPRING SEMESTER 1930

The first day after the holidays, Mr. Moretti, Paulo's bespectacled economics teacher greeted each student coming into the classroom. When everyone was seated, he leaned against the front of his desk and asked, "How many of your parents have money in a bank?"

Most students raised their hands.

"If they still do, my advice for them is to consider withdrawing it, soon."

Paulo raised his hand. "Why, Mr. Moretti?"

Arms folded across his chest, he said, "Banks made too many loans that were invested in the Stock Market. When it crashed those shares were worthless, so that asset became a liability. To protect their reserves, many banks are restricting how much depositors can withdraw. When a bank's reserves drop below a certain level, it becomes insolvent and fails. The bank closes its doors and depositors, your parents, lose their money. Bank failures are increasing and will continue for some time to come."

The room was silent, then another student asked, "Say my parents withdraw their money, what do they do with it to keep it safe?"

"Well, I can only tell you what I'm doing. Your parents must decide for themselves, but I decided to buy a new house."

Paulo asked, "I don't understand? Why a house?"

"Remember when we discussed how banks foreclose and take possession of mortgaged properties?"

Heads nodded.

"Well, then they turn around and try to resell them, to change the property from a liability to an asset on their balance sheets. With the increase in foreclosures and so few buyers, it has become a 'buyer's market'."

"It's supply and demand," said an excited voice from the back of the room.

"Exactly!" said Mr. Moretti, clapping

"What are you going to do with your old house?" a student asked.

"Right now, I'm trying to rent it. If that doesn't work," he sighed, "the bank will foreclose, and I'll lose it."

Walking home, Paulo considered his economics teacher's advice. As he thought about his parents account at a bank downtown near Wanamaker's, he looked up to see a sign tacked to a corner phone pole that wasn't there in the morning. It read, "New Homes for Sale at CRASHED Prices". An arrow pointed up the street.

At dinner, Paulo relayed his economics class discussion. His parents listened attentively and were surprised when he showed them the brochure the real estate agent gave him, when he detoured to look at the new houses.

"Look, Mama, everything is brand new! See how big the kitchen is? It's bigger than our house, has trees in front, and the price is reduced by forty percent!"

"It's nice, Paulo," Anna said. "Let your father see."

Raffaele carefully studied the brochure, then asked, "Anna, you like this house?"

"It's nice, Raffaele," she said quietly.

"Do you want to move, amore mio?"

Anna looked around slowly and shook her head. "No, I like our home."

"But, Pop, what if your bank fails and you lose all your money?"

Raffaele patted Paulo's cheek gently. "Thank you, son—"

"Paulo, your father has always been a good provider for our family," Anna added.

"But—"

"Enough, Paulo. I know what I must to do."

Later that week, Raffaele went to his bank and paid off the mortgage on 1216 E. Price Street. When he told his family, Paulo asked why. Raffaele said, "It's simple. When I bought this house, I promised to pay for it. It's a matter of honor."

At his violin lesson on Saturday, Signore Lombardi could see his student's mind was not on his music.

"What is filling your mind today, Paulo?"

"Uh, nothing…why do you ask?"

"Because I know your moods. You are not thinking about playing your violin, am I right?" He motioned to the chair across from him. "Come and talk with me."

Paulo slouched into the chair.

"Now, what is keeping you from your music?" he asked, his voice serious.

Paulo hesitated before relating what his father had done, shaking his head, "I don't understand. He told me it was a matter of honor."

Signore Lombardi regarded Paulo and smiled. "Your father was the son of a baron in the old country, in a time when a man's honor defined him, determining his character and his reputation."

"Yes, my father has always been different from other men, more certain I guess."

"Your father is a man from another time. He has certain convictions about what is best for his family." Signore Lombardi patted his heart. "His actions come from the heart."

Paulo shook his head.

"Now, let's focus on this. Your Philadelphia Conservatory of Music scholarship is less than six months away and there is much to do, capisci?"

Paulo's senior spring semester was full of competing commitments. Number one was increased violin practice, then keeping up with school-work, playing in the school orchestra, teaching his two students at church, and playing for masses when Father Donati asked.

All February, Signore Lombardi had Paulo practice potential audition pieces for the June scholarship competition.

At the end of the month, his teacher asked, "So, which one do you like?"

Paulo leafed through a folder of sheet music. "I like the Brahms Sonata."

"It's a good early Romantic piece," Signore Lombardi commented.

He scanned another set of sheet music and held up Amy Beach's 'Romance for Violin.' "But I really liked this one."

Signore Lombardi stroked his chin. "What makes you like it?"

Paulo thought a moment. "It's passionate. The melody feels powerful."

Signore Lombardi tilted his head a little. "It is also a difficult, complex piece, and only six-minutes long. Are you sure?"

Paulo grinned. "What better way to show what I can do?"

He submitted his scholarship application in mid-March along with letters of reference from Signore Lombardi, his orchestra teacher, and Father Donati.

His friend and second violin, Dave also applied to audition for the scholarship. The upcoming competition became their only lunchtime topic.

Three weeks later, Paulo came home from school and saw a letter propped up on the sideboard by the front door, addressed to him. The return address read, The Philadelphia Conservatory of Music.

Anna watched him pick it up and asked, "Isn't that—"

Paulo started at the sound of his mother's voice.

"—what been you've waiting for?"

As he walked into the kitchen, he slid his finger under the envelope flap, unfolded the fancy stationary, and scanned the letter. He looked up with a huge smile. "I'm going to play for Leopold Stokowski, Mama."

Anna crossed herself and kissed him on the forehead. "Good for you, Bambino."

The minute his father got home from work, Paulo showed him the letter. Raffaele boomed, "Fantastico!" Hugging him tightly, exclaimed, "You make me proud, Paulo."

The first Saturday in June, the family drove to Paulo's audition. As they neared the Philadelphia Conservatory of Music, Anna turned back to Paulo, "You're so quiet. Are you nervous?"

"No. I'm fine Mama. I'm just playing the piece in my mind."

They arrived at 1617 Spruce Street an hour before his eleven o'clock appointment. Raffaele, Anna, and Vincenzo were ushered in and seated in the rear of the auditorium, as another violinist was setting up to play. Leopold Stokowski sat at the front of the stage with his back to the audience, writing on a small table-desk.

Paulo was led to an individual practice room to wait his turn. After unpacking and tuning his violin, tightening, and rosining the bow, he played warm-up scales. The violinist on stage finished playing. He knew Dave's audition was next, right before his, so he opened the door to listen. After a few moments, Vivaldi's Concerto in A Minor filled the auditorium.

"He's really good," Paulo thought to himself. "All that practice...his technique is a lot more precise...the melody is beautiful."

When his turn came, Paulo walked on stage. Stokowski introduced himself and welcomed him to the competition,

"Well, Paulo Colaluca, I understand you're going to play 'Romance for

Violin', by Beach, is that correct?"

"Yes, sir," Paulo answered, his mouth dry.

"I'm interested in hearing your interpretation. Please proceed."

Paulo put the violin under his chin, grasped the neck gently, arched his fingers over the fingerboard, balanced the bow above the strings, closed his eyes, and began to play. Everything around him faded away. He swayed gently and became one with the melody. The experience of playing the piece here, in front of Leopold Stokowski, felt like soaring. When it was over, he stood still, his eyes close until he heard applause.

The conductor was standing and clapping. "Paulo, you have a great career ahead of you. I look forward to hearing you play in the future."

The next week, he and Dave wished each other well on the competition outcome and reminisced about their year together, music teachers, friends, and orchestra class.

Two weeks later, a second letter arrived, informing Paulo that he won the scholarship. Despite winning, he and Dave remained friends for many years. Dave played solos as Concertmaster/First Violin of the Los Angeles Philharmonic Orchestra. Paulo loved going and hearing him play.

CHAPTER TWENTY FIVE

THE PHILADELPHIA CONSERVATORY OF MUSIC 1930-32

"Good morning." Signore Lombardi closed the book in his lap and motioned Paulo to the seat across from him. "Tell me what you know about the Philadelphia Conservatory of Music."

This was Paulo's first music lesson after receiving the Conservatory award letter. He was surprised. "It's one of the best music schools in the country."

"And..."

"Many famous musicians have studied there."

"And..."

"It also has programs for dancers."

"And...?"

Paulo shrugged. "It's been around for a long time?"

"The Philadelphia Conservatory of Music, or PCM as it's called now, was founded in 1877 by Richard C. Schirmer, a pianist and music teacher trained at the Leipzig Conservatory in Germany. His goal was to bring the traditional European style of music instruction to Philadelphia. At first, he only recruited students from first generation German and European families. His legacy is the reason you were given an audition, capisci?"

Paulo nodded.

"In 1884, he got the state of Pennsylvania to incorporate the Conservatory so it could grant degrees in music. His classical music curriculum offered studies in orchestral instruments, music theory, arranging, composition, voice, opera, and musical education. Students attended concerts, recitals, lectures, and courses on history, foreign languages, and fine arts, to provide them a comprehensive classical education."

Signore Lombardi stood, went to his desk, and opened a drawer. Walking his fingers over files, he opened one and brought a document back to his seat. "This is a prospectus from their 1917-1918 catalog. It declares 'a mere empirical and technical proficiency upon an instrument does not rise to the dignity of an art.'"

He took his glasses off and gazed at Paulo. "You are the best violin student I've ever taught. Your musicality and technique are beyond your years."

Paulo looked down, awkwardly self-conscious.

"When you play, your music soars."

"Thank you," Paulo said softly, then glanced up with a slight smile.

"You, have to understand where you're going to is one of the best conservatories in the world!"

His voice rose. "They believe art is passed best from an accomplished artist to a student. You will learn how to interpret music, give it life, and make it your own."

Paulo nodded, taking in every word.

"You will get to play with string quartets, chamber music groups, orchestras, and at renowned venues in Philadelphia."

Leaning forward in his chair, eyes sparkling, Signore Lombardi said, "Do you understand, Paulo, what a special thing you've won?"

Eyes wide, Paulo said, "I'm beginning to. This scholarship is the door to my dreams."

Over the summer, he continued his lessons with Signore Lombardi, teaching his two students at church, and playing at Mass when Father Donati requested.

The first week in August, Paulo attended an orientation for scholarship students. It included a meeting with the Admissions Office, a tour, lunch with the String Department faculty, and most importantly, the person who would be his Primary Teacher, Mr. Amato. An accomplished violinist, he taught at the Curtiss Institute in Philadelphia before coming to the Conservatory. He volunteered to be Paulo's Primary Teacher, in part, because he too had grown up in Germantown.

At dinner that night, he excitedly shared his day with his parents and brother. "Pop, they have a huge collection of historic violins, including some by Antonio Stradivari and Giuseppe Guarneri!"

"Italians make the best violins in the world," Raffaele said proudly.

"Advanced students can apply to borrow them for special performances or competitions. Can you believe it, Mama? I'll be able to play a Stradivari violin."

"I'm so proud of you, Paulo," Anna said, crossing herself. "Per favore, be careful with them, they are so…prezioso."

"I know how valuable they are, Mama. I promise to be careful."

"The scholarship," he turned back to Raffaele, "will pay for my tuition and all fees! You and Mama don't have to pay for anything."

The Saturday after Labor Day, Paulo went for his usual lesson with Signore Lombardi. When he walked in, he saw a long, wrapped rectangular box on the music stand. He put his violin case down and looked at his teacher.

"It's a going-away present for my best student," Signore Lombardi said with a twinkle in his eye.

"But I'm not really leaving," Paulo said, holding the present.

"Yes, you are. Open it."

As Paulo began to unwrap the box, Signore Lombardi said, "You will have a new, accomplished teacher, helping you develop your talent. It's time for me to let you go."

Paulo stopped unwrapping and looked at his teacher.

"I won't be your primary teacher anymore, but you are always welcome here. Paulo, I want you to tell me about your studies and what you're learning. Now, please, open your gift."

When Paulo lifted the lid, he grinned. With the greatest care, he lifted out a beautiful, polished bow. Hugging his teacher, he croaked, "I don't know what to say—"

Signore Lombardi returned the embrace, then held him at arm's length. Eyes full of tears, he said, "Promise me you will always make the music your own."

"I promise," Paulo said, wiping his own moist eyes.

Most days, Raffaele picked Paulo up, and at dinner Anna was always eager to hear what he had done and learned that day.

The Saturday after his first week, Paulo was up early and, on his way, out the door when Anna called him back, insisting he sit down to have breakfast.

"Mama, I'm still very full of eating every bit last night's delicious dinner. I want to see Signore Lombardi."

With a reproving look, she said, "Paulo, Signore Lombardi is not a young man. He's probably still asleep. Have your breakfast and then call him."

Paulo ate as fast as he thought he could get away with, called Signore Lombardi, and asked to come over.

His teacher's door opened almost immediately at his knock.

"Good morning, Paulo. Come in and tell me all about your first week." For the next half-hour, Signore Lombardi sat in his wingback chair, listening attentively, nodding at Paulo's descriptions. When Paulo stopped, he said, "It all sounds wonderful, but about the music. How well do the other violin students play?"

"They play very well. Better than me," Paulo added softly.

"Excellent!" Signore Lombardi said, excitement in his voice.

To Paulo's confused look, he said, "Haven't you always been the best in your school orchestra?"

'Yes…"

"Do you think these other students were the 'best' too?"

Paulo nodded. "I'm sure of it."

Signore Lombardi leaned forward and held up his index finger. "They're a new orchestra. Each one will push you to grow, perhaps to become a first chair, capisci?"

Paulo's expression changed as he grasped what Signore Lombardi had said, "Oh…My new orchestra."

Signore Lombardi leaned back. "It's the perfect place for you to keep growing."

Paulo's first year overflowed with new expectations and successes. Always an above average student, he worked hard to master his academic classwork. No one out-practiced him on the way to excelling in his performances. He threw himself into learning to play in string quartets, with chamber music groups, and as part of an orchestra. Opportunities to perform in and around Philadelphia, opened his eyes to a life far beyond Germantown. Yet as the year ended, he remained undecided about the next year.

The first Saturday in May, he went to see Signore Lombardi. "Thank you for seeing me on such short notice."

Signore Lombardi waved his hand. "I always enjoy seeing you, Paulo." He studied his former student and said, "You look worried. What is bothering you?"

Paulo rubbed his hands together and said, "I'm not sure. You know me better than anyone. I'm not sure I want to continue at PCM."

Signore Lombardi rubbed his chin as he stared at Paulo. "From what you've shared, I thought you were enjoying it."

"I am, I do," Paulo said quickly, "especially the performing." He looked down. "I just don't see myself spending the next three years cooped up in classrooms. I'm not interested in a degree. I just want to play and improve my playing. Is that so wrong?"

Signore Lombardi smiled. "No, Paulo. You've always worked harder at doing than learning from books. Remember in high school—"

"—I got good grades in school," Paulo interjected.

Signore Lombardi leaned forward in his chair. "Remember gymnastics? You've always loved to learn, but by doing, not only reading about it. Am I wrong?"

Paulo's chin dropped. "No," he admitted, reluctantly.

"Have you talked with Mr. Amato about this?"

Paulo shook his head.

"They want to support young, talented musicians, Paulo. Winning your scholarship says they value you and your talent."

Signore Lombardi rose and motioned for Paulo to come to him. As always when he wanted to make a serious point, he hugged Paulo, then held him out at arms-length.

"Promise me you'll talk to Mr. Amato. Please say it for me."

"I promise to talk to Mr. Amato," Paulo repeated.

"He's there to support you. Come back and tell me what he says." He patted Paulo's cheek. "Be honest about what you're feeling, okay?"

"I will. Thank you, Signore Lombardi."

The next week, Mr. Amato listened attentively to everything Paulo said. The older, professional artist was understanding and said he would consult with the administration about possible options.

The following week, Mr. Amato said to Paulo, "Although your scholarship was for completing a four-year degree, PCM also has a Diploma Program."

He handed Paulo a program description, who read it silently to himself. The Diploma Program is the most advanced non-degree track and provides focused studies for young artists in the pre-professional stages of their careers. Qualification to enter this program is predicated principally on the level and quality of performance and/or achievement, rather than the attainment of specific academic credentials. This program in music concentrations is a two-year program. Young artists must be invited to continue their studies into the second year. A minimum of 52 credits is required to complete the Artist Diploma.

When he finished, Paulo looked at Mr. Amato, who said, "It sounds like what you're asking for, Paulo. Are you interested?"

Paulo grinned broadly. "Yes, very much!"

"Excellent. I've been given permission to formally invite you to continue here in the Diploma Program, beginning in the fall.

When Paulo told his parents about his acceptance into the Diploma Program, he received a mixed response.

Anna spoke first. "I thought your scholarship was for four years?"

"It is, Mama, but—"

"You were going to be the first person in our family to graduate from college with a degree, Paulo."

"I am going to graduate, Mama—"

"Clara's two-year Normal School program gave her a degree," she said, disappointment in her voice.

"Amore mio, favore," Raffaele interjected, "Paulo does not want to be a teacher. He wants to be an artist, someone who plays beautiful music."

"But—"

"Anna, per favore," Raffaele cut her off. "No buts, now Paulo can become a virtuoso, capisci?"

Anna frowned but didn't say any more.

The next day, Paulo went to see Signore Lombardi to tell him the good news.

"Congratulations my boy," Signore Lombardi said, shaking his hand.

Paulo told him about his parent's reactions the night before.

With a wry smile, Signore Lombardi said, "From what you've told me, your father was a serious clarinetist in his younger days. He has a musician's heart."

During Paulo's second year, the Diploma Program in music concentrations, allowed him to change his focus to performance, rather than academics. He thrived, learning new techniques, developing his talent, and playing at renowned city venues.

Paulo was selected to perform at the 1932 spring graduation ceremony for the Diploma Program. His family was there and heard him play Igor Stravinsky's "Violin Concerto in D Major" on a Stradivari.

At the conclusion of the piece, he looked out into the applauding audience. His mother beamed proudly.

CHAPTER TWENTY SIX

AFTERGLOW SHIFT 1932-34

The applause seemed to go on forever. Paulo lost count of how many times he bowed, before touching his lips, sending a kiss, and leaving the stage.

Waiting in the wings, Mr. Amato, grasped his hand and pulled him into a celebratory embrace. "That was an amazing performance."

"Thank you," Paulo said, momentarily lightheaded.

"Go enjoy your family and your weekend, but let's talk first thing Monday, okay?"

Paulo agreed. As he headed for the auditorium floor, Mr. Amato patted him on the back.

On Monday, Paulo paused at his teacher's open door. Mr. Amato motioned him to the two chairs in front of his desk and sat down beside him.

"When Leopold Stokowski awarded you the scholarship, it was for four years. Your change to the Diploma Program used two of those years. Would you be interested in continuing here as a mentor for first-year students in the string department? Your scholarship would continue to cover your tuition and fees, so you could audit classes. We would pay you a stipend from the unused tuition money, to have you share your talents and skills in technique, musicality, and interpretation."

His eyes fixed on Mr. Amato, Paulo finally said, "Like a teacher?"

Mr. Amato's smile spread. "Not in the formal sense, but yes. You wouldn't grade them. You'd be someone they could talk to informally, listening and relating to their concerns—like a trusted advisor."

Paulo thought about his sister, teacher Clara, and despite her superior attitude, he respected her for helping students learn. "Yes, I'd like to be an advisor. Thank you for your faith in me, Mr. Amato. I'll do my best to help them."

As he told his parents about being a mentor, he kissed his mother's forehead, and added, "I'm going to be helping students like Clara. You'll have two to brag about."

Vincenzo snorted, "Why do you want to be like 'Miss Bookworm'?"

Anna stared at him. "You should be proud of your sister."

"She thinks she's better than us—"

"Basta!" Raffaele growled, pointing at his youngest child, "that's enough."

"Vincenzo, you will choose what you want to do in life when the time comes, but this is about your brother," Anna added.

"Paulo Colaluca, you have always been a gypsy talker."

"Mama." He feigned hurt. "You never raised any gypsy children."

Raffaele laughed. "He speaks the truth. You are not a gypsy madre."

Anna gave them both a tight-lipped smile.

During the next two years, Paulo mentored dozens of students. On occasion faculty sought him out to discuss student motivation and progress. Mr. Amato arranged for him to play with orchestras at various venues, serving as an ambassador for the Philadelphia Conservatory Music Programs.

Spring of his fourth year at PCM, he turned again to Signore Lombardi for advice about his future.

"I'm not sure what's next for me. The depression keeps getting worse. Mr. Amato tells me employment opportunities for classically trained musicians have all but dried up, with funding for the arts cut or eliminated."

Signore Lombardi set his glasses on the end table and rubbed his eyes. "Mr. Amato's correct. This is not a good time for artists…or people anywhere, and I don't see it changing soon. I read that President Roosevelt is trying to get Congress to fund something called the WPA—"

"The Works Progress Administration," Paulo said. "If it's funded, the unemployed will be hired for public works projects, like building roads, bridges, schools, and parks."

Signore Lombardi rested his chin on his hands. "Let's hope that happens soon."

"Mr. Amato told me that the directors of conservatories like PCM, The Curtiss Institute, Juilliard, and major orchestras around the country, are lobbying for a similar federal music project, to put professional musicians back to work."

"That would be a good thing for a lot of talented people—for the country too. Let's hope President Roosevelt listens to them."

That night, as Paulo sat on his bed untying his shoes, Vincenzo came out of the bathroom and plopped flat on his back on the other bed, hands behind his head.

"So, big brother, what are you going do when your scholarship ends in a couple of months?" he asked, staring at the ceiling.

"I don't really know yet." Paulo pushed his shoes under the bed. "What are you going to do after you graduate in June?"

Vincenzo turned on his side facing Paulo. "Well, I'm not going to college. Two brains in the family are enough."

"We all know school has never been your thing," Paulo said with a grin.

"While you've been gone these past four years, hobnobbing, I've been stuck here in Germantown. I want to get out and see the world."

Paulo stood and walked to the closet. "Traveling takes money, which takes a job, and finding one right now is hard." He hung up his shirt and pants and went back to sit on his bed. "How do propose finding a job? There's not much call for squeezing a wine press in your father's basement, since Prohibition ended last December," he teased.

Vincenzo slung his pillow at Paulo, who caught it and pushed Vincent backwards on the bed, covering his face with it.

"Hey, I can't breathe!"

Paulo let go and sat next to him, chuckling. "I've missed you, strambo."

"I am not a weirdo. At least I don't carry a violin case around to impress girls."

"Hey, it's worked well. Especially if they're into romantic music."

He bumped Vincenzo with his shoulder, who bumped him back. "I've missed you, too. Mom and Pop are definitely old world, and not a lot of fun to hang out with."

Paulo's tone became serious. "Sounds like we're both in the same boat. You graduate in June, and I'm done with PCM, and neither of us know where we're going?"

Vincenzo's voice softened. "I've been thinking about going in the Navy—"

"What?" Paulo said loudly.

"Jeez, shh," Vincenzo said, a finger to his lips. "I haven't told Mom and

Pop yet."

"And when were you planning on dropping this bomb on them?"

"Not until I turn eighteen."

Paulo faced his brother and leaned forward. "Your birthday is December 4. You'll tell Mama you're leaving home at Christmas time?" he said quietly.

Vincenzo shrugged.

"Her favorite time of the year? Great plan, strambo."

"Don't say anything, okay?"

Paulo nodded solemnly.

"Promise?"

"Okay."

In June, Vincenzo graduated, and Paulo completed his mentorship. Anna and Raffaele invited neighbor friends to join the family in celebrating their achievements on Sunday afternoon after church. Clara and her husband, Andrea, Father Donati and Signore Lombardi came. Angie called from New Castle, and Mr. Amato called Paulo to thank him for his work as a mentor.

That summer, Paulo helped Signore Lombardi with some of his advanced students and continued working with beginning students at Father Donati's church. Occasionally, he played with orchestral groups, like the Doylestown Symphony, which he'd first done in 1932.

Unable to find fulltime employment, Vincenzo continued his after-school, part-time, position at the YMCA.

In early October, Paulo went upstairs to bed and saw Vincenzo sitting at the desk studying something.

"What are you looking at?" Paulo said as he walked toward the closet.

"Nothing," Vincenzo said, hurriedly closing it.

"It's too thin to be a girlie magazine. What'd you buy?"

"I didn't buy it, and it's private."

"Okay, you didn't buy it—and it's private. It must be valuable. Did you steal it?"

"No, I didn't steal it!" Vincenzo crossed the room and put it under his pillow. "There's no privacy in this house."

Paulo hung up his pants and sat on the bed. "Never has been and never will be in this family, little brother. Since when did you and I stop talking about stuff? Did I miss a memo or something?"

Vincenzo met Paulo's gaze. "No, but I know what you're going to say."

"How do you know what I'm going to say?"

"Because you already told me it would hurt Mama."

Paulo took a deep breath. "It's about joining the Navy, right?"

Vincenzo nodded. "I went to the Navy Yard today and talked with a recruiter."

Paulo was flabbergasted. "The Navy Yard downtown by the Delaware River?" How the hell did you get there?"

"On two buses," Vincent said smugly.

Paulo held out his hand. "Let me see it."

Vincenzo grudgingly handed him the brochure. On the cover under the Navy's insignia was a picture of the battleship USS Pennsylvania. Inside were descriptions of the different programs the Navy offered and colorful pictures of naval ships.

"Very nice. What did the recruiter say about you joining?"

"Petty Officer Costa said because I was a high school graduate, I'm an excellent candidate. I must pass a physical, complete an aptitude test, and be eighteen to enlist," Vincenzo answered confidently.

"So, you're really going to do this?"

"Yes, and I told him about you, too, your scholarship to PCM and everything."

"What? Why'd you do that?"

"Because older brother, the Navy has an Admiral's Orchestra. Bet you didn't know that, did you?"

Paulo looked at him skeptically.

"Well, they do. When the Admiral visits a country, he invites important people aboard, and entertains them. The Admiral is like a diplomat for America."

Paulo looked at Vincenzo with new respect. "I see."

"Petty Officer Costa would really like to talk to you, Paulo. Think about it. You could keep playing, get paid for it, and travel the world!"

Paulo did think about it, for a very long time before falling asleep. The next day he went to see Signore Lombardi and told him about his conversation with Vincenzo. Paulo sat pensively, then said, "The depression keeps getting worse, Signore Lombardi, and there are fewer and fewer opportunities for me to play."

"It is a very difficult time for everyone, especially artists."

"Do you know anything about the Navy Admiral's Orchestra?"

"The military has always had bands. They march in parades and play at ceremonial events. I've not seen or heard the 'Admiral's Orchestra' perform, but if it travels with the Admiral and is used to entertain important people in foreign countries, I'm sure the musicianship is excellent. Vincenzo's right you know. You would be able to play, be paid for it, and travel the world. It is a different opportunity than those you've had at the Conservatory."

"But I've worked hard to be the best violinist I can be. I don't want to waste my time playing in an orchestra that's not professional, even the Admiral's Orchestra."

Smiling, Signore Lombardi said, "Do you remember your high school orchestra? Few were as dedicated as you. Your friend Dave was, but I don't remember you talking about anyone else. Did your orchestra's playing improve?"

Paulo chortled. "Yeah, but it was like pulling teeth."

"My point is your dedication, your mentoring, and your teaching raised the orchestra's level of playing to a higher level of artistry. Am I right?"

Paul nodded.

"You have a God-given gift, Paulo," Signore Lombardi said, pointing at him, "that you've been sharing since I've known you. You can do the same thing in the Admiral's Orchestra, and play on a much bigger stage than the Conservatory."

The next day, Paulo got a phone call from Mr. Amato, who said Signore Lombardi contacted him.

"Paulo, I want you to know that the Admiral's Orchestra is an excellent ensemble. The Navy recruits only the best musicians. Some of our graduates played in the orchestra during their time in the service. I would encourage you to consider this as a serious professional opportunity." Mr. Amato gave him the number to arrange an interview and audition, then asked to know how things turned out.

Paulo thanked him for his help, hung up, and sat down, feeling a little overwhelmed. With a deep breath, he called and made an appointment to meet with the officer in charge.

At dinner, Paulo told his parents about the opportunity to play in the Admiral's Orchestra. To his surprise, both parents were quick to support the idea, voicing immigrant patriotism for their adopted country, and pride in Paulo's wanting to serve in the Navy. Raffaele raised his wine glass to salute him—more than once, and this time, Anna dabbed at happy tears.

CHAPTER TWENTY SEVEN

THE NAVY 1934-38

*T*wo weeks after calling the office of the United States Navy Band, Paulo had an appointment for an interview and audition. He took the train to the Washington Navy Yard in Washington, D.C., where he met with the Lieutenant in charge, Charles Benter, at his office in the Sail Loft building.

Lieutenant Benter immediately asked, "Tell me about your training before you won the scholarship, and your experiences at PCM."

Paulo summarized his training with Father Donati, Signore Lombardi, and Mr. Amato, spoke with pride about the students he'd mentored, then added, "Finding out about this opportunity was serendipitous. If accepted, it will be a definite change from where I thought I'd be playing."

"And where was that going to be?" Lieutenant Benter asked.

"My plan was to join a professional orchestra, work toward being the first chair violin, and someday become the concertmaster."

The Lieutenant nodded, seeming impressed. "According to what Mr. Amato told me, you have the talent and discipline to do both. What are you playing for me today?"

"Violin Concerto in A Minor, by Antonio Vivaldi."

Lieutenant Benter smiled knowingly. "It's a beautiful piece of Baroque music."

Paulo followed him to a rehearsal room. The Lieutenant sat quietly. At the end of the piece, the Lieutenant clapped.

"Tell me why you want to play in the United States Navy Band?"

Paulo considered his answer. "My father and mother are both immigrants from Italy and are patriotic naturalized citizens of this country, their adopted country. I was born here but never thought much about the special birthright they gave me. My mother cried tears of joy when I talked with them about joining the Navy. My father, an accomplished clarinetist, kept pouring wine and saluting me until," Paulo laughed, "I was buzzed."

Lieutenant Benter covered his mouth and chuckled.

"Suddenly, joining the Navy and representing our country through my music became important, something I wanted to do."

The Lieutenant studied Paulo for several moments. "How would you like to play in the Admiral's Orchestra, aboard the USS Pennsylvania?"

Paulo sucked in his breath. "The Admiral's Orchestra?"

"You are an exceptional talent, Paulo, and would add to the orchestra's quality, professionalism, and the Admiral's ambassadorial impact."

November 5, 1934, Paulo enlisted in the Navy as an Apprentice Seaman, for a four-year tour of duty. He passed the physical, and immediately started his recruit training. Completing the eight-week Boot Camp, he reported to the Navy Music School for another ten weeks of study in music theory, ear training, and instrumental performance.

Lieutenant Benter met with him at the end of Music School training on March 5, 1935. "You've done very well in your course work." Shaking Paulo's hand. "You've earned the rating of Seaman 2nd Class and are hereby assigned to the Admiral's Orchestra aboard the USS Pennsylvania."

"Yes!" Paulo said, making a fist, then quickly recovering. "Thank you, sir."

"The USS Pennsylvania is the Navy's flagship for the fleet, currently sailing in the Pacific engaged in Fleet Exercises. I'm sending you to Coco Solo Naval Air Station in Panama, aboard the USS Ranger. There you'll catch a ride on the first westbound ship scheduled to connect with the USS Pennsylvania. I'm not sure how long you'll have to wait. You leave March 29 and arrive at Coco Solo April 6. You'll have a week's shore leave to say goodbye to your family and friends. Being at sea means you won't be seeing them for some time. Any questions?"

"No Sir. Thank you for this honor. I'll do my best to represent the Navy well."

"I know you will, Paulo. You're dismissed."

Lieutenant Benter returned Paulo's salute.

As Paulo walked up the steps of 1216 E. Price Street, duffle bag over his shoulder, he saw his mother's face at the kitchen window.

"He's home. Paulo's home!" Anna cried out.

The front door opened, and Vincenzo was in Navy dress blues. "Hello, fellow Seaman," he said with a little smirk.

Paul dropped his duffle bag and they embraced. "When did this happen? How did you convince Mom and Pop?"

Vincenzo grabbed Paulo's duffle. "I'll tell you later. Right now, go hug Mama."

Paulo went into the kitchen, where Anna stood by the sink, dabbing her eyes with a dishtowel. "Why are you crying?" he said, embracing her. "I'm home."

She looked up at him with a weak smile. "Because you are home."

"And, you have a whole week to fatten me up, before I ship out." He squeezed her chin playfully. "So, what's for dinner tonight?"

"What would you like?" Grabbing his chin, she squeezed back.

"Surprise me, Mama. Right now, I want to talk to Vincenzo about how he convinced you to let him enlist."

Anna gestured with her hand indicating she didn't want to talk about it.

Paulo kissed her on the forehead and went upstairs. "So, how'd you, do it?"

"I waited until my birthday, then told them the present I wanted most was to be like you and enlist in the Navy. Naturally, Mama came unglued, saying I was her baby, I was too young, something terrible could happen to me, etc. To my surprise, Pop supported me, saying 'he'd been in the army in the old country, and it helped him grow up.' And that was it. Boot Camp completed. I'm waiting to start Aircrewman School."

"Flying?" Paulo said, disbelieving.

"Yep." Vincenzo grinned. "I want to fly, big brother."

The rest of Paulo's week at home was filled with congratulations and goodbyes from family and friends—and his mother's delicious food.

On March 28, 1935, he returned to the Washington Navy Yard and boarded the USS Ranger leaving for Panama the next day. Nine days later he arrived at the Coco Solo Fleet Air Base on the Atlantic side of the canal. His transfer papers were processed and because he was in transit to the USS Pennsylvania, he was temporarily billeted in the building where the Coco Solo Base Band was housed.

"I'm Phil Johnson, Musician 2nd Class, and I've been assigned to show you to your room and get you squared-away."

"Thanks, I'm Paulo Colaluca, Seaman 2nd Class, pleased to meet you."

Phil glanced at the violin case. "You're a violinist?"

Paulo nodded. "I'm supposed to join the Admiral's Orchestra on the USS Pennsylvania. I'm here to catch a ride on a westbound ship that will connect with it."

"Okay, I was wondering. The Base Band is woodwinds, brass, and percussion. No violins, but you're welcome to rehearse with us anytime."

Phil led Paulo to his room, introduced him to the Band Director and members of the Band, then gave him a tour of the base.

That evening Paulo ate with and enjoyed the camaraderie of the other band musicians.

Lieutenant Benter's parting comment, "I'm not sure how long you'll have to wait," turned out to be prophetic. As the Navy's Flagship for the fleet, the USS Pennsylvania was constantly engaged in peacetime training exercises, port visits, and foreign cruises. Naval ships coming through the canal were typically not scheduled to connect with it directly.

Paulo's lack of any specific duties on the base didn't last long. Three days after his arrival, he was assigned to train at the Squadron Gunnery School as a rear gunner, in a Curtiss Falcon Fighter-Bomber Biplane. He would fly in the second cockpit behind the pilot and shoot the camera guns at drone targets. Upon landing the film would be analyzed and graded. Paulo's scores were among the best in the squadron, until he realized that his proficiency might get him reassigned permanently. At that point he began shooting at the clouds and blamed his poor performance on blurry vision from constantly squinting into the sun. His gunnery training ended soon thereafter.

Paulo waited at the Coco Solo Air Station for the next nine months. During that time, he experienced many firsts, like how to live in a tropical climate, where the average temperature was 86 degrees, with 190 days of rain a year, that produced 150 inches of dampening rainfall, a moldering existence.

He saw how easily others wasted their money on frivolous pursuits. His frugality propelled him into becoming a source of loans with vigorish rates of interest. His business sometimes required forceful collection of overdue loans, so he recruited two large Naval MPs to assist him, on whom he affectionately bestowed the nicknames 'Moose' and 'Ox'. Paulo liked to think he was teaching his comrades about money management.

December 3, the captain of the base met with Paulo. He informed him he was promoted to Seaman 1st Class and talked with him about his situation.

"I understand your concern, with the length of time it's taking to get you on the Pennsylvania," the captain said, looking at Paulo's transfer paperwork. "I know what ships are coming through the canal, but I'm not generally privy to where they're going. What ship to put you on must come from further up the chain of command, and obviously there's been a snafu."

Paulo looked puzzled. "Snafu, Sir?"

With a wry smile, the captain said, "It means 'system-normal-all-fucked-up.' I'll push this up the line and find out what damn ship I'm supposed to put you on. Be patient, okay? Obviously, one traveling violinist in this man's Navy is not a high priority to someone. I'll do my best to get you where you're supposed to be. As of now, I'm assigning you back to the band."

"Thank you, Sir," Paulo said, saluting smartly. He returned to his life of rehearsing with the band's chamber music ensemble, morning tennis matches, loansharking, and courting Rosa, the dark-eyed Navy Nurse who loved his romantic serenades. She was his first serious lover.

On December 11, orders were issued for Paulo's transfer out, but it was not until January 11, 1936, that Paulo was awakened in the middle of the night and told he was being transferred to the USS New Mexico, via the USS Nitro, an ammunition ship coming through the canal on one of its transits between the east and west coasts. He had Moose and Ox hurriedly collect what they could of outstanding loans and handed the business over to them.

Paulo was able to contact Rosa. They embraced on the dock before he boarded, kissing, and tearfully promising to stay in touch, both knowing it was unlikely.

Once on board, Paulo was taken to the bridge. The Commander of the USS Nitro looked him over and smiled. "Well, I'll be damned! So, you're what all the fuss is about. I've never had a violinist on the Nitro before. You must be one hell of fiddle player, son, for them to want you in the Admiral's Orchestra."

He handed Paulo an official looking form. "Somebody up the line is watching over you. This is your notice of promotion to Musician 2nd Class."

As Paulo read the form, the Commander, with a twinkle in his eye, said,

"Would you be willing to play for my crew, while I'm getting you to the New Mexico?"

"Sure," Paulo said, then corrected himself, "Yes, Sir. How long will that take, Sir?"

"Twelve to fourteen days, depending on the weather. I promise to get you safely on the New Mexico, but I don't know how long before you get to the Pennsylvania."

Two weeks later, when the USS Nitro rendezvoused with the USS New Mexico, Paulo, was warmly welcomed on board by the members of the Captain's Orchestra. Once again, as part of a full orchestra, he enjoyed the connection with other violinists. Rehearsals were lively fun, and the esprit de corps among the musicians went beyond his experience.

On March 6, 1936, Paulo was officially promoted to Musician 2nd Class.

Three weeks later, Paulo finally reached the USS Pennsylvania, docked at the Puget Sound Naval Shipyard in Bremerton, WA, for overhaul.

For the next two and half years, Paulo played in the Admiral's Orchestra as the first chair violin and concertmaster. In a letter to his mother, he described life on board.

April 25, 1936
Dear Mama,

How are you and Pop? I hope safe and well. Have you heard from Vincenzo? I'm enjoying finally being on board the USS Pennsylvania. The orchestra is first rate and more fun than the conservatory. The musicians have separate sleeping quarters from the rest of the crew. Our only assigned duty is to rehearse and play for guests when the ship makes a port call. A canopy is put up over the fantail on the stern of the ship (that's the back end, Mama), and ringed with lights for nighttime performances. My first performance with the orchestra was in San Francisco. We played for important city people who were on board as guests of the Admiral. After dinner, there were speeches and the evening ended with dancing. The Admiral proudly introduced the orchestra. I met Mayors, the Governor, and an Archbishop. It was exciting to be playing for an audience again. I'm doing well here, Mama.

Love,
Paulo Colaluca
Musician 2nd Class
USS Pennsylvania.

What he didn't share was, he never had to stand watch, or do any scraping, painting, or other ongoing maintenance of the ship, and was free to roam around when he wasn't rehearsing. Few of the thousand other sailors on board knew who he was or what he did.

In May, the USS Pennsylvania took part in Fleet Problem XVII exercises off the west coast of the United States, Central America, and the Panama Canal Zone, preparing for anti-submarine warfare. She returned to San Pedro in June and spent the rest of the year in other training exercises between the west coast and Hawaii. The training program ended in San Pedro on November 18.

One afternoon, as Paulo sat on the fantail with other musicians, he asked, "Is the weather like this all the time?"

"Pretty much, why?" Jack, the trumpet player replied.

"I was raised in Philadelphia. By this time of year, we'd have two feet of snow and it'd be freezing ass cold."

Jack laughed. "You poor bastard. We get some rain in the spring." He looked out at the ocean. "I grew up in Gardena, a little town up the coast from here. It snowed maybe a half inch once when I was a kid. That's it."

Paulo nodded, thought of his parents in Philadelphia, and then how nice it felt to be warm.

The USS Pennsylvania remained in port until February 1937, when she started a tour along the west coast. In each port of call, Paulo led the orchestra entertaining the Admiral's guests. In April-May she participated in Fleet Problem XVIII doing exercises to practice the tactics of amphibious warfare. First, they were in Alaskan waters, then around the Hawaiian Islands, and finally in the vicinity of Midway Island, before returning to Puget Sound for maintenance, then back to San Pedro in September.

While on shore leave, Paulo met two brothers, Harry and Bill Sweet, on the beach one morning as he was working out on the low bar and rings, and they were lifting weights. They invited him to their house for a home-cooked meal. That evening he met their older sister, Loucille Light.

During dinner, Paulo told them about being in the Admiral's Orchestra on the USS Pennsylvania, and the many dignitaries he played for around the world. When he looked across the table, Loucille was gazing at him intently.

"And what about you, Loucille, tell me about yourself," he asked, smiling.

"Well, nothing so glamorous as your worldly adventures. To be perfectly frank, I'm back living with my parents while I divorce my husband."

"That son-of-a-bitch better never show his face around her again," Harry interjected.

"The bastard broke her arm!" Bill added, hitting the table with his fist.

"That's enough," Art, her father commanded.

"It's water under the bridge and best forgotten," her mother, Almyra said quietly.

Loucille looked at Paulo and smiled. "They're very protective."

Almyra touched Loucille's arm. "Why don't you and Paulo walk down to Bluff Park. It's a lovely evening—"

"Mama, I'm sure he's seen the ocean many times—"

"Not from Bluff Park," Paulo said quickly and grinned at her.

They strolled the three blocks to the narrow green belt, that ran along the bluff overlooking the beach and ocean below. They each shared easily about their growing-up years. Paulo had never met a woman like her. Born and raised on a farm in Liberty, Missouri, near the Kansas border, she'd grown up tending barnyard animals, and attending a one-room schoolhouse.

"One of my favorite childhood memories, was hearing the far-off whistle of the train my father worked on, and running through fields to wait by the tracks, so I could jump up on the cowcatcher when they slowed down for me. I'd sit on the front of that huge, hissing, black locomotive, my hair blowing in the wind and ride it into town. My mother used to call me 'her little Indian princess.'"

Paulo looked at her quizzically.

"I'm a quarter Choctaw and an eighth Mohawk," she said smugly. "Which means I'm slow to anger but can go on the warpath."

In addition to being almost divorced, Loucille was eight years older than Paulo. She was raven-haired, unpretentious, slow to smile, fun to be with, and loved the music he brought into her life. There was a 'settled' quality about her. He was captivated.

The USS Pennsylvania spent the rest of the year going up and down the coast to San Francisco. Every time Paulo came back to San Pedro, they dated.

On November 16, 1937, Paulo was promoted to Musician 1st Class.

On February 3, 1938, Loucille's divorce became final.

The ship made a short trip to San Francisco in February 1938, before taking part in Fleet Problem XIX in April and May. The exercises were designed to give the fleet added experience in the use of submarines, destroyers, and aircraft in scouting, attacking, and seizing advanced fleet bases.

At the end of April, during a brief layover in San Pedro, Paulo met with Loucille's father, and asked for her hand in marriage. Arthur Sweet, a large man, a head taller than Paulo, gave him his boisterous, bear-hug permission. That evening, Paulo and Loucille walked around the horseshoe-shaped, colorfully lighted Rainbow Pier by the Long Beach shoreline. Paulo stopped halfway around, took her hands in his, told her he loved her, and proposed.

With an elfin smile, Loucille gazed at Paulo, and nodded. "Yes, I'll marry you, my romantic Italian," she said, and kissed him tenderly.

Not wanting to wait for California's required blood tests results, Paulo and Loucille drove to Yuma, Arizona, on Saturday, April 30 and were married by a Justice of the Peace.

Driving back on Sunday morning, with Loucille's head resting sleepily against his shoulder, Paulo thought of his parents, especially his mother, and not telling them he was married. Growing up, he listened to his mother's ideas about marriage. He knew his mother's dream was to watch him walk down the aisle in her church and be married by the priest to a good Italian girl. Anna would not understand his choosing to marry outside the Catholic faith, and Loucille was not the "good Italian girl" she hoped he would marry.

"I'm gonna have to tell them," Paulo said to himself.

"Tell who, what?" Loucille said, half-watching the landscape flow by.

"My parents…about getting married."

Loucille sat back up and stared at him. They had told each other about their childhoods and growing up, and laughed together at family foibles, but his confession was a surprise. She was hurt.

"You haven't told them about us getting married?"

"It's complicated."

"Are you ashamed of me?" she said, turning away.

He reached to touch her arm, but she pulled away.

"Loucille, I am not ashamed of you. I love you." He took a deep breath. "My mother's from the old country. She wanted to be a nun for Christ sakes. I'm her eldest son. In her mind, I'm supposed to marry a nice Italian girl, in a Catholic Church wedding, and have lots of little bambinos to carry on the family name. That's always been her dream, but it's not mine. You're my dream, I love you."

When she finally turned back to him, he saw tears on her cheeks. "You must tell her first thing when we get back. Do you understand?"

Paulo nodded.

"Promise?"

"Yes, I promise."

Loucille wiped her tears with the back of her hand and touched his arm. "I do not want to be the daughter-in-law she hates for the rest of her life."

As soon as they got back to her father's house, Paulo called.

When Raffaele answered, he said, "Pop, it's me. Sorry to call so late, but I wanted you and Mama to be the first to know…I got married yesterday."

"Married?"

Paulo could hear his mother's voice asking who was calling.

"Paulo. Said he got married yesterday. Here, you talk to him."

"You got married? Who is she? What's her name? Is she Italian? You never said anything about getting marriage?" Hesitating, Anna asked. "Paulo, did you have to get married?"

"Mama, stop! The answer to your last question is no. And she's not Italian. Her name is Loucille. She's from Missouri. I love her. I'm sorry I didn't tell you beforehand."

"Where did you get married, Paulo?"

"In Yuma, Arizona."

"By a priest?"

"No, Mama, a Justice of the Peace."

"I see. Here, talk to your father."

"Paulo, does this woman make you happy?" Raffaele asked.

"Yes, Papa, very much. She's wonderful."

"That's what's important, Paulo. What is her name?"

"Loucille."

"May I speak with her?"

With a smile, Paul handed the phone to Loucille. "My father wants to talk to you."

With both hands, she hugged the receiver to her ear.

"Loucille, my name is Raffaele. I'm pleased to meet you. I wish you and Paulo happiness, and a long life together."

"Thank you, Raffaele. I know we will meet face-to-face someday."

"That would be nice. Per favore, I want to say goodbye to Paulo."

"Yes, Pop?"

"She sounds nice. Treat her with respect, Paulo. Don't worry about your mother. Give her time. She loves you very much, capisci?"

"Okay. Goodnight, Pop, and thanks."

"I like your father," Loucille said. "He seems like a gentle soul."

He nodded. "He can be, and like I said before, it's complicated."

In May, the USS Pennsylvania rejoined and completed Fleet Problem XIX. They returned to San Pedro and stayed until June 20, 1938, when the USS Pennsylvania embarked on a two-month cruise along the west coast. Just before the Pennsylvania went to Puget Sound for maintenance on September 19, 1938, Paulo was transferred to the cruiser, USS Houston.

When asked if he wanted to be discharged where he enlisted, he said, "I'd like to skip the winter in Philadelphia, Sir. San Pedro will be just fine."

Back at the base, he called his PCM teacher, Mr. Amato.

"Hello, Paulo, how wonderful to hear from you. How are you? Navy life good?"

"Yes, sir, it's good, but coming to an end in November. I've loved playing in the Admiral's Orchestra. It's a first-rate ensemble. The camaraderie is special, and seeing the world was…well, eye opening."

"After being stranded in Panama, I'm glad everything worked out for you. What are your plans after you're discharged?"

"That's why I called. I got married in April and wanted to ask you about musical opportunities in civilian life. I'd really appreciate your advice."

"Well, first, let me congratulate you on getting married. What's the lady's name?"

"Loucille Sweet, and she is that, and a whole lot more."

"Is she a musician, too?"

Paulo laughed. "No, she's a farm girl from Missouri, but she loves my music."

"I'm happy for you Paulo. Finding someone to love with your whole heart is a gift in this life." He paused. "Now, as to civilian opportunities in music, as I'm sure you're aware, the depression continues to worsen. Municipal orchestras all over the country have been hard hit and many have closed their doors."

Paulo sighed, "I knew things were bad generally, but I was hoping—"

"Try getting in touch with the Works Progress Administration."

"The WPA? Don't they build roads and bridges?"

"Yes, but part of Roosevelt's 1935 New Deal legislation's WPA relief programs is the Federal Music Project. The goal is to employ professional musicians and help them become self-supporting again. Contact your local WPA office and see what's available. If I hear of any orchestral openings, I'll let you know."

"Thanks so much, Mr. Amato," he said, hopeful of continuing to play.

"Take good care of your new bride. She sounds wonderful."

"Will do, and thanks again for the advice."

The WPA office, told him he could only register if he was on the relief roles in the city or county where he lived, and to call back after his discharge.

Paulo could not wait or go on the relief roles to get a job. There was no way he was going to let Loucille support him with her working as a receptionist in an insurance agent's office.

During evening mess in early October, Paulo talked to Willie, a trombone player, and fellow Pennsylvania shipmate, awaiting discharge two weeks before him.

"Willie, what are you going to do after you're out?"

"Probably help my dad and hopefully play some gigs around town."

Paulo chortled. "Violinists don't play gigs. I've got to find a real job."

Willie frowned. "What kind of job are you looking for?"

"Right now, pretty much anything."

"Would you ever consider driving a laundry truck?"

Paulo looked across the table, surprised. "Where did that come from?"

"My father owns a laundry company here in San Pedro and he's always looking for drivers. The work is hard, and drivers never stay long. I'll introduce you—if you're interested."

Reaching to pat Willie's cheeks affectionately, he said, "I'm definitely interested."

At the end of the week, Willie took Paulo to meet his father. After introductions, the short, gray-haired man lowered his spectacles and looked Paulo up and down. "Woodrow says you're quite the violinist."

Paulo glanced at Willie and mouthed "Woodrow?"

"He likes 'Willie' instead of his real name," Mr. Kolinsky scowled at his son.

"Woodrow is a very dignified name," Paulo said, looking at Willie mischievously.

"His mother and I thought so, too." Mr. Kolinsky looked at Paulo, eyes twinkling. "Never had a violinist driver before." He picked up a large white sack of laundry and tossed it to Paulo, who caught the bag in both arms with a "whuf" of surprise.

"Think you can handle a hundred of those a day?"

Paulo grinned. "Only a hundred? Yeah, no problem."

Woodrow's father assigned him the downtown route, to start the week after he was discharged.

Loucille was skeptical. "Are you sure, Paulo? You are a violinist, sweetheart."

"One with no immediate musical prospects and a beautiful wife to support."

The week before his discharge they rented a small wood-frame house in San Pedro. The light blue exterior and dark blue trim were fading, especially on the weathered posts supporting the covered porch over the front door, and on the single car garage behind the house. Inside were a tiny kitchen, breakfast nook, a Murphy bed in the front room, and a cast iron, claw-foot tub in the bathroom.

Paulo received an Honorable Discharge on Friday, November 4, 1938, with five ratings: Able Seaman, Seaman 2nd Class, Seaman, Musician 2nd Class, Seaman 1st Class, and Musician 1st Class.

CHAPTER TWENTY EIGHT

THE BREAK SIGN 1938-40

The following Monday morning, Paulo left early and walked to Mr. Kolinsky's office. The air was brisk, but nothing compared to Philadelphia's frigid winters.

"Did you walk here, Paulo? Where do you live? I like that you're early, but you understand I don't pay overtime."

"We don't have a car yet and live nearby on Gaffey Street."

Mr. Kolinsky clapped his hands. "Well, let's get you working so you can buy one. I'll ride the route today and introduce you to our customers. Woodrow will go with you the rest of the week."

The laundry truck was a step van. Reminding Paulo of a milk truck, it was white with rounded, blue fenders over the wheels, sliding doors on both sides, hinged doors on the back, and "Kolinsky Laundry Service" on each side.

The downtown route included businesses catering to the varied needs of lonely servicemen. Miss Velma's was his first stop. A three-story Victorian with multiple bright colors adorning the body, trim, and doors, with rose beds bordering the front yard.

A young woman answered the doorbell and ushered the two of them into the parlor.

Velma sat behind a small, four-legged, rosewood desk. "Good morning, Mr. Kolinsky. What a pleasant surprise." As her eyes surveyed Paulo appreciatively, the tall, lithe, fiftyish, striking woman closed her lilac morning gown and stood.

"Velma, meet your new route man, Paulo Colaluca. He played in the Admiral's Orchestra with my son, Woodrow."

"What did you play, Paulo?" Velma said, shaking his hand, but not letting go.

"Violin…first chair violin…concertmaster, actually."

"Really?" With a squeeze, she finally let go. "You must be very good."

"And he just got married this past weekend," Mr. Kolinsky said emphatically.

Velma smiled. "Girls please come here," she said in a calm, yet authoritative voice.

Three young, attractive women came into the parlor, and stood in a line facing the men, their morning gowns modestly closed.

With her hand lightly on Paulo's shoulder, Velma said, "Paulo is our new laundry man. He just got married, so he's off limits. Do you understand?"

The girls smiled at Paulo and nodded.

Velma shooed them away. "Mr. Kolinsky, I'll do my best to make sure you don't lose another driver."

"Thank you, Velma. I'll show Paulo the laundry routine and we'll be on our way."

Velma and Paulo exchanged smiles as Mr. Kolinsky led him around to the back door and showed him where laundry was left for pickup. Paulo put the four sacks in the back of the truck.

As they drove, Mr. Kolinsky described Paulo's schedule. "Laundry is picked up and returned the next day."

Paulo whistled, "That's fast!"

"Times are changing. People who can afford electric washing machines are buying, ones who can't are going to these new laundromats. We have to compete."

The remainder of the week, Woodrow—Willie, went on Paulo's routes and introduced him to customers.

Friday, a fast-walking Willie met Paulo as he came to work.

"Guess what?"

"You've taken up speed walking?"

"I got a job playing in the house band at The Majestic Ballroom on the Pike!"

"When did this happen? Why didn't you ever say something earlier?"

"Right after I was discharged, I saw an ad in the newspaper," Willie went on in a rush. "I went in for an audition, but never got a call back so forgot about it. Last night, the bandleader called. One of the bone players left town and was I still interested? I almost jumped through the phone!" Willie saluted like he was back in the Navy. "Yes, Sir, I'm interested. When do you want me to start? Paulo, tonight, me, Woodrow Kolinsky, will play with a big band! Can you believe it?"

Paulo clapped him on the back. "Congratulations! Willie, they're lucky to have you. What nights do you play?"

Willie stood still. "I don't even know…but I'll find out. Will you and Loucille come?"

"Let me know the nights and we'll be there," Paulo said, heading to the office. "Come on, we gotta get to work."

While Paulo and Loucille dated, he was at her parent's house frequently and got to know them well. Her father, Arthur moved his family to California a few years earlier to trade farming for a steady paycheck with the Long Beach City Parks Department. A groundskeeper at the sprawling 200-acre park at 7th Street and Park Avenue, his responsibilities included the 18 and 9-hole golf courses, a lawn bowling green, and the Blair Field baseball stadium.

Almyra, Loucille's mother, was a hard-working, down-to-earth Midwestern woman and mother of five, who lost a baby daughter to whooping cough back on the farm. In California, her younger sons, Harry and Bill, became star athletes at Wilson High school. Both received full scholarships to play football at USC, but couldn't keep up academically, losing their scholarships after one semester. Almyra took to Paulo right away, loving his music and that he was educated. She was thrilled when he proposed to Loucille and believed they were penny-wise for getting married in Yuma. Paulo was solicitous with her, gentle with her daughter, and was never late to family dinners. She loved his "Italian" stories and adventures. Paulo became another son to her.

Shortly after they were married, Paulo asked Loucille if she knew how to cook any Italian dishes.

"Spaghetti," she said, proudly. "You boil noodles, cut up hot dogs, put them in tomato sauce, and mix it all together. My brothers loved it."

Paulo stared at her.

"What?" she said, perplexed.

"That might be Missouri spaghetti, but it's not Italian, sweetheart."

Loucille frowned. "So, how do you make Italian spaghetti?"

"Not like that." He grinned, and quickly added, "You're a good cook, sweetheart. I love your fried chicken, potato salad, and apple pies. They're delicious, but—"

Petulantly, she said, "If you show me how, I'll make what you like."

With a hug, he kissed her forehead. "I watched my mother cook when I was growing up, but in our house the kitchen was strictly her domain. I excelled at eating everything she made. I can't make it, but I can tell you how it's supposed to look and smell. I make great Italian sandwiches, though."

Loucille gave him a flirty smile. "Would your mother give us her recipes?"

"She'll have to write them down first. I never saw her use any, but I'll ask."

"She can't cook your favorite foods?" Anna said, a sarcastic edge in her voice.

"Mama, she's a good cook of American food, and wants to learn how to cook Italian for me. Will you please send her some of your recipes?"

"Of course. For you, Paulo anything. What do want her to cook?"

He looked at Loucille, sitting in the breakfast nook. "Mama, I love everything, but could we start with your pasta fagioli, your bracioli, and Pop's special meatballs?"

"Si, bambino. I'll write them, but be patient, I'm still slow with it."

"Thank you, Mama. I'll call you soon as they get here."

"Paulo, is she good to you?" Anna said softly.

"Yes, Mama, all the time. I love her very much."

"That's good." Quietly, she said, "Tell her I said 'Hello'. Goodnight, Paulo."

The recipes came a week later. They listed the ingredients, and instructions to add a "pinch" of this or that, approximate cooking temperatures and times based on how the food looked and tasted.

The first time they made pasta fagioli, Paulo finished his second bowl, patted his stomach, and announced, "I'm in heaven."

They called Anna that night and the first time they made each of her recipes. Eventually, she and Loucille talked directly about cooking Paulo's favorite foods.

"I want to invite Harry and Bill for dinner," Loucille said one January evening. They sat close together on their thrift store love seat, her fingertips tracing the floral pattern of the upholstery.

"You might want to invite them for lunch and maybe by dinner time—"

She shoved into him. "Come on, they're not that bad."

"Oh, really? How many times have they been late for dinner at your mother's?"

"Well, I want to cook them an authentic Italian meal."

"Fine, just make sure they know we eat at six, okay?"

Loucille invited her brothers for their "authentic Italian dinner" at six and called to remind them a week before.

"Hi, Harry. I just wanted to remind you about our dinner, Saturday night."

"At your house, right?"

"Yes, my house, six o'clock sharp. Okay?"

"I'll be there," he assured her.

She hung up and called Bill to remind him, too.

Saturday morning, she and Paulo walked the few blocks to the market on Gaffey Street to buy ingredients for Anna's recipe for rigatoni and meatballs in marinara sauce.

As his father always did, Paulo asked the butcher to put bread through his grinder before grinding the steak for the meatballs. Next came rigatoni noodles, more spices for his mother's sweet spaghetti sauce, French baguettes, everything for an antipasto salad, extra Parmesan cheese, and two bottles of Chianti.

"I hope I didn't forget anything," Loucille said on the walk home.

"Any more and we'd need a wheelbarrow," he joked, a heavy grocery bag in each hand.

That afternoon, they stood next to each other at the kitchen counter, bumping hips and laughing, as they made the meatballs, antipasto salad, and garlic bread. Preparations completed, they tidied the house, set the kitchen nook table…then took a bath—together.

"I hope my brothers like it," she said, toweling off, as Paulo wiped steam off the window.

"What's not to like?" He pretended to snap his towel at her. "They'll never go back to spaghetti and wienies again," he said, smirking.

At five-thirty, she put a two handled-pot of water on to boil, checked the simmering meatballs, lowered the heat, and opened a bottle of Chianti.

The two of them sat in the nook, Paulo raised his wine glass. "To my wife the Italian cook, Salute."

Loucille smiled shyly and took a sip of wine. At five-forty-five, she put the rigatoni in to cook and turned on the oven.

Five minutes later, she furtively looked out the kitchen window. In another five minutes, she went to the front door, stepped on the porch, and scanned the street.

"Something must be holding them up," Paulo heard her say.

She came back in, put the bread in the oven, stirred the rigatoni, and held one out on the wooden spoon for Paulo to taste.

He blew on the steaming noodle, put in his mouth, and chewed slowly. "Al dente. Perfetto. It's perfect sweetheart," he said, hugging her.

She drained the rigatoni, put them in a big ceramic serving bowl, and ladled meatballs and sauce on top, while Paulo put the antipasto and garlic bread on the table.

As they waited for her brothers to arrive, Paulo finished his glass of wine.

"I even called to remind them," Loucille said at six-fifteen, tearing up. She could tell Paulo was also upset.

"Let's eat before the food gets cold, okay?" he said, his anger growing.

"You go ahead, Paulo, I'm going to wait."

Angrily he said, "This is exactly how they treat your mother."

Loucille got up and looked out the window, again.

"Please, come and eat your delicious dinner," he said, putting another fork full of rigatoni in his mouth.

She shook her head and continued to look out the window, arms crossed across her stomach.

Paulo ate quickly, got up and began putting the food away.

"What are you doing?" she said.

"Those two need to know they can't treat you like this, Loucille. They're not eating here tonight."

"What? "I can warm it up—"

"No, you're not, Loucille!" he said angrily, dropping his plate and silverware in the sink with a bang. He walked into the front room and pulled the Murphy bed down.

She stood in the kitchen doorway with tears in her eyes, and watched him change into his pajamas, lock the front door, and turn off the porch light.

"I'm sorry, but I'm not waiting for those two and pretending everything's okay." He motioned for her. "Come to bed. Please." He got into bed.

Loucille wiped her tears with the back of her hand and turned off the kitchen light.

She went in the bathroom and returned in her nightgown. Paulo turned off the nightstand light. Loucille laid down with her back to him, sniffling.

Hands behind his head, Paulo lay there seething.

Loucille stopped sniffling when she heard a knock on the door, followed by "Hey, we're here." Paulo glanced at the alarm clock on the nightstand, got up, turned the porch light on, and opened the front door.

Harry and Bill blinked in the sudden brightness.

"Aren't we supposed to have dinner with you guys tonight?" Harry asked, surprised at seeing Paulo in his pajamas through the screen door.

"The invitation was for six o'clock, it's damn near seven-thirty. You do know how to tell time, don't you?"

"Hey, we got hung up, okay?" Bill said defensively.

"Your sister spent all day making a real Italian meal for you, and you two inconsiderate jerks didn't even call when you knew you were going to be late." Paulo opened the screen door and stepped out on the front porch.

"Don't you ever disrespect your sister like this again. Do you understand?" he said through gritted teeth

Both nodded, kept their heads down, and took a step back.

"The only reason I won't beat the shit out of you both, right here, right now, is because we're family." He shook his head. "Now get the hell off my porch." He turned, went inside, slammed the door, and shut off the porch light.

When he got back in bed, Loucille was still turned away from him, but wasn't crying. "Nobody's ever going to treat my wife like that. Those two, especially, needed to know that."

At dinner Monday, Loucille said, "My mother called me at work today,"

"Almyra called you at work?" Paulo stopped eating. "Is everything ok?"

Loucille smiled. "Mother told me my brothers showed up early for Sunday dinner. When she asked if they'd enjoyed their authentic Italian dinner with us, she'd never seen them so flustered. Finally, Harry fessed-up about being late and the dressing down you gave them. She wanted me to thank you for what you did and invited us to family dinner next Sunday."

"I like your mother more and more," Paulo said, with a grin.

Married life agreed with Paulo. Loucille was loving, fun to be with, and frugal with money. She continued working as a receptionist for Mr. Ziskin, the Prudential insurance agent, riding the bus every day to downtown Long Beach.

Paulo enjoyed working for Mr. Kolinsky, who encouraged and mentored him about running a business, and liked getting to know his eclectic group of customers.

He and Loucille mutually decided their first big purchase would be a car. Paulo wanted his boyhood dream car, the convertible Kissel roadster, but Loucille wanted something practical that wouldn't put them in debt.

Their "dream" car sat in the driveway of an elderly couple, one they'd seen while walking to the market as they did each Saturday.

A "For Sale" sign in the rear window caught their attention. The dark blue, 1932 Buick roadster was a hardtop, with roll-up windows, a rumble seat, and wire wheels. Well cared for, with low mileage, it shined in the morning sun and best of all, it was in their price range. They talked to the owners, hurried to their bank on Gaffey Street, and were back with the cash before noon. With groceries in the rumble seat of the first car either of them had owned, they took their maiden excursion.

"Where would you like to go this afternoon, Mrs. Colaluca?" Paulo asked, as he pulled into the garage.

"First I want to show Mom and Dad," she said excitedly, "and after that anywhere. Where do you want to go?"

Paulo thought a moment. "Let's drive up to the top of Signal Hill. It's supposed to have a great view of the city."

"Ever been there at night?" Loucille said with a coy smile.

"Why ever would I go at night, my love?"

"Because you were a handsome, Italian sailor, and it's the best place in Long Beach to make-out!"

Paulo's hand went over his heart, feigning hurt by her words.

"P-l-e-a-s-e," she said. "If I've been up there a few times, I'm sure you have."

Paulo winked at her. "Well, it's nice to know I married an experienced woman."

"And don't you ever forget it, my handsome wop," she said with an exaggerated wink back, grabbing a bag of groceries from the rumble seat.

Paulo loved to drive. Sunday drives became adventures up and down the southern California coast. Sometimes, Loucille packed a traditional picnic lunch of fried chicken, deviled eggs, and pie, or Paulo stopped at a market to buy an impromptu picnic of bread, cold cuts, cheese, and potato salad. Finding a park or shady spot with a view, they laid out the checkered wool blanket they kept in the car, and simply enjoyed being together.

*

The lead on the evening news Friday, September 1, 1939, was of a German "Blitzkrieg" or "lightning war." Germany had invaded Poland with highly mobile forces that rapidly overwhelmed the Polish army.

*

The following Monday, Paulo picked up the laundry from Velma's. As he pulled out from the curb, a car slammed into the driver's side of the step van. The impact knocked Paulo across the inside of the Kolinsky Laundry truck.

Velma and her girls heard the crash and came running. They pulled him out through the passenger-side door and laid him on the grass median.

Paulo was in shock, moaning and holding his left leg.

Velma called Mr. Kolinsky, who called the police and then rushed to the scene.

An ambulance transported him to San Pedro General Hospital on Sixth Street, where X-rays showed a fracture of the left tibia. In surgery, his leg was set and put in a cast. Paulo stayed in recovery before being placed in a room.

After Mr. Kolinsky called Loucille, her boss closed the office and drove her to the hospital. A nurse came out of Paulo's room as she arrived.

"How is he? Is he all right?" she said, fighting back tears.

The nurse put her hand on Loucille's arm. "Are you Loucille?"

"Yes."

"He kept calling your name in recovery and saying he loved you. It was very sweet. He's going to be fine. He'll be here a few days to make sure there are no complications. He's asleep, but you're welcome to sit with him as long as you like." The nurse smiled and walked down the hall.

Loucille went in and sat next to his bed. The cast on Paulo's left leg went from his groin down to his ankle and was elevated on pillows. She wiped tears from her cheeks as she listened to him breathe.

Family or friends took Loucille to visit Paulo in the hospital every night. At the end of the week, he came home on crutches. Being confined to bed for most of each day gave him a lot of thinking time. As much as he liked Mr. Kolinsky and enjoyed his customers, especially unconventional ones like Velma, driving a laundry truck would not be his career.

A week out of the hospital, he causally remarked at dinner, "I really think the accident was a sign."

Loucille stared at him. "A sign?"

"Yeah. It barreled into me and said, 'Paulo, it's time to move on with your life.'"

She reached across the table and squeezed his hand. "I'm glad to hear that, Paulo. You have so much talent. You're smart and good with people. I don't know about the sign, but you need something that challenges you and gives you a purpose in life."

The next day, when Mr. Ziskin asked her how Paulo was, she shared their discussion.

Mr. Ziskin smiled, reminiscing. "He sounds like me back in the day. Before I became a Prudential agent, I was in a dead-end job like Paulo, wanting something more for myself and my family. Helping people protect themselves, and their loved ones, has given me a lot of satisfaction over the years and provided a good income, too."

"How does somebody become an insurance agent?"

Mr. Ziskin counted the steps. "You have to study the state licensing manual, take the exam, and if you pass, you get finger-printed, and submit an application. Tell Paulo if he's interested, I'll be happy to talk to him."

"Thank you so much, Mr. Ziskin. I'll tell him tonight."

Paulo was excited that evening at what Loucille told him, immediately barraging her with questions.

"Whoa, I've told you everything he said. If you call him tomorrow, I'm sure he will answer all your questions. Does it sound like something you'd like to do?"

He thought a moment. "Helping people get insurance is about protecting who they love and what's valuable to them. I like the idea of doing something important."

Paulo called the next day, and after they talked, Mr. Ziskin sent a copy of the State Licensing Manual home with Loucille, for Paulo to study.

For the next month, Paulo studied the California Department of Insurance Licensing Manual with the same focus and perseverance he'd applied to learning new musical compositions. Each night after dinner, Loucille quizzed him on the section he studied that day. Mr. Ziskin patiently answered his questions and encouraged him.

In mid-October, a follow-up X-ray showed his fracture was healed, so the cast was removed, and he was able to drive again.

Paulo took the next scheduled Licensing Examination early in November. After four weeks, he received an official letter with his results. He immediately called Loucille.

"I got my results," he said excitedly. "I passed with a score of ninety-five percent!"

"Oh, Paulo, I'm so proud of you," she said, tearing up.

"Were going out to dinner tonight to celebrate. I'll pick you up at work. Please tell Mr. Ziskin. I couldn't have done it without his help and encouragement—and all your help. I love you, sweetheart. See you soon."

Paulo was fingerprinted and sent in his application for a license the next week. When his license arrived in January 1940, Mr. Ziskin helped him apply and get a position with the Prudential Insurance Company. The Regional Manager described the southern California communities that were underserved and promising places for Prudential to open an office. The closest one was north and west of Long Beach. When the manager pointed to it on a map, Paulo's mind flashed back to sunning himself on the Pennsylvania's fantail in November 1936. *He was talking to Jack, the trumpet player, about winter in Philadelphia. His friend had laughed and shared about a childhood half-inch snowfall in his hometown.* The manager's finger was tapping on Gardena.

On Saturday, Paulo and Loucille drove to investigate this latest "sign" about their future. The Chamber of Commerce was welcoming and provided all sorts of information.

Gardena was now a city, incorporated in 1930. It was tiny, only 5.8 square miles. Japanese immigrants began farming strawberries, raspberries, and blackberries in the area, before the turn of the century. Back then it was known as "Berryland". The public library was still the "Strawberry Flats" branch. Commercial development was just beginning along the major streets on its borders: Western Avenue, Vermont Avenue, and Redondo

Beach Boulevard.

Gardena High School, built in 1901, was renamed the Gardena Agricultural High School in 1908. It had a working farm, livestock, and a curriculum to better reflect the local economy. Its two elementary schools, 156th Street and Denker Ave., were built in 1917 and 1932 respectively.

Paulo and Loucille drove up and down residential streets, some without curbs and sidewalks, seeing single-family homes set back from the street, often with empty lots on either side. The downtown street was three blocks long with no chain stores, one Post Office, and had a railroad spur running through it. Numerous berry farms dotted the area, owned and operated by Japanese residents.

By the time they stopped for a late lunch, Loucille was smitten.

"It reminds me of where I grew up," she said, as they waited for their order. "There's a feeling of openness, especially with the farming. Everyone's been so friendly. I feel comfortable here, Paulo."

They returned Sunday. A realtor gave them a list of homes for sale or rent, along with a map, and told them to come back if they saw any they liked.

They drove by several, before stopping in front of a three-bedroom home at 1561 158th Street. The street was paved, but without curbs or sidewalks. The pale blue house had white shutters, an attached single car garage on its right side, and appeared empty. It sat in the middle front of a two-acre lot. Two-foot weeds covered the yard, which they stepped over and onto a sidewalk that led to the covered front porch and peered through the windows. Another sidewalk went around to the side of the house and ended at the backdoor stoop. Holding hands, they continued carefully through the tall grass to the stand of bamboo at the back of the lot. Only bamboo and empty lots lay on both sides of the property.

Back in front, they leaned on the car, surveying everything.

Loucille spoke first. "This would be a good place to raise a family."

Paulo looked at her, surprised.

"We've talked about this, Paulo. We both want children, right?" She waved her hand back and forth, "This would be a wonderful place to raise them."

He smiled at her. "Been talking to my mother?"

"No, but every mother wants grandchildren."

Paulo surveyed the property again. "I'd like to get my parents out of

Germantown winters." Pointing behind the house, "I could build a home for them right there."

"And they could watch their grandchildren grow up," she said, hugging him.

At the realtor's office, they signed a rental agreement with an option to buy, paid him the first and last month's rent, and got the keys to the property.

Loucille gave Mr. Ziskin her two-week notice.

Paulo met with Prudential's regional manager to let him know he was moving to Gardena, so that area would no longer be underserved and was given his new agent materials. While Loucille finished her two weeks, Paulo drove to Gardena every day, got the utilities turned on, joined the Chamber of Commerce and the Gardena Lions Club, began cleaning the house, and mowed the lawn. On weekends, they shopped for appliances and furniture, started painting inside, and introduced themselves to neighbors.

Since getting married they both worked and saved their money, but money was tight the first few months. The first life insurance policies he sold were for himself and Loucille. Quickly, Paulo became known in the community. With his ability to communicate, his professional manner, and by going door-to-door, he brought in more and more clients as the year progressed.

Paulo's marketing plan for his new business was simple. Let people know the Prudential Insurance Company was there to help them *"plan for the future by protecting the ones they loved."*

Like all the other things he did in life, Paulo attacked the challenge with tenacity and charm. In addition to going door-to-door, he made presentations to every service club, business, PTA, and church group in Gardena. As his client list grew, he offered incentives for referrals, and expanded his outreach into neighboring communities.

Loucille ran their home office, answering the phone, making appointments, keeping his schedule, processing paperwork, and making sure he looked professional going out the front door.

*

In May, Germany invaded the low-countries and northern France, leading to the evacuation of British and French troops from the seaport of Dunkirk on June 4.

From July through September the war news was all about the "The Battle of Britain". After months of bombing Britain's air bases, military posts, and its civilian population, the Luftwaffe failed to gain air superiority over the Royal Air Force, causing Hitler to abandon Operation Sea Lion and not invade England.

*

By the end of 1940, three things had happened that helped Paulo move closer to achieving the goals he voiced to Loucille a year earlier when they leaned against their car in front of a blue house with an overgrown lawn.

First, after a year of perseverance in building his insurance business, it was supporting the two of them—and making a profit.

Second, they exercised the option in their rental agreement and bought the blue house at 1561 158th Street.

Third, Paulo was recognized in December, as the top selling new agent for the southern California region. The framed award came with a $500 dollar check.

On the way home from the presentation ceremony at Prudential's Los Angeles office, Loucille held the award in her lap and kept smiling at Paulo.

"I'm so proud of you." She leaned over and kissed his cheek. "You're amazing."

"We're amazing!" He held up a hand and using his fingers, ticked off, "You answered calls, scheduled appointments, handled the paperwork, and made sure I always looked professional." He held up his pinkie and winked at her, "Your late-night secretarial services were…ah, very motivational."

Loucille pushed on his shoulder. "Stop it," she said, turning red.

"Seriously, Loucille, we did it together."

Loucille held up the check. "A down payment on the house for your parents?"

His smile broadened. "That would certainly start the ball rolling."

Since asking his mother for her recipes, he and Loucille called Raffaele and Anna regularly when they lived in San Pedro, typically on Sunday afternoons, to check on them, and get family news.

After they moved to Gardena, the Sunday phone calls continued, and before Christmas, Paulo broached the idea of them coming to live with Loucille and him. It was tradition in Italian families for first sons to care for parents.

Raffaele was nearing retirement, and as a first son himself, understood Paulo's request and was willing to come. Anna was adamantly against it. She had all sorts of reasons for not leaving Germantown: her church, her friends, Clara, and Vincenzo.

Paulo and Loucille spent Christmas day, 1940, with her parents. Almyra outdid herself. When Art sat down at the head of the table, the mid-afternoon meal spread before them included turkey, ham, green bean casserole, mashed potatoes, yams, deviled eggs, homemade cranberry sauce, and pumpkin pie. After they recovered with a nap, Loucille and Paulo went to the Pike to see Woodrow play at the Majestic Ballroom.

CHAPTER TWENTY NINE

INFAMY 1941

"*Happy* New Year, Pop! Welcome to 1941. How are you and Mama?"

"We're good, Paulo," Raffaele said, his voice scratchy.

"You don't sound good. Are you sick?"

"No, no, a little cold, that's all."

"What's the weather like back there?"

"Cold, lots of snow this year."

"It's sunny and warm here, Pop. I want you and Mama here and out of that miserable weather. You would love it."

"I know, Paulo, but your mother—"

"Pop, please! We have a Catholic church. When was the last time you saw Clara or Vincenzo?"

"Um, Clara came by before Christmas and left us a present. Anna, when did Vincenzo come to see us?"

Paulo heard his mother say, "For Thanksgiving, don't you remember?"

"I heard, Pop," he said, pausing to control his tone. "I just won an award from the Prudential Insurance Company. It came with a check for the down payment, so I can build a house for you and Mama, right behind mine, and take care of you."

A long silence followed before Paulo heard his mother ask, "What's he saying?"

"Pop, put Mama on the phone."

"Hello, Paulo, how are you?"

"I'm fine, Mama. I told Pop I now have the money to build a house for you."

"But—"

"No buts, Mama. Winters there are hard on you both. It's freezing there and sunny and 70 degrees here. Mama, the Italian tradition is the first son takes care of his parents. We're three thousand miles apart and it's my responsibility, not Clara's or Vincenzo's. Besides, it's what I want to do."

Silence.

"Mama, I love you and want take care of you and Pop," Paulo said, his voice and tone gentle.

Raffaele came back on the line. "She's crying and shaking her head, Paulo. Let's not talk about this anymore, per favore."

Before calling his parents each Sunday, Paulo checked the paper's national weather map. Each time when he asked about the weather, invariably his father said it was better than reported.

As the year progressed, daily news of German and Japanese aggression around the world, combined with America's fear of being drawn into war, fueled isolationism. People thought about what they had and how to protect it, making insurance more important and Paulo's business grow.

At breakfast, after checking the weather before his Sunday call to his parents, Paulo looked out at the blue sky and May clouds. "Maybe if we go ahead and build the house, they'll come for a visit."

Loucille smiled. "Persistence is your middle name."

"Once they're here and see how nice—"

"And devious is your first name," she added.

"Devious has negative connotations. I'm just being indirect," he added impishly.

"Well, Mr. 'Indirect', let's not bring it up again, okay? Your mother's not ready and you, of all people, know she doesn't like to be pushed."

In June, Vincenzo called, to report he was being transferred to the new Naval Air Station at Willow Grove, north of Philadelphia. He would be part of a new classified, anti-submarine warfare program.

"The damn German U-Boats are killing us in the North Atlantic. Allied shipping losses are going up every month!" Vincenzo growled.

"That's what I keep reading. I know it's classified, but can you tell me anything about what you're going to be doing?"

"Only, that I'm finally going get to fly, big brother? It's my dream come true. I told Mom and Pop, but I'll be out of contact for a while and she's gonna worry."

"Count on it, little brother." Paulo laughed. "She has gray hair from you growing up."

"And from you, too, big brother. Seriously, we are going to war. It's a matter of time. I'm glad you're out of it. Gotta go. Will call when I can. Thanks for taking care of Mom and Pop. I love you." The line went dead.

*

June 22, 1941, Germany invaded western Russia with over three million troops in Operation Barbarossa. Despite extensive territorial gains and inflicting serious losses on the Red Army, by December 5 the mission to destroy Soviet fighting power failed to force a capitulation.

In July, when Japan moved to take the rest of Indochina, the United States froze all Japanese assets, and on August 1 established an oil embargo. Diplomatic negotiations with Japan, begun earlier in the year, continued into the fall.

*

At the end of July, Vincenzo called. "Remember, in spring, I said 'war is coming'? Well, it's here big brother. Our Navy's been helping the British escort convoys since April. At first, we could report it when we saw a German submarine. This week, Roosevelt authorized us to shoot at them. My squadron is being transferred closer to the action. We'll be flying anti-submarine patrols over those convoys." He went on more softly. "I have a friend who works at the Pentagon. He tells me that General Motors, Chrysler, and Ford have retooled their plants to turn out fighter planes, tanks, and bombers."

"Really?"

"We're gonna be in a war with Germany or Japan soon, big brother. You know the Japs have already invaded Manchuria, China, and the Soviet Union, right?"

"They're halfway around the world from us, Vincenzo."

"Yeah, and this summer we stopped sending them oil that they need to fuel their huge Navy and expand their empire. They're not happy with us. Hey, gotta go. Stay safe there on the west coast, big brother. Hug Loucille for me. I'll call when I can. Love you."

Paulo was staring out the window when Loucille came in.

"Who was that on the phone?"

"Vincenzo."

"What did he say?" His face told her it was serious.

*

On September 8, the German army began a genocidal siege of Leningrad.

*

Paulo and Loucille spent Thanksgiving with her parents. While relaxing on the couch after another of Almyra's delicious holiday meals, a special news bulletin came over the radio. Operation Barbarossa, Germany's invasion of the Soviet Union, had come within 200 miles of capturing Moscow, but the army had bogged down and stopped advancing due to the early Russian winter.

*

Sunday, December 7, as Paulo and Loucille read the Sunday paper, a special announcement interrupted the music playing on the radio.

This is KTU in Honolulu, Hawaii. I am speaking from the roof of the Advertiser Publishing Company Building. We have witnessed this morning the distant view of a brief full battle of Pearl Harbor and the severe bombing of Pearl Harbor by enemy planes, undoubtedly Japanese. The city of Honolulu has also been attacked and considerable damage done. This battle has been going on for nearly three hours. One of the bombs dropped within fifty feet of KTU tower. It is no joke. It is a real war. The public of Honolulu has been advised to keep in their homes and await results from the Army and Navy. There has been fierce fighting going on in the air and on the sea. The heavy shooting seems to be — one, two, three, four. Just a moment. We'll interrupt here...We cannot estimate yet how much damage has been done, but it has been a very severe attack. And the Navy and Army appear now to have the air and the sea under control.

Paulo stared at Loucille. "Jesus Christ, Vincenzo was right. We're at war." Throughout the afternoon and evening, announcements interrupted regularly scheduled radio programs. The Metropolitan Opera was interrupted with the announcement that Japan declared war on the U.S. and Great Britain. During the Jack Benny Program, a local announcement was made to Californians requesting that civilians not get hysterical, and they should report for volunteer duty.

First Lady Eleanor Roosevelt, used her Sunday evening broadcast to discuss the situation. President Roosevelt interrupted a Sherlock Holmes mystery to announce that he would address Congress the next day and make his report to the country.

*

Paulo and Loucille made repeated attempts to call family members, but phone lines were tied up. Finally, late in the evening, they talked to everyone except Vincenzo.

*

By day's end, the government moved swiftly to solve the "Japanese Problem" in Hawaii and on the west coast, by having the FBI arrest selected "enemy" aliens, including 1,200 Japanese Issei (first generation) immigrant men in California. This included businessmen, Buddhist priests, Japanese language teachers, and other community leaders. More than 5,500 Issei men were eventually picked up and held as potential threats to national security.

*

"December 7th is a date which will live in infamy," announced President Roosevelt during his December 8 radio address to the country. The USA was at war. Indignantly, he vowed that the "unbounding determination of our people...will gain the inevitable triumph—so help us God." Britain joined the United States in declaring war on Japan.

That same day, Japan invaded Southeast Asia, including British Malaya and the Philippines.

*

In the days that followed, Paulo and Loucille learned first-hand, which of their Issei friends had been arrested and taken away, and the devastating impact on the families they knew.

By the end of that week, Loucille finished writing Christmas cards to Paulo's clients, their family, and friends

"Thank you for organizing our Christmas cards," he said. "I'll take them to the Post Office. What would I do without you?"

She just smiled.

Paulo and Loucille spent Christmas day with the Sweets. Loucille and Almyra were inseparable, as they prepared dinner. Shooing the men out of the kitchen, they talked and giggled like schoolgirls.

*

A special bulletin on the evening news announced that Hong Kong had surrendered to the Imperial Japanese Army.

*

Sunday morning, Loucille returned from the bathroom and curled up in bed next to Paulo. She walked her fingers across his chest.

He rolled on his side and kissed her gently. "You're awfully frisky—"

Her finger pressed against his lips. "Shh. I want to tell you something. I think I'm pregnant, Paulo."

A smile spread across his face. "Really?"

"I've missed my period twice," she whispered, her lips on his, "Will you help me make sure?"

"Gladly," he said, embracing her.

Afterwards, as he was shaving, Paulo felt Loucille's arms around him. "Thank you," she said softly, squeezing him. "That was wonderful."

"Anytime beautiful, anytime."

"I want to see Dr. Storken and have him confirm it."

"Breakfast first, okay? I need sustenance you animal."

She poked him in the ribs.

"Hey, it was your idea!"

"Well, you didn't hold back. So, Romeo, what would you like for breakfast?"

Paulo came into the kitchen, leafed through their address book, and gave Loucille Dr. Storken's emergency number. Nurse Green answered, and after Loucille explained the reason for the weekend call, she congratulated her and scheduled an early appointment for the following day.

The minute she hung up, Paulo took the phone and started dialing.

Loucille stopped him. "Who are you calling?"

"My parents and then yours, to tell them the good news."

"Not until we're sure, okay?"

Paulo put the phone back in the cradle. "Sure, sweetheart, whatever you want. Will you let me take you out to dinner at least?"

"I'd love a romantic dinner with you," she said, giving him a long, slow kiss.

Dr. Storken called the following Friday and asked to speak to Loucille. "The results of your test came back sooner than I expected and were positive. Congratulations, you are pregnant."

Loucille nodded excitedly and mouthed, "Yes" to Paulo.

"Your pelvic exam was normal," Dr. Storken continued, "so call my nurse next week and schedule a four-week follow-up appointment. Congratulations again, to you and Paulo. Happy New Year."

At home, Loucille held out the handset. "Okay, call your parents."

"Call Almyra first, she's closer."

After that call, with the accompanying joyful tears, it was Paulo's turn.

"Hi, Pop, I'm calling to tell you—"

"What's wrong?"

"Nothing's wrong."

"It's not Sunday."

Paulo chuckled. "You're right, Pop, it's not Sunday. It's Friday. Loucille has something she wants to tell Mama, okay?"

"Sure, sure, Paulo. Anna, Loucille wants to talk to you. Come, take the phone."

"Hello?" Anna said.

"Anna, Paulo and I just found out. I'm going to have a baby."

"A baby? When? A boy or a girl?" Anna asked rapidly.

"Sometime in August or September. I'm hoping for a boy."

"Raffaele," Anna said, crying, "she's going to have a baby! Take the phone."

"Is she all right?" Loucille asked Raffaele. "I thought she'd be happy?"

Raffaele chortled. "Oh, she's happy. She's waving a handkerchief and smiling. That's wonderful news, Loucille. Can I talk to Paulo?"

"Is Mama, okay?" Paulo asked.

"Yes, they're happy tears. Congratulazoni, Paulo. I must go. Your mother wants to call Clara to tell her the news."

"Sure, Pop. Do you think Mama will come to see the baby?"

"I think maybe, yes."

During breakfast the next morning, the phone rang.

"I want to talk to Loucille," Anna said.

"Sure, hold on." He motioned to Loucille. "Mama wants to talk to you."

"Good morning, Anna. How nice—"

"I will come to see the bambino."

Loucille looked at Paul. "Thank you, Anna. That makes me very happy."

Anna's tone softened. "Babies are a special blessing."

"It's just…I want everything to be—"

"Everything will be fine."

"I hope so, Anna."

"Do not worry, mia figlia. Now, I want to talk to Paulo."

"Are you coming for a visit, Mama?"

"Yes, but not to live, Paulo, capisci?"

"Yes, Mama, I understand."

"Is Loucille worried about the baby?"

"I don't think so. It was a surprise to both of us, Mama. Why are you asking?"

"How do you say…intuizione?"

"Intuition?"

"Si, I have an intuition she is worried. Take care of her, Paulo."

"I will, Mama," he said, looking at Loucille.

"I love you, Paulo. Goodbye." The phone clicked off.

"What does 'mia figlia' mean?" Loucille asked.

"It means 'my daughter' in Italian, and coming from my mother, a lot more."

CHAPTER THIRTY

WAR AND DEATH 1942

Millions of men volunteered to fight after Pearl Harbor. The military offered salaries equal to what 80% of civilians were earning, and included disability, death benefits, and widow's pensions. The result was people didn't buy personal insurance as before.

Undaunted, Paulo continued to grow his business by increasing personal outreach and client referrals.

*

Japan captured the principal rubber producing areas of the Far East, eliminating 90 percent of the world's natural rubber production. The Office of Price Administration (OPA) began wartime rationing December 1941, beginning with tires, followed by automobiles in January 1942.

*

Hearing Paulo pull into the driveway, Loucille met him with a kiss at the front door. "Welcome home handsome. How was your day?"

"Good." He set his briefcase down and hugged her. "I sold a policy and got a referral I'll follow up on. Your phone calls are really working. You give our clients a friendly reminder that we didn't sell them insurance and walk away when the world's falling apart. And they save wear and tear on our five tires per car ration. I'm not sure the Ration Board would see selling insurance as an essential service and let me recap them when they wear out."

"I like making the calls. The wives tell me all about their families. It's interesting."

Seeing him glance into the kitchen, she asked, "Are you hungry?"

"Starved. Your delicious sandwich was almost six hours ago," he said, inhaling the enticing aroma from the kitchen. Moving past her, he added, "What's for dinner?"

"Eggplant parmigiana and salad."

Opening the oven, he smacked his lips, "It smells delicious."

"Go sit down and I'll feed you," Loucille said, turning him toward the kitchen table.

"Tell me about the new client," she said, bringing food to the table.

"Met him after lunch. He owns a neighborhood market in Hermosa Beach and wants a policy to protect his wife and three kids. Nice guy, ten years older than me, and a Navy man who loves living at the beach. He referred and introduced me to an employee."

Paulo took a bite of eggplant and sucked in his breath. "Hot, hot."

"Slow down or you'll burn your tongue," Loucille advised.

Paulo took a gulp of water and blew out slowly. "I delivered my debit notes this morning, to give clients a heads-up that an invoice is coming and ate my lunch on the pier. The ocean was shades of green in close to the beach, and sparkling blue to the horizon. I reminisced about my Navy days. I enjoyed them," he grinned, "once I got over being seasick."

The last Friday in January, Paulo took Loucille to her follow-up appointment with Dr. Storken. Their blood tests to determine if their Rh Factors were compatible showed they were not. She was Rh negative. Paulo was Rh positive.

"Have you had any previous pregnancies?" Dr. Storken asked Loucille, as he took her history.

Tears welled in her eyes, as she glanced at Paulo and then back at Dr. Storken. "I had a miscarriage during my first marriage."

"Do you remember what year that was?"

Loucille stared at him in disbelief. "1936. November. My first husband was abusive. The miscarriage happened after he broke my arm. That's why I divorced him."

"I'm sorry, Loucille," Dr. Storken said softly. "Because you and Paulo have different Rh Factors, you will likely develop antibodies in your blood, during this pregnancy. The baby's blood type will be from Paulo, and your antibodies might cause problems for your baby."

"Is there something we can do to prevent that?" Paulo asked.

Dr. Storken shook his head. "There is no way to prevent the antibodies from developing, but we can reduce their effect on the baby by ensuring any transfusions Loucille receives are Rh negative."

"I'm so sorry, Paulo. I didn't know," Loucille murmured through tears.

"No one knew, sweetheart," he said, touching her knee.

Sunday afternoon, while Loucille napped, Paulo called his parents.

"Hi, Pop. How are you doing?"

"Good, Paulo. Are Japanese invading California? Are you and Loucille safe?"

"Well Pop, people are jumpy, but it's all rumors. We're perfectly safe here in Gardena. Civil Defense spotters are in towers and in patrol planes, flying up and down the coast. Lights are blacked out at night, and with Japan over five thousand miles away, you don't have to worry, okay? Can I talk to Mama?"

Anna came on the line. "Paulo, how are Loucille and the baby?"

"Your intuition was right, Mama. At the doctor this week, we learned she and I have different blood types. She's what's called Rh negative and I'm Rh positive. The baby will have my blood type, but if her blood mixes with the baby's at birth, there could be problems. Loucille blames herself and thinks she's done something wrong."

"She has done nothing wrong, Paulo," Anna said forcefully. "Loucille is strong and will be a good mother. I will light a candle every Sunday at Mass and pray every day for your baby to be healthy. God will provide."

His mother's certainty washed over him.

"Can I talk to her?"

"She's asleep, Mama, I can wake—"

"No. Tell her she's done nothing wrong. Babies are a gift from God, and just love the perfect soul he gives her, capisci?"

"I understand. I'll tell her, Mama."

"You take care of yourself and mia figlia."

When Loucille woke up, Paulo relayed his mother's comforting words.

"I love your mother. I need to do what I can and leave the rest to the Almighty."

Paulo knew that besides her mother, Loucille's two best friends in Gardena were Mrs. McKeever, an elderly widow who lived directly across the street, and Katherine Scott who also lived across from them and a few doors towards town on 158th.

Katherine, or Katsey, was expecting her first child soon. She and Loucille saw each other almost every day, walking to the other's house, for coffee or lunch, to talk about their pregnancies, families, or the latest war news.

At dinner, he again brought up the idea of building the house for his parents.

Surprised, Loucille said, "Your mother's just coming for a visit, when the baby's born."

"But if she could see the house, walk around inside, know it was here anytime they wanted to come out, it might get her comfortable with the idea."

He waited for Loucille to respond as she studied his face.

"Wanting to have your parents close and take care of them is one of the things I love about you. If you think the time is right, let's build their home."

The next day Paulo called George, one of his first Gardena customers. A general contractor, George became a friend while repairing their leaky garage roof. Paulo told him his plan to build a two-bedroom house for his parents behind their home.

Later in the week, George brought preliminary plans. They agreed on a floor plan, stucco exterior, and asphalt shingles. George promised to be finished in July.

Next day, Paulo met with another of his clients, the Bank of America manager downtown on Gardena Blvd., and took out a construction loan. George began work the following week, and construction continued through the spring and into summer.

*

In February 1942, automobile manufacturers converted their plants to produce tanks, aircraft, and weapons.

Sunday, February 15, the evening news reported that Singapore had fallen to the Japanese, causing the largest surrender of British-led military personnel in history.

Thursday, February 19, Roosevelt signed Executive Order 9066, authorizing the deportation and incarceration of over 110,000 Japanese Americans, including United States citizens. These people were to be removed from their homes and transferred to ten internment camps in the west.

That same day, the Imperial Japanese Navy and Army Air Forces attacked the Royal Australian Air Force base in Darwin, on the northern coast of Australia. Deploying 242 planes, the air raids killed 235, wounded 400, and sunk eight Allied ships. The raids continued through May 1943.

February 23, 1942, a Japanese submarine shelled an oil storage facility at night near the Ellwood Oil Field, north of Santa Barbara. Though there was little serious damage, it sparked invasion panic along the California coast, and in the hearts of Paulo's parents and sister, who all called the next day.

*

At the end of February, Paulo took Loucille for her monthly checkup with Dr. Storken, who told them everything was progressing normally. Sunday, they visited with Katsey and her husband, Bill, to see their new-born son, Billy Joe.

When Katsey let Loucille rock Billy Joe, Paulo watched her soften into mothering mode, as she cooed to the swaddled bundle in her arms.

*

In March, the first of ten internment camps for Japanese Americans opened at Manzanar in California's Owens Valley.

On March 1, 1942, dehydrated dog food replaced canned food.

*

At her end-of-March appointment, Dr. Storken had Loucille insert the earplugs of his stethoscope and place the end on her stomach. She looked at Paulo with wonder.

"That's a strong heartbeat," Dr. Storken said. "He's right on schedule." Motioning Paulo to come closer, she said, "Listen. You can hear our baby."

He inserted one of the earplugs and put his arm around her. Trans-fixed, they listened to their baby together for the first time.

*

In April 1942, to buy a new tube of toothpaste, you had to turn in an old one.

*

April first, Paulo took Loucille to visit her mother, who was expe-riencing abdominal pains. Almyra said it was indigestion, but the pains worsened overnight, so they returned next day, and Loucille convinced her mother to see a doctor. Tests and X-rays identified a large mass. Surgery was scheduled for the following day.

Loucille and Paulo joined Art, Harry, and Bill in the hospital waiting room early in the morning. When the surgeon finally came out of the OR, the look on his face told them what they dreaded.

Loucille began to cry.

"I'm so sorry, but the cancer has metastasized—"

"There's nothing you can do?" Art asked.

The doctor shook his head. "It's inoperable."

Loucille got up and headed toward the Ladies Room, sobbing.

"Is she 'Loucille'?" the doctor asked.

Paulo nodded.

"Right before she went under, her mother said, 'Loucille, I love you'. They must be very close."

"You have no idea," Paulo answered.

The doctor looked at Art. "How your wife lasted this long with the intense pain is remarkable. We will control it and make her comfortable, but in her weakened condition," he paused, "I would make final arrangements if I were you. She'll be in recovery for a while and then you can see her."

Loucille was by Almyra's bedside when she woke late in the afternoon.

"Why didn't you tell us you were in pain, Momma?" Loucille said, squeezing her mother's hand.

Almyra smiled weakly. "They weren't that bad…until now. What did the doctor say?"

Tearing, Loucille said, "The tumor is in inoperable, Momma…but they can help with the pain."

Almyra looked at the ceiling. "I guess the good lord wants me home."

Loucille put her face down on the bed and sobbed.

Almyra reached over, tenderly rubbing her daughter's head. "You're going to be fine, honey. You will be a wonderful mother, and I promise to watch over you and the baby every day." She closed her eyes. "I'm going to rest now."

When Almyra woke again in the evening, she saw Paulo and motioned for him to come around to the other side of the bed. She grasped his hand and smiled up at him. "Hold that baby for me every day and tell him I love him from heaven."

"I will," he said, tears welling.

"You are the best thing that's ever happened to Loucille. Promise me you'll take care of yourself, my beautiful daughter, and especially my precious grandbaby."

"I promise." Tears became unstoppable and ran down his cheeks.

She snuffled. "You're like a son to me, Paulo. I love you."

"I love you, too, Almyra,"

She let go of his hand and looked at Loucille. "I'm going to rest now, sweetheart. I love you very much."

Almyra slipped into a coma that night and died the next day with the entire family at her bedside.

Paulo called his parents and told them of Almyra's passing.

"I'm so sorry, Paulo," Raffaele said.

"Can I talk to Mama?"

When Anna came on the line, he choked up. "Mama, Loucille is devastated. Her mother was her best friend; they talked practically every day. I don't know what to do."

He heard his mother snuffle and blow her nose.

"I will come for mia figlia before the baby comes…and for you, Paulo."

"Thank you, Mama, I love you."

"And I you, Paulo. Goodbye."

Almyra was laid to rest the following week in Sunnyside Cemetery in Long Beach.

After the funeral, Paulo drove Loucille to the Point Vicente Lighthouse on the Palos Verdes Peninsula, parked at an overlook, and held her while she cried.

*

On April 9, 1942, the Bataan Death March began. The Japanese Army forced 70,000 defeated American and Filipino soldiers to march 65 miles through the jungle, to a concentration camp. At least 10,000 prisoners died during the forced march.

CHAPTER THIRTY ONE

WAR AND BIRTH 1942

Lieutenant James Doolittle led 16 B-25 bombers, launched from the USS Hornet, to successfully attack Tokyo in revenge for Pearl Harbor on April 18, 1942. The raid proved that the Japanese homeland was vulnerable, boosting American morale.

Civilians began receiving ration books on April 27, 1942.

A nationwide "Victory Speed" limit of 35 miles per hour was ordered beginning May 1942 with the goal of reducing gasoline and rubber consumption. The slower people drove, the less gas and rubber they would need. It lasted until August 1945.

Another restriction, also enacted May 1942, was Southern California's Civil Defense Authority imposed "Dim Out" restrictions, ordering residents to turn off all lights that could be seen from the sea at night. Japanese submarines prowled the California coast—one even shelled a Santa Barbara oil refinery. U.S. naval commanders were concerned about further attacks. They worried that shore lights would silhouette American merchant ships, creating easy targets for anyone manning a periscope. Residents pulled their shades, neon signs flickered off, and motorists learned to drive in the dark. Orders included any light shining upward, even those as far inland as San Bernardino; the goal was to dim an umbrella of light that hovered over Los Angeles, visible 150 miles out at sea. Anyone violating the order was subject to criminal penalties and expulsion from the West Coast.

Every Southern Californian, even one previously insulated from wartime hardship or injustice, realized these were extraordinary times. Suddenly, daily—and nightly—life had changed. Beach bonfires were banned.

Movie premieres at Hollywood's Chinese Theater took place under a black canopy. The Los Angeles Angels, the Hollywood Stars, and the entire Pacific Coast League rescheduled night games to the afternoon.

Sugar was the first food rationed on May 4, 1942.

The "Battle of Coral Sea" on May 4, 1942, prevented the Japanese from seizing Australia and stopped their southward expansion. Both Japanese and Allies used their carrier-based airplanes instead of their ships as weapons, beginning a new kind of naval warfare.

*

Riding to her appointment with Dr. Storken the first week in May, Loucille suddenly said, "Oh…"

"What?" Paulo glanced over at her. "You all right?"

"He's moving again, a little flutter." Patting her belly, "Yes, I know you're there."

Nurse Green greeted them warmly and led them to the exam room.

"How are you feeling this beautiful spring morning?" Dr. Storken asked.

"Fine, just fine. He's fluttering, like you told me he would."

He put his hand on her stomach and after a moment smiled. "Right on schedule."

"It reminds me of a baby bird," Loucille said.

Dr. Storken laughed. "Well, your little bird will get stronger. His movements will become pokes and kicks and be more frequent."

*

Gasoline rationing began in 17 eastern states on May 15, 1942. By the end of the year, President Franklin D. Roosevelt made this war effort mandatory in all 48 states.

*

Unless he had client calls to return, Paulo and Loucille cleaned the kitchen together after dinner, then snuggled on the sofa, listening to the radio for war news, followed by their favorite weekly programs. Paulo liked The NBC Symphony Orchestra conducted by Arturo Toscanini and the Bell Telephone Hour concert series. Both enjoyed The Mercury Theatre on the Air drama series with Orson Wells. Favorite comedy shows included Burns and Allen, Fibber McGee and Molly, Amos and Andy, The Jack Benny Show, Abbott and Costello, and the Fred Allen Show.

*

In June of 1942, companies also stopped the manufacturing of metal office furniture, radios, television sets, phonographs, refrigerators, vacuum cleaners, washing machines, and sewing machines for civilians.

*

The first week in June, Loucille told Dr. Storken that the baby was now more active at certain times of the day. "He likes early mornings and late afternoons."

Making a note in the chart, he said, "He'll continue moving a lot for the next few weeks so it's time to see you more frequently."

"Can you arrange to bring her in every two weeks, Paulo?"

"Is anything wrong, doc?"

Dr. Storken assured them everything was right on schedule; more frequent monitoring the next two months and weekly the last month was normal.

Relaxed, Paulo took Loucille's hand. "Whatever you want, we'll be here."

*

June 4-7 the Japanese lost a four-carrier task force during the Battle of Midway. This decisive defeat of the Japanese proved to be the turning point, putting Japan on the defensive for the remainder of the war.

A Japanese submarine got to the mouth of the Columbia River on the Oregon coastline on June 21, surfacing and firing unsuccessfully on Fort Stevens.

*

Mid-June Loucille told Dr. Storken the baby moved several times a day, but by the end of June, she reported a change. "He's decided to kick and jab more now."

"How often does he move in an hour?" Dr. Storken asked in mid-July.

"I don't know, I've never counted." She glanced at Paulo.

"He's pretty active Doc. Why are you asking?" Paulo said, concerned.

Dr. Storken smiled. "The baby's fine. At this stage of development, they usually move ten times in two hours. Please keep track of his activity for our next appointment."

*

The German advance into Russia was finally stopped during the Battle of Stalingrad that began July 17, 1942, turning the tide of the war in favor of the Allies, although it raged on until February 2, 1943. One of the bloodiest battles in history, the combined military and civilian casualties totaled nearly two million.

*

Construction on the back house was completed the last week in July. George added flowerbeds on both sides of the front door, tilled a small patch of ground behind the house, and bordered it with red bricks for a small vegetable garden.

Paulo and Loucille planted flowers by the front door, took pictures of the house, inside and out, and sent them to Raffaele and Anna.

The end of July, Loucille handed Dr. Storken a typed chart titled 'Baby's Movements' as she walked into the examination room. Across the top of the neat grid were the hours in a day, and down the left side were the days of the week since her last appointment. Numbers filled most of the boxes from early morning to late at night.

"Very impressive. May I assume the chart was your idea, Paulo?"

"You may."

"And the numbers are mine," Loucille added proudly.

"He's consistently moved around ten times every hour. This final month he'll gain body fat and have less room to move. Loucille, you're going to feel less forceful movements and more stretching and twisting."

With a grimace, she patted her stomach. "How much bigger is he going to get? I already feel as big as a barn."

"The weight you've gained is within the normal range," he assured her.

Paulo put his arm around her. "And you're still beautiful to me, sweetheart."

She put her head on his shoulder. "Thanks, but I still look like a barn."

"Until the baby's born I want to see you weekly to monitor everything."

"Pop, did you get the pictures I sent you and Mama?" he asked on his weekly call.

"Yes, Paulo. The blue house is beautiful, and the flowers—"

"What did Mama say?"

"She thought it was nice. She showed them to Clara who said it was... how do you say...bello?"

"Cute!" Paulo stiffened. "Clara thought it was cute?"

"Yes, and adorable," Raffaele added brightly.

"Cute and adorable. As always, I get skeptical judgments from my endearing sister. Let me talk to Mama, okay?"

"Hello, Paulo."

"Mama, we're excited that you and Pop are coming next month. Do you know when you'll arrive?"

"Clara's taking care of all the arrangements for us, Paulo. She hasn't told us yet."

"That's okay, Mama, I'll call her. What'd you think of your Gardena house?"

"It's nice, Paulo. Clara says it's—"

"I know, cute and adorable." He took a deep breathe. "Mama, I love you. I'll call you after I talk to Clara. Let me say goodbye to Pop, okay?"

"Paulo, what will you plant in the garden?" Raffaele asked.

"Pop, out here you can pretty much plant year-round. You're the gardener in the family. Tell me what you would plant. I'll make a list."

"For Loucille, herbs first: basilica—"

"Basil, got it," Paulo said, translating as he wrote each item:

"Origano,"

"Oregano."

"Salvia,"

"Sage."

"Menta,"

"Mint."

"Timo,"

"Thyme."

"Rosmarino,"

"Rosemary."

"And whatever vegetables you like to eat."

"Thanks, Pop. I'm sure my wife, the farmer, will fill the garden in no time. I'm excited for you to see your garden next month. I love you."

"And I you. Addio, Paulo."

Paulo dialed Clara next. "Hi, Sis—"

"I know what you're calling about, Paulo," her tone frustrated. "The military takes priority over civilians, so I'm still trying to confirm their tickets past Chicago. I'll call as soon as I know their itinerary, okay?"

"Sure, Clara, thanks."

"You're welcome. Goodbye."

Clara called back on Tuesday. "Mom and Pop will leave here on Thursday and arrive in Los Angeles mid-afternoon on Monday. Pop's excited about the train trip, Mama's worried, as always."

"Thanks, Sis, I really appreciate you helping with all of this."

"That's what big sisters do for little brothers. Sorry I was short with you on Sunday. Any idea when you'll be sending them back?"

They're not even here yet, he thought. "No, depends on when the baby's born. I'll let you know after the baby arrives. Thanks again for all your help."

"You're welcome. Give my love to Loucille. Goodbye, Paulo."

*

The Battle of Guadalcanal began August 7, 1942, and lasted seven bloody months, ending February 7, 1943. This first major offensive in the Pacific theater was a decisive Allied victory. Strategically, possession of a Guadalcanal air base was critical in controlling the sea lines of communication between the United States and Australia.

*

During the week, Paulo and Loucille finished their guest bedroom preparations for his parents, cleaned the house, and shopped for food. The next Monday they drove to Union Station and waited for Anna and Raffaele's train to arrive. On the way home, Raffaele sat in the front with Paulo and excitedly described all he'd seen coming across the country. In the back seat Loucille and Anna talked quietly about the baby.

The following Friday, Dr. Storken listened to the baby's heartbeat a long time. Returning his stethoscope to his lab coat pocket, he said, "He's developed a murmur."

"What's that?" Loucille and Paulo said in unison.

"When the heart pumps it makes a 'lub-dup' sound. If there is an extra whooshing or swishing sound could be an issue with a heart valve."

Loucille clutched Paulo's hand.

Dr. Storken put his hand on her shoulder. "Many babies are born with a murmur. Most are what's called 'innocent' murmurs and go away as the baby grows. If the murmur continues or gets more pronounced, it can be treated. Let's wait and see what develops, but because of your Rh incompatibility, I'd like to have your baby born at Community Hospital in Long Beach in case there are any complications. Okay?"

They nodded. Paulo's arm protectively around Loucille, he said, "Sure, Doc, whatever you think is best."

Dr. Storken met Loucille's gaze and smiled. "Don't you worry, I'll be there to deliver your baby."

Paul Jr. was born at 2:19 pm on Friday, August 28, 1942. The delivery was normal with no complications. He weighed 6 lbs. 13 oz., was 21 inches long, and had dark brown eyes and hair. At first, he didn't nurse and lost weight in the hospital, but at home gained it back—and more. Paulo nicknamed him Biff. Loucille called him Sugar Puss.

CHAPTER THIRTY TWO

WAR AND SEA 1942

That evening Dr. Storken came to Loucille's room where she was cradling the baby, Paulo by her side.

"Everything was normal, but I detected an innocent heart murmur. Remember I told you many babies are born with heart murmurs, and they aren't serious and outgrow them over time. I will monitor it as he develops."

"Is this because I'm Rh negative?" Loucille asked, a catch in her voice.

"No, Loucille," he said, patting her arm. "You did not have any transfusions, so it's unlikely your Rh negative antigens were passed to the baby. Right now, what matters is for you and Paul Jr. to rest. I will check in on you tomorrow." He paused and added to Paulo, "Resting includes you. Goodnight and again, congratulations. He is a fine-looking boy."

"Thank you," Loucille said, kissing the baby's forehead.

Aunts, uncles, grandparents, and friends flooded in over the weekend, bringing congratulations and gifts. Once Anna knew her mia figlia and new grandson were fine, she insisted on returning to Germantown. Paulo tried but could not convince her to stay.

Loucille and baby remained in the hospital for a week. Paulo was with them all day Saturday and Sunday, and after making his debit rounds, came at dinnertime every day that week. On a whim, because the Long Beach Community Hospital was close to San Pedro, he finished work early and drove by their first home. At the harbor, he parked and watched a Navy ship come into the shipyard. The smell of saltwater and metallic sounds of construction brought memories of his youth and the Navy.

In the weeks following the Pearl Harbor attack he thought about re-enlisting and talked with Loucille about it several times.

She was steadfastly against it.

"You're older, married now, and building a business. We are established here and going off to war is not part of our plan."

When they discovered she was pregnant Paulo dropped the subject. However, people Paulo knew continued to join the war effort or enlist, and he got letters and sporadic phone calls from Vincenzo about the war.

With Loucille and baby home, although Paulo was attentive, caring, and doting, she sensed his mind was often elsewhere. With the baby asleep between them, she broached the subject.

"Paulo, we need to talk," she said quietly.

He started, his eyes popping open. "Did I forget to do something?"

"Yes, to tell me what you're thinking. I know your mind is elsewhere."

He turned and looked at her. "What are you talking about?"

"Paulo, you are everything a wife could ask for, but now that the baby's here, where do you go? I see you gazing far off. What are you thinking about so intently?"

"You really want to know?" he said, tentatively.

Loucille put a finger to her lips when she felt the baby squirm at the sound of Paulo's voice. She whispered, "Of course I want to know. You're my husband, the love of my life, and the father of our child."

"I want to re-enlist," he said, with a tight-lipped smile.

Loucille sighed, kissed the baby's forehead, and sat up on the edge of the bed.

Carefully, he got out of bed and went around to her, knelt, put his head in her lap, and wrapped his arms around her waist.

"I don't want you fighting somewhere halfway around the world. I want you here, close to home. They're crying for people to work in the factories and shipyards."

Loucille's eyes welled with tears. "Please, Paulo, think about it."

"I have thought about it, ever since Pearl Harbor. Loucille, I'm a Navy man and been all over the world. You know how hard a nine-to-five job is for me. I don't want to build a ship. I want to be on a ship, helping to win this damn war."

He rose and pulled her up into his arms, then stepped back and wiped the tears from her cheeks. "I need to do this. It's important for me…and you and Biff…for our country. I want to be a part of stopping them. Do you understand?"

She clung to him. Once he made up his mind about something, she knew there was no stopping him. Although sad, she understood he needed to re-enlist.

The following afternoon, Paulo drove to the Navy recruiting office in Long Beach. The young recruiter looked at his discharge papers and said he would not be given credit for his prior service or rank but could start as an Apprentice Seaman. "I'm sorry Sir, but there's not much use for violinists in this war," he added, suppressing a smile.

"I can do more than play the damn violin," Paulo said, his anger rising.

The recruiter then made it worse by adding, "Sir, we thank you for your prior service, but now that you're older there are lots of jobs available in war production."

"Older?" Paulo's glare silenced the recruiter. He took his discharge papers out of the young man's hands and walked out onto the sidewalk, seething. Across the street, the recruiting office for the United States Maritime Service caught his eye.

"If the Navy doesn't want me, perhaps the Merchant Marine will," he said aloud.

The older rotund recruiter looked at Paulo's discharge papers. "Paulo Colaluca…Italiano?"

"Si…Yes," Paulo said, smiling.

"My wife's Italian. She can be a handful. You married?"

"Sweet farm girl from Missouri."

The recruiter grinned. "Lucky man. Now, we don't have bands on our boats, but I can give you credit for your prior service and rank, Paulo." He motioned across the street. "Unlike those Navy kids across the street, the Merchant Marine values experience. I'll start your paperwork while the doc gives you a physical." He motioned down the hall behind him then stood and shook Paulo's hand. "Welcome aboard, Sailor!"

An hour later, Paulo walked out as a proud Able Seaman, United States Maritime Service.

Over dinner, he told Loucille the two different receptions he got.

"What happens next?" she asked anxiously, hands clasped, fingers intertwined. "How soon do you have to leave?"

Reaching across the table, Paulo took her hands in his. "I'm not going anywhere right away, sweetheart. As a Navy veteran I'll attend an abbreviated training next week. My reporting date is not until October 5."

"What about your debit, your clients?"

"Tomorrow, I will call my manager and see how he want's me to handle things, so I can let our clients know who will handle their accounts."

He squeezed her hands. "Can I tell you a secret? I'm surprised at how excited I am to be going to sea, again." With a faraway look in his eyes, added, "When Vincenzo and I were teenagers, we took the trolley down to the Philadelphia Navy Yard, to hang out. Those huge ships came and went, the noise from the shipyard was thunderous, and the smell of the ocean strong. Sweetheart, we were hooked on the sea years ago."

The next morning, Paulo called his parents. Raffaele was proud of him. His worrier mother, not so much, but gave him her blessing.

Clara thought he was being impulsive. "You're always determined to do things your own way, Paulo." She started to cry.

"Clara, why are you crying?"

"Both of my impetuous brothers are going in harm's way. What did you expect me to do? Cheer? I love you, Paulo." She hung up.

Vincenzo congratulated him. "Hey, with both of us in this war, it will be over before you know it, big brother. I love you. Take care of yourself."

Loucille's family was surprised, but supportive and her father and brothers promised to look after Loucille and the baby while he was at sea.

"I certainly don't want to lose one of our best agents, but I understand," his manager said when Paulo met with him the next day. "If I were twenty years younger, I'd join up too. Will you consider continuing to service your debit when you're not at sea?"

Paulo was surprised, but before he could say anything the manager continued.

"The war is making it difficult to recruit and hire suitable new employees. I know Loucille could handle the paperwork and phone contacts, if she's willing."

"I'm sure she would be. She knows all the families, sometimes better than I do," Paulo said.

"Tell Loucille she can call me anytime if she has questions, okay?"

The manager shook Paulo's hand. "Thank you, and take care of yourself, sailor."

For the next few days, Paulo, Loucille, and Biff drove around his debit and told his clients about enlisting in the Merchant Marine. While he was at sea, Loucille would run the office.

Loucille met the families she'd come to know over the phone, and

Paulo proudly introduced Biff, who, when he wasn't sleeping loved riding in the car.

The last week of the month, Paulo drove Loucille to her post-birth checkup. "I commend you for patriotism," Dr. Storken said, shaking Paulo's hand.

"Loucille and Biff are doing well," the smiling doctor said after the exam.

"What about the murmur?" Loucille asked, concerned

"It's still there, but unchanged, a good sign that it is an innocent murmur he'll outgrow. Don't worry about this healthy boy. I will check him again in six months."

*

October 5 Paulo boarded a Liberty ship in San Pedro harbor and shipped out on a three-month contract. The ship joined a convoy escorted by Navy destroyers setting a zigzag course to confuse the enemy about their destination. Prior to sailing, the Master of the ship received a top-secret piloting diagram and the communication signals to be used within the convoy, but not to be shared with the crew.

The officers on merchant ships included: the Master/Captain, Chief Mate, 2nd Mate, and 3rd Mate. As an Able Seaman, Paulo was assigned to the 2nd Mate's deck crew. His responsibilities included standing a daily, rotating four-hour watch, maintenance of the deck, hull and superstructure, the lifeboats, and monitoring the cargo, mooring operations, and anchoring the ship. A 2nd Mate also serves as the ship's navigator, so when Paulo stood watch, he sometimes served as helmsman or lookout.

Paulo's time in the Navy prepared him for the cramped quarters, constant engine noise, and life at sea, but not for the size of the crew. The USS Pennsylvania's crew had been 1,159 (56 Officers, 72 Marines, and 1,031 Enlisted men). Liberty ships sailed with crews of 38-62 Merchant Mariners, and 21-40 United States Navy Armed Guards. It quickly fostered a sense of camaraderie onboard.

The busiest time for deck crew sailors was in port, taking on cargo and later off-loading it. At sea, when not standing a watch and other daily duties were completed, sailors relaxed and got to know one another.

Some exercised on a jury-rigged high bar set up on the forward deck. Early in the voyage, after seeing how many chin-ups he could do, Paulo kipped up on the bar, did a handstand, and dismounted to whistles and clapping from shipmates.

An older sailor, with close-cropped gray hair called the "Swede", smiled broadly at Paulo. "You were gymnast, ya?" He had the muscled arms and weathered face of someone long at sea.

"Back in high school," Paulo said, rubbing his shoulders.

"You can you do this, ya?" The Swede kipped up on the bar, went into a handstand, did one giant swing, then another, and a third one, before landing a fly-away dismount.

"A long time ago," Paulo said, nodding and impressed.

"You young, ya?"

Paulo smirked. "I'm thirty, but watching you makes me feel old."

"I am sixty years. We practice. You do big swings again, ya?"

"Ya, Swede, we practice," Paulo answered, feeling the Swede's vise-like grip as they shook hands.

Whenever Paulo stood watch, especially as a helmsman, he took special notice of the convoy's zigzag course as it continued south by east across the Pacific Ocean. Familiar with the basic elements of navigation from his friendship with a navigator on the USS Pennsylvania, he decided they were en route to Australia.

*

The "Battle of El-Alamein" began on October 23, 1942, a turning point of the War. The North African campaign, between the British Empire and the German-Italian army, raged on until British Commander Montgomery finally defeated German Commander Rommel in May 1943, stopping Germany's advance into North Africa.

Nearing Australia, the convoy divided, sending ships westward towards Darwin and Fremantle, and the rest south to ports along the Eastern Coast. Paulo's ship off-loaded cargo at Brisbane, Sydney, Melbourne, and Hobart, Tasmania.

Japanese air raids continued across northern Australia since the bombing of Darwin in February. The entire population of the country was engaged in preparing for and worrying about the next attack.

Coffee was added to the ration list in the United States on November 29, 1942. Gasoline rationing went into effect in December. That month, eight additional items were rationed by the government: typewriters, bicycles, shoes, rubber footwear, silk, nylon, fuel oil, and stoves.

*

Paulo arrived home the week before Christmas to celebrate baby Biff's first Christmas with Loucille, her father, her brothers' families, Mrs. McKeever, and Katsey and Bill Scott, and their boy, Shug. Paulo's parents and siblings sent gifts, and despite the war's restrictions, there was laughter and heartfelt sharing of their life's blessings.

During his two weeks home, Paulo followed up on the Christmas cards Loucille had sent, calling each of his clients to wish them happy holidays.

The week after Christmas, Paulo and Loucille planted their live Christmas tree in the front yard. A bundled-up Biff watched from his baby carriage.

"How long will you be gone this time?" Loucille asked, patting dirt around the base of the tree.

"It's another three-month contract. I should be home by Easter."

God please protect him, she prayed to herself, and stood, brushed the dirt from her hands and embraced him. "Come home safely, you hear me. I'm not going to raise your son alone."

Paulo grinned at Biff. "If his hair gets any longer, we might have to change his clothes from blue to pink."

Loucille snorted and took Paulo's face in her hands. "He's all boy…just like his father."

*

Unknown to the public, on December 28 President Roosevelt approved funding for the top-secret Manhattan Project, to develop the atomic bomb.

*

Paulo boarded a Liberty ship in San Pedro harbor on December 30, joined a convoy the next day, and sailed for an unknown destination.

CHAPTER THIRTY THREE

WAR AND SEA 1943

During his voyage to Australia, Paulo had increased his understanding of navigation. Intrigued with the ability to plot the ship's exact location in the middle of an ocean that spread from horizon to horizon, he asked to stand watch as a lookout or helmsman. On his next voyage to India, he requested, and was approved by his ship's Captain, to stand similar watches, continuing to plot the convoy's destinations each time it left a port.

While Paulo was at sea, Loucille was busy. She raised Biff, visited neighborhood friends, and stayed in touch with her family, calling Raffaele and Anna with news about their grandson and handling the occasional phone calls and correspondence regarding their Prudential clients.

A farm girl at heart, the huge yard of their Gardena home was special to Loucille. They loved dogs, so after moving in, Paulo brought home a bright-eyed, cuddly, German Shepard puppy. They named her "Lady", and in no time, she grew into an affectionate, adored member of the family.

In nice weather, Loucille sat outside in a weathered Adirondack chair and nursed Biff, Lady lying quietly at her feet. Head on her paws, she lifted her head uttering a low growl, only when someone walked by.

On a crisp sunny day in late January, Loucille wheeled a bundled-up Biff in his baby carriage, down 158th Street to Western Avenue to the corner, tented outdoor vegetable market. Lady was leashed to the carriage as Loucille meandered the aisles picking out produce.

A gray-haired matron noticed Biff's profusion of black ringlets and said, "What an adorable little girl." She smiled at Loucille and reached to pat Biff. Instantly, Lady emitted a low growl and grasped the woman's wrist, holding it gently but firmly in her mouth. The woman froze, her eyes wide, momentarily speechless.

"Lady, no! I'm so sorry," Loucille said, flustered and embarrassed.

Lady released the woman's wrist, sat back on her haunches, panting quietly.

The matron took a step back, hand to her mouth, "I wasn't going to hurt her."

"I know," Loucille said, touching her arm. "She's just very protective of him."

The matron peered into the carriage. "Oh, with those beautiful curls, I thought she...I mean he, was a girl."

Loucille smiled. "A lot of people make that mistake."

At Christmas Paulo had made it clear he felt Biff's hair was too long. After the incident at the market, Loucille knew it was time for a haircut, so no one would mistake him for a girl. In February, unable to bring herself to do it, she enlisted her friend Katsey to take him to Fred's Barbershop, and make a real boy out of him.

Once the ship rounded the Cape of Good Hope and entered the Indian Ocean, Paulo was able to determine that the convoy's destination was Bombay, India. The port was busier than anything Paulo experienced in the Navy during peacetime. The frantic crush of off-loading war materiel in Bombay was unbelievable. Trucks, jeeps, and tanks, sat on the wharves in endless rows, behind them crates of all sizes, filled with bombs, ammunition, guns, parts for planes and vehicles, and medicines. Everything was piled to the sky, waiting transport inland.

Paulo watched a young Indian boy jump into a two and a half-ton GMC truck, known as a "Jimmy 6x6," mistakenly put it into reverse and back it off the dock into the bay. When the boy popped up, workers cheered. Nobody seemed to care about the sinking truck.

Bombay's sights and sounds fascinated Paulo. Thinking of his father, he watched carvers make beautiful, polished sculptures of animals from any type of wood requested. He ordered half a dozen small elephants to be carved from different woods and picked them up two days later. Each elephant came with ivory tusks and eyes.

Biff was not a fragile baby. In February, Cousin Charlie, a rambunctious toddler, upset his bassinet. Other than tears that Loucille wiped away, he was fine.

In May, he fell out of his buggy with no apparent injury.

At six months, Biff started taking milk in a bottle. When the weather was nice, Loucille put a blanket on the grass by the back porch, placed him on his side, and watched him out the kitchen window as she washed lunch dishes. Lady laid on her stomach, paws almost touching the blanket. When Biff fell asleep, she inched forward, chewed on the bottle's nipple, and licked any milk that dribbled out.

*

As the war continued to rage, meats, fats, canned fish, cheese, and canned milk were rationed across America in March, 1943.

*

Paulo's ship returned from India and docked in New York on March 29. Train travel was too time-consuming for Paulo and his shipmates who lived on the West Coast. Wanting to make the most of their month's leave, they pooled part of their wages, and bought one the few new cars still available, a yellow Buick convertible. Taking turns behind the wheel they drove cross-country, stopping only for gas and food. Four days later, on April 2, they arrived in California.

Paulo called Loucille before leaving New York, but not from the road. As he got out of the top-down, dirty yellow car in front of the house in the early afternoon, Loucille rushed out the front door, crying and embracing him. He introduced his shipmates and Loucille invited them in, but they thanked her and declined, eager to get to their own homes. Everyone waved as they pulled away from the curb. One shipmate yelled, "See you soon, Wop!"

With their arms around each other's waists, Loucille's head resting on Paulo's shoulder, they walked into the house.

"Why didn't you call and let me know you'd be home today—"

He put his finger to her lips. "We drove straight through, sweetheart, stopping only to pee and get gas. I wanted to surprise you."

She kissed him long and hard.

"It was worth it for that kiss." He looked around. "Where's my boy?"

"Napping," she said, and pulled him down the hallway.

Paulo picked Biff up gently and held him at arm's length. "How's my big boy?"

Biff rubbed his sleepy eyes, looked at the bearded man, and smiled.

Paulo kissed him on the cheek, then held him to his chest, as the three of them walked to the kitchen. Paulo ran his fingers through Biff's curly black hair.

"You can see I had his hair cut while you were gone. What do you think?"

"It's definitely an improvement," he said, pressing a curl between thumb and forefinger, "but, not Navy regulation."

Loucille grimaced. "He's just a baby—"

"Boy," Paulo interjected, "and I don't want anybody confused about that, okay?"

That afternoon, a second haircut made Biff's black ringlets a memory.

Throughout April, Paulo drove around his debit reconnecting with clients, answering questions, and sharing his overseas travels. Loucille and Biff rode along enjoying the special time with Daddy in the almost spring-like-weather.

One afternoon, they put Biff in bed for a nap and soon heard a whump sound, then crying coming from his room. He'd pulled himself up and over the side of the crib rail and fallen.

Paulo picked him. "There, there, you're okay," he said, rocking him up and down.

"What are you trying to do? Scare us to death?"

Loucille touched the red bump on his head tenderly. "Does it hurt?"

Biff nodded with a sad smile. Paulo lowered the mattress in his crib.

For Easter on April 25, Biff got three Easter baskets, a blue bunny from Daddy, and a doll with moving eyes that he repeatedly tried to punch out.

Paulo sailed out of Los Angeles harbor on May 2 for a three-month voyage to what turned out to be Durban, South Africa via the Panama Canal, serving as the Navigator's Mate.

Durban was a strategically important British and Allied port for convoys en route to the Middle East and other theaters of war. German and Japanese submarines were active along the eastern coast of Africa, eliminating safe anchorage outside the harbor, resulting in multiple ships docked side-by-side at each berth, slowing turnaround time.

*

During the Battle of Sicily, July10 to 17, the Allies diverted German divisions from France. Victorious, this led to the overthrow of Fascist dictator, Benito Mussolini.

*

The day before Biff's first birthday, August 27, Paulo returned to Los Angeles harbor. Colds and runny noses were running through the neighborhood, so Loucille decided against a party. Instead, Paulo took her and Biff for a long drive followed by a quiet dinner at home. Biff ate at the table in his highchair and had his first birthday cake with one blue candle. Loucille couldn't take pictures as no film was available.

Two days before he sailed again, on September 16, Paulo was issued his official Identification Card by the LA Captain of the Port and awarded Certificates he earned on his voyages: Certificate of Service to Able Seaman, Certificate of Efficiency to Lifeboat Man, and his Seaman's Certificate of Identification.

The following day, he joined the Sailors Union of the Pacific and on September 18, left Los Angeles harbor for a five-day coastal run on the S.S. James Otis, serving as the Navigator. Arriving back in Los Angeles on September 22 he went ashore for one night at home, then reported back aboard for his second voyage to India.

Since moving to Gardena, Loucille was part of an informal babysitting network, occasionally watching young children for neighborhood friends when they needed to run a quick errand or go to an appointment. After Pearl Harbor when women began working in jobs supporting the war effort, childcare became a necessity for some of her friends. Loucille applied to the Department of Social Welfare and was issued a license on October 6, 1943, to provide childcare for up to four children over the age of two. It added joy to her life while Paulo was away and provided more playmates for Biff.

*

Following the Allied victories in North Africa and Sicily, the S.S. James Otis sailed in convoy via the Panama Canal, across the Atlantic, into the Mediterranean, and through the British controlled Suez Canal to the Port of Bombay. The harbor and docks were crammed with war materiel that stretched even further inland than before. Despite the feverish pitch of activity on the docks, nothing was driven into the bay. Paulo found the carvers he met on his first voyage and purchased gifts for Loucille, and more wooden elephants for his collection. While his ship was moored in Bombay, the BBC broadcast the news of an Allied offensive in the Pacific.

*

The Battle of Tarawa (November 20-23,1943) began the U.S. Central Pacific Campaign against Japan. In a bloody invasion, they seized the heavily fortified Japanese-held island of Betio in the Tarawa Atoll in the Gilbert Islands. It was strategically important in planning for MacArthur's return to the Philippines.

At the same time stateside, additional items were rationed: lard, shortening, food oils, butter, canned, bottled, and frozen processed foods, dried fruit, firewood, coal, and jam and jellies.

*

With Paulo overseas, Christmas at the Colaluca house in 1943 was different. Determined to make Biff's second Christmas special, Loucille invited all his aunts, uncles, and cousins from her side of the family, and neighborhood friends to drop by during the holidays for cookies and eggnog. She also convinced Raffaele and Anna to come for an extended visit.

Despite fears of Japanese submarine attacks, Civil Defense "Dim Out" restrictions, rationing, and the constant news of war, Christmas 1943 was a time of connection and celebration at 1561 158th Street in Gardena.

CHAPTER THIRTY FOUR

WAR AND SEA 1944

His second voyage to India was the longest time Paulo was away from home in the war. During his six months at sea, his convoy sailed through the Panama Canal, across the Atlantic Ocean, and into the Mediterranean. The Allied victory in North Africa the previous May10-17, 1943, led to the Battle of Sicily, the subsequent invasion of Italy, and defeat of the Fascist Dictator, Benito Mussolini. It allowed convoys to sail through British controlled Suez Canal to India.

War Department planners understood that communication between service men and their families was vital for the morale of both the military and loved ones back home. Overseas fighters couldn't make phone calls, so letters were the only means of staying in touch. Mailbags took up valuable space on cargo ships and planes. The solution was "Victory Mail" or V-Mail. Taking up one-thirty-seventh of the space as the same letter on paper saved five million pounds of cargo space in two years according to military estimates.

V-Mail, never mandatory but successful, was a single page, printed front and back. On the back were instructions and space for return and mailing addresses. One wrote their message on the front within the margins, return address again at the top—all bold and in dark ink for the best reproduction. The form was folded in half, sealed, and sent off.

At the V-Mail processing center, each letter was censored, photographed, and reproduced on microfilm. The roles of microfilm were transported overseas, where the letters were printed again at one-quarter size and mailed to their destination. Original letters were stored until confirmation was received that the shipment arrived, insurance in case a cargo ship was sunk by a U-boat, or a cargo plane went down in bad weather.

V-Mail had its disadvantages. Letters had to be short, enclosures impossible. The scent of perfume did not photograph. Lipstick prints, dubbed the "Scarlet Scourge" by postal workers, gummed-up the scanning machines.

As he had in the Navy when they were courting, Paulo wrote regularly to Loucille. She looked forward to Paulo's letters but preferred delivering her expressions of love in-person when he was home. Every postmark signaled he was alive as of that date. Sitting on their sofa, cuddling Biff, she read Paulo's words aloud, with a smile and sometime tears.

Paulo wrote about a time the ship was at anchor in good weather, when crewmen were suspended over the sides in bosuns' chairs, engaged in the endless job of scrapping and painting the hull. Hard, sweaty work, sometimes a sailor "accidentally" fell into the water to cool off. At the call "MAN OVERBOARD," an Officer came on deck, to look over the railing and issue the swimmer below the amused warning, "Sailor, you're only allowed one accident a day."

The S.S. James Otis convoy returned from India the way it came, with an additional layover in London before ending the six-month voyage in New York. Paulo was discharged March 29, 1944. Knowing no cars were available to buy, he rushed ashore to buy a train ticket home. When Paulo said he wanted a ticket on the fastest train to California, the elderly, tight-lipped agent looked at him and shook his head.

"Young man, there are no seats available on any of my trains for at least a week. There's a war going on you know."

"Yes, sir, I know. I just got off the S.S. James Otis, back from India. Been gone six months in this war, and I really want to see my wife and son." That brought a smile. Motioning toward the platforms, he said, "Son, I wish I could help you, but the only way you could get on one of these trains now, is if you bought a whole railroad car."

"How much would that cost?" Paulo asked.

With a skeptical look, the agent said, "Four-thousand dollars for forty seats."

"Does that include food?"

"No son, but there are canteens, run by the Red Cross, Salvation Army, or local groups where you can get a free meal at stops along the route."

"Start the paperwork, I'll be back," Paulo yelled, running out the door.

With a smile and a head shake, the agent watched Paulo disappear in the crowd.

Paul knew most of the S.S. James Otis crew lived on the West Coast and were trying to get home. He raced back to the ship to catch as many men as possible before they disembarked to spend their pay. Standing at the end of the gangplank, he explained his idea and collected ticket money. Some helped track down crew members he missed.

Paulo was met with wide, astonished eyes when he returned and handed the agent four thousand dollars. He whistled softly. "This is a first for me."

"Which car is ours?" Paulo asked.

"Loucille, sweetheart, I'm in New York, waiting for the Pennsylvania Railroad to hook the car I bought to their next train to Chicago," Paulo told Loucille.

"You bought a train car?"

"Yeah, I—"

"A whole train car?" she blurted, "How could you afford—"

"Slow down, okay? There are no cars and it's a week's wait for a train ticket. The agent joked the only way I could get on a train sooner would be if I bought a whole coach, so I went back to the ship and got the guys to buy in. I'll be home in a few days."

"You are unbelievable, you know that?"

"What can I say? You married a schmoozer."

Paulo's coach arrived in Chicago three days later, and reconnected to a Sante Fe train bound for Los Angeles. During their week-long journey, the close-knit group played cards, talked about their months at sea together and their families, and read papers to catch up on the news at home. And they slept—a lot.

When the train pulled into Union Station in Los Angeles, Loucille, Biff, and her brother Harry were on the platform, along with the wives, girlfriends, and families of most of his shipmates. Many kisses, hugs, and tears later, the group moved into the terminal and out into the sunlight. The men's shouts that they'd see each other on another voyage, morphed into goodbye waves, as they drove off.

Harry dropped them at home. Paulo showered off the train ride, changed into civilian clothes, and played outside with Biff and their German Shepard, Lady.

As she prepared dinner, Loucille watched from kitchen window, listening to excited voices and barking. He was home again, safe. With a serene smile she continued preparing his favorite meal of antipasto salad with rigatoni, meatballs, and wine.

After dinner Paulo asked Loucille and Biff to sit on the sofa, then brought out his weathered Navy duffle bag to hand out their gifts. For Loucille, he had jewelry and a large, beautiful scrapbook. A strong black cord tied the darkly stained front and back wooden panels together, holding the pages tight, and "Good Junk" carved in raised, blonde block letters on the front.

Paulo paused. Ceremoniously reaching deep into his duffle bag, he brought out a small, hand-carved, brightly painted, red wooden plane, white truck, and blue ship for Biff. His final gifts were the new carved elephants to add to their collection.

Early Easter Sunday morning, April 9, Paulo masterfully hid eggs that he, Loucille and Biff colored the past two days. It took Biff almost an hour and required three baskets to find and collect all the eggs. After breakfast, Biff found a basket from the Easter Bunny on his bed filled with candy treats, and a stuffed, white, corduroy rabbit with red-button eyes.

The next week, Paulo, Loucille, and Biff drove around his debit reconnecting with his clients. Some lost loved ones in the war. Friday evening, after Biff was in bed, he and Loucille sat on the sofa. Somberly, he said, "I don't want to do this anymore."

Loucille looked back with pursed lips but stayed quiet.

"Dealing with those beneficiaries this week was…hard. I've seen my share of men die in war but dealing with the death of my clients is worse."

He leaned over and put his head in her lap.

Gently smoothing his hair, she whispered, "I love you, Paulo. Whatever you want to do is fine with me."

"I don't know what I want to do yet…but it's not selling insurance."

The next week, Paulo met with his Prudential Manager in Long Beach. He leaned forward in his chair. "I'm shipping out again at the end of the month, but I want to let you know I plan to resign when I get back."

The surprise on the Manager's face became a frown. "You're one our best agents. Why do you want to resign?"

"With all due respect, I want my life to be about more than selling insurance. The war and seeing the rest of the world, makes me want more. Life's too short to delay one's dreams."

"I can only imagine what you've seen in the Merchant Marine. One reason you've been so successful as an agent, is that you really care about your clients. You are that proverbial Prudential 'Rock' for families. When do you expect to be back?"

"I signed up for a three or four-month voyage, but you never know what might happen at sea. Seems like German and Japanese submarines are still everywhere."

"Will Loucille continue to monitor your debit's accounts and be available to answer clients' questions?"

"Yes, sir. Just like always."

"Good. I'll start on finding your replacement." The Manager extended his hand. "Thank you, Paulo, for your service to our country and to Prudential. I'm going to miss you." With sadness, he added, "Take care of yourself out there, son. Let's hope this god-awful war ends soon."

When he drove in his driveway at home, Loucille and Biff were in the front yard, putting the half shells of their colorful Easter eggs on the tips of the little fir Christmas tree they planted after Biff's first visit from Santa Claus.

Paulo knelt by them. "What are you two up to now?"

"I thought we needed to celebrate." She looked at him expectantly.

With a smile, he said, "My insurance career is over. You two want to ride with me one last time tomorrow to say goodbye to our debit families."

"Biff, want to go for a ride with Daddy tomorrow?"

Paulo picked up his delighted son, kissed his cheek, and hugged Loucille. "I like it...an Easter Christmas tree. Wait until the neighbors see it!"

Friday, April 28, Paulo sailed from Los Angeles on the Liberty ship, S.S. Benjamin Bonneville. Once the convoy cleared the Port of Colon, at the eastern end of the Panama Canal, and started across the Atlantic, Paulo quickly plotted they were headed for Africa.

The convoy off-loaded first at Simon's Town naval base, on the Atlantic side of South Africa, to resupply the Allied submarine base and squadrons of sub-hunting Catalina flying boats. At sea heading to the next port news reached the crew about the June 6 D-Day Invasion and the Normandy landings on beaches in France. Their slow progression off-loading stops continued at Cape Town, Port Elizabeth, Durban, Mozambique, then finally in Mombasa, Kenya.

Coming out of Mombasa's deep-water Kilindini Harbor, the Bonneville experienced propulsion problems, causing it to lag behind the convoy. Alone and sailing southward at reduced speed, they neared the end of the Mozambique Channel, between Madagascar and the east coast of Africa. When an Axis submarine surfaced and fired a shot across their bow, their Captain refused to stop, and the Bonneville's crew returned fire with their four-inch deck gun. The submarine submerged and fired a torpedo. The explosion lifted the forward part of the ship out of the water, throwing many of the crew, including Paulo overboard. He landed on a piece of wooden flotsam, and lost consciousness.

When he opened his eyes, Paulo was on the ship's deck, lying on his side, on a heavy wool, gray blanket. He raised his head to look around when a searing pain made him gasp and shout, "SHIT!"

"Easy, Paulo," the corpsman said, "you've got a pretty bad gash on your tailbone. I dressed your wound and gave you a shot of morphine. Lie still until it kicks in and we'll move you below."

"We're still afloat?" Paulo asked through gritted teeth.

"Don't ask me how. The forward compartments are flooded and we're down by the bow, but the captain is heading for the shore in case we must beach her. You just lay still and thank your lucky stars you're here and not out there."

"Is everybody okay?"

"No. There are casualties. Lie still. I'll be back to check on you."

With the throbbing of the engines and his pain fading, his eyelids grew heavy, and he drifted off.

Water-tight hatches in the forward compartments held over the next hours as the captain guided the ship toward Africa's eastern shoreline. He beached the Bonneville, pushing her bow slowly into the sandy bottom. His earlier S.O.S. received, Durban dispatched a sub-hunting Catalina patrol bomber, a salvage tug to tow the ship, and an armed cutter escort. Once in Durban, Paulo was transferred to Addington Hospital where his wound was treated, and he convalesced for three weeks.

On his release, he rejoined the crew, who were housed ashore. Waiting for the Bonneville's repairs to be completed, there was time for sightseeing, and the opportunity to drive into the bush to hunt for a day, where

Paulo, the city kid from Germantown shot a water buffalo.

With Daddy in Africa on August 28, there was no party for Biff's second birthday, but Loucille and Biff had company for lunch and dinner. Uncle Harry and Aunt Eleanor came for lunch with their girls, Sandra, and Judy, and brought Biff, a beautiful bedspread. Harry took Biff for a ride to the grocery store. Mrs. Keever dropped by in the afternoon and gave him a Bubble Ball Bank with 25 cents inside. Uncle Bill, Aunt Thelma, and their boys, Lee and Charlie, came for dinner with a little wagon with blocks for the birthday boy. Grandad and Grandma Colaluca sent him five dollars. Also in the mail, came a winter suit, shoes, and a pair of socks, from Aunt Angie.

Paulo was discharged from the S.S. Benjamin Bonneville in New Orleans on October 18. The wound he received from being blown overboard had not healed satisfactorily, so he was transferred to the US Naval Hospital in Long Beach.

*

The U.S. Navy landed four Sixth Army divisions ashore on Leyte Island in the Philippines on October 20. General Douglas MacArthur gave his famous "I have returned" radio message to the Philippine people and began his relentless battle to drive the Japanese out of southwest Asia.

The Japanese knew if Leyte were lost, the rest of the Philippines would soon follow and sent five naval forces to drive off the American fleet and land more troops for fighting on the island.

The air and sea "Battle of Leyte Gulf" raged October 23 to 26. The biggest and most multifaceted naval battle in history, it involved hundreds of ships, nearly 200,000 participants, and spanned more than 100,000 square miles. Some of the largest and most powerful ships ever built were sunk, and thousands of men went to the bottom of the sea with them. The Japanese gamble cost them almost their entire fleet. The Imperial Japanese Navy, as an offensive force, was eliminated.

*

On October 25, Paulo underwent back surgery to successfully remove bone fragments from the wound.

In the hospital, he received his Captain/Master's papers, and the War Shipping Administration Certificates confirming active service with the

United States Merchant Marine. He was awarded the following:

Pacific War Zone Bar

Mediterranean Middle East War Zone Bar

Atlantic War Zone Bar

The Merchant Marine Combat Bar

After his discharge from the hospital, Paul came home to convalesce. When he called his parents to invite them for Christmas, Anna tearfully insisted on coming sooner to see him, and Clara reluctantly arranged their train reservations.

*

November 3, 1944, the Imperial Japanese Army launched the first of over 9,300 Balloon Bombs, using the Jet Stream to carry them to the west coast of America. Nicknamed Fugos, the Japanese word for fire, the intention was to cause mass disruptions by killing people, destroying buildings, and causing forest fires. The hydrogen balloons were thirty-feet in diameter and carried either a 30-pound, high-explosive antipersonnel bomb or 26-pound incendiary bomb. Depending on high-altitude weather the balloons could cross the Pacific Ocean in 1-3 days. November 4, a Navy patrol craft discovered a balloon floating off San Pedro, California.

To avoid public panic, The Office of Censorship sent a message to newspapers and radio stations nationwide, asking them to make no mention of balloons and balloon-bomb incidents. They did not want the enemy to get the idea that the balloons might be effective weapons or have the American people panic. Cooperating with the government, the press did not publish any balloon bomb incidents.

*

Anna and Raffaele arrived a few days before Thanksgiving.

In early December, Paulo met the new Prudential Agent who would replace him, and took the young man around the debit to meet his families. After the tour, he and Loucille turned over all their client records. As the young man drove away, they waved goodbye and felt both sadness and relief.

*

The "Battle of the Bulge", the last major Nazi offensive against the Allies in World War II began on December 16. The surprise attack in the

Ardennes Forest between Belgium and Luxembourg, was Hitler's last-ditch attempt to split the Allies in two in their drive towards Germany and destroy their ability to resupply themselves from the Port of Antwerp.

*

The Colaluca's 1944 Christmas was special for several reasons: Paulo was home safe and sound, his and Loucille's debit clients were in the hands of a new agent, it was Biff's third Christmas—who was ready and waiting for Santa, and Rafaele and Anna decided to make Gardena their home permanently. The extended Colaluca and Sweet families were healthy and looking forward to the holidays.

To prevent nighttime submarine attacks, West Coast Civil Defense continued dimout restrictions, limiting traditional Christmas shopping, open-houses, and other festivities mainly to daylight hours. After work, families walked to neighbor's homes in the evening to drop off presents and socialize.

The week before Christmas, the house at 1561 158th Street welcomed many friends and relatives who dropped by almost daily for eggnog, cookies, hugs, and hear about Paulo's trip to Africa, especially the submarine attack, and to see pictures of the water buffalo he shot. People laughed and children played out in the yard with Lady. For a while the war was out of mind and far away.

December 27, Paulo left on his last Merchant Marine voyage sailing from San Pedro harbor on the S.S. North Wind, for a thirteen-day coastal run north.

CHAPTER THIRTY FIVE

WAR AND SEA ENDS 1945

The thirteen-day assignment, ending in San Pedro on January 8,1945, was Paulo's last. At home, he explained his reasons to Loucille.

"This last trip up the coast on the North Wind gave me time to think. My back is not completely healed from being blown overboard, and I still get tinges of pain. Being away from you and Biff is too hard for me. I'm tired of seeing war's brutality up close."

Sitting by him on the sofa, Loucille turned, took his hands in hers, looked into his eyes, and said, "Paulo, I can't even imagine what you've seen in war, and then come home to face the deaths of people in your Prudential families." Her voice drifted off, tears fell, and she embraced her beloved husband.

"I feel like a coward," he whispered in her ear.

Loucille held him at arms-length. "YOU are NOT a coward! You are the bravest man I know. You've served twice. Paulo, In my book you're a hero."

They sat silently before Paulo said. "I plan to resign from the Merchant Marines."

"Really? You can do that?"

"I'm not in the military. I'm a Merchant Mariner, a civilian serving during wartime. I choose the ships I sail on, sign a contract, and I can quit after each voyage."

"You won't have to leave any more?" she asked hope rising.

"No."

She sat in his lap, wrapped her arms around his neck, and snuggled into him. "I love you, Paulo." Softly, she added, "You must tell your parents.

Your mother's been on pins and needles waiting for you to come home."

Paulo walked back to his parent's house and told them of his decision.

Anna cried and Raffaele embraced him. "That's good for you and your bambino."

When Paulo resigned from the Merchant Marine the next day, he and Loucille began talking excitedly about their life and what to do next.

*

The month-long Battle of the Bulge ended January 25, 1945, when the American army prevailed. After the defeat, Germany retreated for the remainder of the war, the turning point in the European Theatre.

The Allies invaded the island of Iwo Jima on February 19, 1945, a battle that lasted until March 26. In this most brutal battle in the Pacific Theatre to date, Japanese soldiers fought to the death.

*

Paulo rejoined the Gardena Lions Club and talked with his mentors and friends, asking their advice on job prospects, particularly managerial positions.

At the end of February, Paulo and Loucille decided, reluctantly, to get Biff a smaller dog to play with. They loved Lady, their friendly and overly protective German Shepard, but she was just too rough a playmate for their two and half year-old. After finding her a great home with one of Paulo's former client's family who had older children, they bought a small, white female with brown spots. Biff called her Ginger-Dena.

CHAPTER THIRTY SIX

THE CHICKEN 1945

Early in March, Loucille called into the bedroom. "Time to rise and shine sleepy head."

Biff rubbed his eyes and yawned.

She sat on his bed and slipped her fingers under his pajama top.

He giggled and rolled on his side. "Stop. It tickles."

"Really?" She pulled his top down. "I had no idea."

He sat up and held his elbows close to his sides.

As she wiggled her fingers, he squirmed out of reach. "Okay, I won't tickle you anymore. Until this afternoon."

"Mommy, no," he protested.

"All right, Mr. No Fun. Let's get you dressed. Your Granddad already knocked on the door, looking for his helper."

"Feed the chickens." He bounced up.

"Like you've done every day since he got them," she said. "Let's get you dressed. What do you want to wear today?"

Biff took a pair of brown corduroy overalls out of his low white dresser. From the middle drawer, he grabbed a red flannel shirt and brought the clothes to his mother.

Loucille helped him put on his clothes, socks, and shoes. Looking him over, she pronounced, "You make a very cute little farmer."

Biff beamed. "I help Granddad," he said over his shoulder, hurrying down the hall and bursting out the kitchen door. He galloped to the back house and looked through the screen door. "Granddad?"

"Is that my helper?" Raffaele called out.

"It's me."

Raffaele came to the door. "Well, good morning. How are you today?"

Biff grinned. "Me ready."

Raffaele picked up a shopping bag by the door and came outside. "The chickens are waiting." He took Biff's hand. "Think they're hungry?"

"Always hungry."

"That's true."

They went across the lawn to the chicken coop in the back yard.

Raffaele set down the bag, and picked up the end of the coiled hose lying under the raised, wire-mesh coop. He put the end of the hose through the wire-mesh into the ceramic water bowl. "We'll turn on the water, just a little bit." The chickens clucked quietly from the other side of the coop.

Biff watched carefully as Raffaele did each step: recoil the hose, lift a package of chicken feed out of the shopping bag, unlatch the door on the coop, and fill the other bowl. The chickens clucked louder and moved to the feed. He relatched the coop door and looked at Biff. "There's something else for them in the bag. Will you get it out?"

Biff reached in the shopping bag and pulled out slices of stale bread.

Raffaele pointed. "Put it inside." He opened the coop door part way.

Biff stood on his toes, reached up, and put the bread in the coop. When a chicken pecked at it, he pulled his hand back quickly.

Raffaele latched the coop door. "Don't be afraid. They don't bite."

"They peck you."

Raffaele smiled. "Sometimes." He tousled Biff's hair. "Thank you, helper."

Biff held his Granddad's hand as they walked to the front house.

Loucille stood inside the screen door. "Raffaele, please join us for breakfast."

Biff looked up at Raffaele. "Want to, Granddad?"

He shook his head. "Thank you, but another day." Tilting his head back toward the chicken coop. "I have another chore to do this morning. Thanks for asking."

Raffaele looked down at Biff. "Have your breakfast, bambino. I'll see you later."

A half-hour later, Biff finished his breakfast and stood in front of the kitchen sink, holding out his hands.

Loucille turned on the faucet. "Did you like those pancakes?"

"Specially the syrup."

She wet the red-striped dishtowel in the warm water and wrung it out. "Let's clean those hands and your cute, sticky face."

"Cute?" He tilted his head to one side.

She wiped his hands. "Cute means you're ... well, adorable."

He scrunched up his face.

She sat him up on the counter. "How about this? Cute means you're sweet."

"Like candy?"

"Sweeter than candy?" She wiped his cheeks and around his mouth. "How else can I explain it? Cute means you're going to grow up to be handsome. Like your father."

"Like Daddy?"

"Yes, like Daddy." She ran her fingers through his thick curly hair and hugged him. He still smelled like maple syrup.

"Where Daddy?"

"He went to an early meeting today. He'll be back later."

She lifted him down and held his hand until they got to the hallway. "How about you go play in your room while I finish cleaning up the kitchen?" She smiled.

Biff raced down the hall.

The morning sun slanted into his bedroom at the back of the house. He sat on the floor placing wooden alphabet blocks around Floppy, his long-eared, white rabbit. When the circle of blocks was complete, he went to the toy chest under the corner windows and took a wooden tugboat off the lid.

Ginger barked and kept barking.

Biff crawled up on the chest and looked out.

Ginger was bounding around Raffaele. He was standing in front of the chicken coop at the back of the yard. When he turned, he was holding a chicken by the neck. He swung it and made a quick jerking motion. The body of the chicken fell to the ground. The head was in Raffaele's hand. The body ran into the chain link fence and fell over.

His Granddad grabbed and held on to Ginger's collar.

Biff put his hands over his ears and yelled. "Mommy, Mommy!" before curling up in a ball on the toy chest.

"What's wrong?" She picked him up and glanced out the window. "Oh—"

Biff buried his face against her neck.

Raffaele picked up the headless bird and walked back toward his house holding its feet. Blood dripping from the neck. Ginger barked and ran around him. He saw them at the window and waved.

Loucille sat down on the toy chest and rocked him. "I'm sorry you saw that."

They heard Granddad tell Ginger to be quiet before his screen door banged shut. Ginger stop barking.

Loucille continued rocking him. "I know chickens are your pets, like Ginger-Dena, but Granddad raises them for food. Sometimes he kills one so Grandma can cook it."

Biff didn't say anything.

"I have an idea." She stood him on the floor in front of her. "You know, I bet Mrs. McKeever has a new batch of peanut butter cookies."

He looked at the window.

"Shall we go, and see?"

He continued to stare at the window and said softly, "Okay."

His mother took his hand and held it as they crossed the street to Mrs. McKeever's house.

When they got to the front porch, Biff crawled up the tall steps of the two-story wood frame house. "Miz Keever?" He peered in through the screen door.

"Well, hello?" came a cherry voice from inside. "It's nice to see you."

Biff reached for the door handle but couldn't quite touch it.

Mrs. McKeever, her gray hair pulled back in a bun, pushed the screen door open. "Come on in. Would you like a cookie?" she said.

He nodded.

"Loucille, have a seat on the porch. I'll bring us some sweet tea."

Biff headed to the kitchen at the back of the house, Mrs. McKeever right behind him.

The screen door squeaked open when Biff came out, followed by Mrs. McKeever. He had a peanut butter cookie in each hand.

Loucille sat in the porch swing, tracing the outline of a big yellow flower on the cushion next to her.

Biff laid a cookie in his mother's lap and went to the end of veranda, sat on a wooden hobbyhorse next to the railing, and rocked.

Mrs. McKeever put a lacquered tray down on the small wicker table in front of the swing, handed his mother a glass of tea, sat beside her, and looked down the porch at Biff. "How's my little cowboy this morning."

He heard her but just stared across the street.

"He's awfully quiet this morning," Mrs. McKeever said.

Loucille took a sip of tea and said, "He's had a rough morning."

Biff kept rocking and listening to his mother and Mrs. McKeever talk.

"What happened?" Mrs. McKeever picked up her glass.

"He just saw his grandfather ring a chicken's neck."

"Oh, my. Poor thing. When I was a little girl, my mother used to—"

Loucille put her hand up and shook her head.

Mrs. McKeever nodded. "Of course." She took a sip of tea.

"Up until now, Biff thought the chickens were pets." Loucille smiled at him.

He stopped rocking.

Loucille looked and saw Raffaele back outside and in the garden. She turned to Mrs. McKeever. "Thank you for letting us come over unannounced."

"You're welcome anytime Loucille and remember, love will overcome fear."

"Biff, it's time to go." She stood.

He got off the rocking horse and walked to her.

"What do you say to Mrs. McKeever?" she said pointing at the tray of cookies.

"Thank you."

Mrs. McKeever smiled at him. "Would you like to take one home with you?"

He shook his head.

"Well, thank you for coming to see me." She leaned down, kissed the top of his head, and then hugged his mother.

When they got across the street, Loucille pointed at the garden. "Want to go help your Granddad?"

He shook his head. "No."

"Well, let's go see if the mailman brought us any letters." Taking his hand, they walked to the mailbox in front of their house.

CHAPTER THIRTY SEVEN

THE AFTERMATH 1945

When they came in the back door, Loucille suggested he play in his room, and Biff started down the hall. She sat down at the kitchen table to open the mail.

Biff came back. "I play out here?"

"Sure, sweetheart. Let's bring some of your toys out here."

She took his hand and walked to his room Loucille watched him go to the toy chest, glance at the window, but not look out. All morning, she noticed he played where he could see her. After lunch, he snuggled in her lap on the sofa looking at picture books. She let him take his nap on the sofa.

Raffaele knocked quietly on the screen door as Loucille sat at the kitchen table making her weekly shopping list. With a finger to her lips she said, "Biff's asleep in the front room."

"Will you, Paulo, and the bambino come eat with us tonight? Anna's making chicken cacciatore."

"Sounds delicious, but Biff saw you kill the chicken this morning and it really scared him."

He met her gaze and shook his head. "I thought he was inside."

"He was, but he heard Ginger barking, crawled up on his toy chest, and saw you wring the chicken's neck. He yelled for me, and I found him curled up crying."

"The head, it was not supposed to come off."

Loucille nodded. "Sometimes it happens."

"I love the bambino."

"I know. I'll tell him we're invited when he wakes up. I'll let you know."

"He's my only grandson."

"And you're the only grandfather he knows. She pushed a strand of black hair behind her ear. "I think he thought the chickens were pets, like Ginger."

Loucille was reading her Better Homes and Gardens, when Biff woke up and crawled into her lap. Loucille put her arms around him and rested her chin on top of his head. "I want to tell you a story. Okay?"

"Uh-huh."

"When I was a little girl, I lived on a farm. There were all kinds of animals on our farm. We had horses, and cows, and pigs, sometimes goats, and chickens."

"You have elephants?"

Loucille smiled. "No. No elephants. They live in the jungle, not on farms." Some animals on our farm helped us, like the horses who pulled our plow so we could plant things, and the cow gave us milk."

"Like the milkman?"

"Yes, but our milk came in a shiny bucket, not in bottles." She held her hands out as if holding one. "All the other animals, pigs, goats, and chickens, we raised to sell to people who bought them for food. They weren't pets."

Biff's gaze went to the back door. "Is Ginger-Dena a pet?"

"Yes, she'll always be a pet. We don't eat dogs." Loucille scrunched up her face.

Biff scrunched his face back at her. "Never?"

"No. Never." She held him away from her. "I know what you saw this morning scared you. The first time I saw my mother do that I got scared too."

He put his arms around her neck and whispered, "Don't want to help Granddad."

She hugged him, sighed. "I know. You don't have to help."

He pulled back, and asked very seriously, "Never?"

She rubbed noses with him. "Never, ever."

At a knock at the back door, Loucille put Biff down on the sofa and went into the kitchen. Raffaele stood on the stoop.

"I came to see if you're coming to dinner," he said through the screen.

Loucille turned and looked at Biff on the sofa. He was shaking his head.

Turning back to Raffaele, she said, "I don't think tonight's a good night for us. Some other time."

"Please tell him I'm sorry I scared him." Raffaele's shoulders sagged as he walked slowly back toward his house.

Loucille closed the back door and went to the sofa. "Did you hear what your grandfather said?"

Biff nodded.

"He didn't mean to scare you. He loves you very much."

Later, when Paulo came home and picked him up, the first thing Biff said was, "Don't like Granddad."

Paulo looked at Loucille, who explained, as Biff's arms squeezed his father's neck.

"Can Daddy tell you a secret?" he whispered.

"Uh-huh."

"I get scared sometimes too."

Biff looked at him.

"Yep, I do. It's okay to be scared, but don't let it stop you from doing what you want to do. Do you like feeding the chickens?"

Biff nodded.

"Then be brave and feed the chickens."

"He hurt the chicken."

Loucille took a deep breath. "Yes, but do you know why?"

Biff shook his head.

"Because Grandma was going to cook it. Granddad raises those chickens for food."

Biff stared at her. "Food?"

"Yes. You like Grandma's red sauce on noodles, don't you?"

Biff nodded slowly.

"Grandma puts chicken in the sauce to make cacciatore," Paulo added.

"Catch-in-tory?"

"Yes, chicken cacciatore."

"Chicken's head too?"

"No, no. Not the head."

"Feathers?"

Paulo smiled. "No."

"Only chicken?"

"That's right, only chicken," Loucille repeated.

Paulo put Biff down. "I'm going to go tell Granddad and Grandma that we'll have dinner with them another night, okay?"

Biff nodded.

The next morning at breakfast, Biff said, "I want to play with Ginger-Dena."

Loucille looked out the window as she washed the breakfast dishes and turned to Biff. "Your grandfather's outside sitting in his patio chair. You're not scared of him anymore?"

"No."

"Okay, have fun with Ginger." She opened the back door. "I bet your grandfather would like to know you're not scared."

Biff looked out the screen door. "Can you tell him?"

"You were the one who was scared," his father said. "You need to tell him."

Biff opened the screen door a crack and looked at Raffaele again.

"I know it's hard, but I think you're brave enough."

Biff pushed the screen door open, went down the steps, and walked along the side of the house touching the stucco. Ginger came up and licked his face.

Biff giggled and pushed her nose away. He took hold of her collar and lead her down the sidewalk. At the back corner of his house, he stopped.

Raffaele waved. "Good morning."

Biff waved back.

"How are you bambino?"

"You scared me."

Raffaele patted the arm of the other patio chair. "Come and sit."

Biff walked to the chair, crawled up, and sat down. "I'm not scared."

Raffaele leaned forward. "I'm sorry I scared you. Can we still be friends?"

"Uh-huh," Biff said smiling shyly.

"Well, friend, will you come to my house for dinner tonight?"

"Is Grandma cooking catch-in-tory tonight?"

Raffaele chuckled. "No chicken cacciatore tonight. Your grandma's making rigatoni and meatballs."

"I like Grandma's meatballs."

Raffaele rubbed his stomach. "Me too."

"Can Mommy and Daddy come?"

"Let's go ask." He spread his arms. "Can I have a hug first?"

Biff hugged him and they walked toward the front house, holding hands.

Loucille stepped out onto the back stoop.

Biff let go of Raffaele's hand and ran to her. "Mommy, can you and Daddy come to dinner tonight?"

"I'm available," Paulo said from inside.

"We'd be delighted, Raffaele." Loucille sat down on the steps. "What time would Granddad and grandma like us to come?"

Biff turned and looked at Raffaele. "What time, Granddad?"

"Grandma said six o'clock." He smiled at Biff. "See you later, friend."

Biff grinned back. "See you later."

The sky turned sunset orange as the three of them walked to the back house. Biff knocked on the door. "We're here."

Raffaele opened the door. "Come in."

Biff galloped past him into the kitchen.

"Hi, grandma." He breathed in the familiar smell of garlic, oregano, and basil, coming from the pot on the stove. "Mommy said you put chickens in your catch-in-tory?"

Anna glanced at Loucille and Raffaele in the doorway behind him. "Let me think," she said, smoothing her apron. "Sometimes. Why do you ask?"

"Do I like catch-in-tory?"

Eyes twinkling, she said, "Last time you had seconds, so I think you liked it."

Biff grinned. He turned and looked at Raffaele. "I help you tomorrow?"

CHAPTER THIRTY EIGHT

ONTARIO, VJ DAY, AND BUFF
1945

In mid-March, Paulo met the owners of the Karakul Fur Farm, a commercial sheep ranch 50 miles northeast of Gardena, in Ontario, CA.

They took him on a tour of the farm, followed by a lengthy conversation about their hope of introducing the sheep's thick, black wool into apparel markets. Immediately after Paulo described his managerial and sales experiences, the owners offered him the position of Karakul Fur Farm Manager, to begin the first week in April. Paulo accepted.

A few days later, he drove Loucille and Biff out to see the farm. "What'd you think?" he asked, as they walked to his office after seeing the barns, pastures, and tree-shaded grounds.

"It's a farm-girl's dream come true," Loucille said, with a lilt in her voice. "I've never seen wool as thick as this."

"Karakuls have been raised since 1400 BC in Central Asia. They're sturdy animals, and the wool can be used for clothing, carpets, and felting."

"Can I have one, Daddy?"

Paulo picked him up. "I don't think our yard is big enough. How about we keep one here for you to feed whenever you visit? Okay?"

Biff nodded. "A little black one, okay?"

"Sure. They're all black when they're born but turn white as they grow."

At the end of March, when Loucille put Ginger's bowl down by the back porch steps, she wasn't waiting like always and she didn't come when called. Loucille walked around behind the house and peered into Lady's oversized doghouse.

"Oh, my God!" she exclaimed.

"What?" Paulo yelled back.

"Ginger's nursing four puppies."

Paulo came running, knelt, and looked. "She must have been pregnant when we bought her. What'd you want to do? Shall we take her back?"

"No! They're adorable. Biff would never forgive us. We'll keep them. Think of it as five for the price of one."

"Jesus." He laughed. "This is what I get for marrying a big-hearted farmer."

Easter was on April 1, 1945. Early in the morning, Paulo hid three baskets of eggs for Biff to find, and a week later, he, Loucille and Biff decorated their little fir tree in the front yard with the colorful eggshells.

*

The Battle of Okinawa also began on April 1, with the largest Allied amphibious assault ever undertaken in the Pacific Theatre. The bloody fighting lasted 82 days, finally ending on June 15. The Japanese Imperial Army lost 100,00 men, the Allies lost 50,000.

The Battle for Berlin began April 4 when the Soviet Army reached the outskirts of the city and invaded.

*

In mid-April, as he was shaving, Loucille came up behind Paulo and clasped her hands around his chest looking at him in the mirror with a dreamy smile on her face.

"Well, good morning," he said, as she squeezed into him.

"I have something to tell you."

"Okay…"

"I'm pregnant."

Paulo put down his razor, turned around, wrapped his arms around her waist, and pulled her close. "Are you sure?"

"Un-huh. I'm very regular and have missed two periods. I'll make an appointment with Doctor Storken but I'm pretty sure."

Paulo lifted her onto her toes and kissed her tenderly. "I love you, wife. I've never gotten a new job and baby all in the same month. I must tell my parents—"

"No," she put a finger to his lips. "Not until Dr. Storken says yes. Okay?"

"I won't tell anybody until you say I can."

Dr. Storken's examination confirmed Loucille's hopes for another baby a few days later, and Paulo proudly let family and friends know of their joy.

*

The Japanese also ended the Fugo Balloon Bomb project in April 1945. Allied bombing had destroyed two of their three facilities for making hydrogen. By then, balloon sightings had been reported in Alaska, Hawaii, Oregon, Kansas, Iowa, Washington, Wyoming, Idaho, South Dakota, Nevada, Colorado, Texas, Northern Mexico, Michigan, the outskirts of Detroit, and the western provinces of Canada. In Southern California, A P-38 Lightning shot down a balloon near Santa Rosa. Another was seen over Santa Monica, and pieces of a balloon were found in the streets of Los Angeles.

Adolf Hitler and his bride, Eva Braun, committed suicide on April 30, as the Soviet Army closed in on his last headquarters, the Fuhrerbunker, located beneath the Reich Chancellery in Berlin. The German Army surrendered May 2.

On May 8, Great Britain and the United States celebrated "V-E Day". Cities in both nations, as well as formerly occupied cities in Western Europe hung flags and banners and rejoiced in the defeat of the Nazi army.

*

One evening after Biff was asleep, Paulo asked Loucille to sit on the sofa.

"I've made the daily drive from Gardena to my office at the Karakul Fur Farm every day all month. How would you feel about moving to Ontario?"

"What? Why?"

Loucille's eyes brimmed with tears.

"Sweetheart, I worry every day that I'll be too far away to help if, God forbid, you have an emergency during your pregnancy." Taking her hands in his, he added, "Okay, we don't need to decide right now. I just wanted you to know what I'm feeling."

Loucille sniffled and nodded.

The next day, Loucille took Biff across the street to visit Mrs. McKeever and for him to have a few of his favorite peanut butter cookies.

Biff climbed the familiar front porch steps and knocked on the screen door. "Miz Keever I'm here." He knocked again.

A voice from inside called out. "Is that Biff Colaluca at my front door?"

Grinning at his mom, he said, "I here for p-butter cookies."

The door opened, "Well, come in. There are fresh baked ones on the kitchen table. Help yourself."

Biff hurried past her as Mrs. McKeever motioned Loucille inside.

"I need your advice. Do you have a few minutes to talk?"

"Of course. Would you like tea?"

From the dining room table, Loucille watched Biff munch a cookie in his left hand, while sorting through the toys in the large wooden box by the fireplace with his right.

"What's on your mind, Loucille?" Mrs. Keever asked, as she placed the tea tray on the table and handed her a cup.

Loucille recounted her discussion with Paulo. "I'm happy here, I love our neighborhood, and we have friends here. I really don't want to move."

Mrs. McKeever sipped her tea. "Mmmm...I love tea, but it's so hard to find nowadays. Do you like it?" she said, pointing at Loucille's cup.

"Ah, yes, thank you."

"Loucille, you know how fortunate you are, right? Not only did Paulo come back from this terrible war, but he returned in one piece. Like so many young men, he's trying to find his way after living through that nightmare. My husband returned from WWI in one piece, but struggled a very long time to find his way."

"I'm so sorry..."

"No need to be, he worked it out and we had a good marriage. I guess what I want to say is, Paulo's a good man. He's a hard worker, and he obviously cares deeply about you and Biff. Most likely he's going to try a few things before he finds where he wants to be, or what he wants to do."

Gently, she added, "Between you and me, Paulo doesn't strike me as the farmer type."

Loucille laughed. "No, this is so unlike him."

"Just be patient. He'll work it out."

Biff walked in with crumbs around his mouth and crawled up into Mrs. McKeever's lap. "Another cookie, please?"

"Of course, and please get one for your mother too."

After lunch that afternoon, Loucille stood at the sink, watching Biff out in the big side yard, play with Ginger and her puppies. Now six weeks old, the puppies were wagging their tails, tumbling over each other, and exploring. They'd named them Fuzzy, Spotty, Midget, and Stinker. Stinker got his name because he was filled with mischief.

At nap time, Loucille called Biff to come in. A few moments later she heard what sounded like "bonk" and an anguished howl. Biff had pulled the screen door open, backed off the steps, and fallen on his back on the sidewalk. When Loucille reached him, he was conscious, but struggling to breathe.

"You knocked the wind out of yourself, sweetheart," she said as calmly as she could, while feeling the back of his head, arms, and legs.

Biff stared at her, eyes wide with fear, gasping, and trying to catch his breath. He managed a shallow breath, exhaled, inhaled, and started crying.

Loucille cradled him in her arms and carried him to the sofa. She called Dr. Storken's office and told Nurse Green what happened.

Dr. Storken came on the line. "As a precaution, can you bring him in to rule out the possibility of a concussion?"

Loucille called Katsey, who came and drove them downtown.

"He doesn't have any symptoms of a concussion," reported Dr. Storken as Biff sat on the examination table. "Otherwise, he's fit as a fiddle, just an active little boy. From what you described you might want Paulo to change that screen door." He lifted Biff down to the floor and gave him a lollypop.

The doctor looked at Loucille, and said, "Your next prenatal visit isn't until next week, but with your history, even at this early stage of your pregnancy, you should not lift anything. If your friend can watch Biff, I like to examine you to make sure you are okay too."

Following the examination, Dr. Storken told Loucille her pregnancy was proceeding normally and warned her again about not lifting.

"Why didn't you call me?" Paulo said, vexed.

"I did, but by the time I got home from Dr. Storken's, you'd left the office and were on your way home," Loucille said, defensively.

Softening his tone, he said, "I'm sorry. This is what I don't like about being so far away from you and Biff and why I want us to move to Ontario." He hugged her close. "I love you two more than anything but can't protect you when I'm so far away. Understand?"

She nodded against his chest.

That evening, after Biff went to bed, they decided not to sell their

Gardena property for two reasons. First, Paulo wanted to make sure his new position would work out, and second, they didn't want to deal with having to move his parents. Raffaele was understanding and agreed to stay to take care of the property. Anna cried about not seeing them every day but was mollified with the promise of weekend visits.

"I don't want to move," Biff said, clutching his favorite stuffed animal, Bear, when Paulo and Loucille told him.

Loucille pulled him close. "I know, but we're a family and must go with Daddy."

"Why can't I stay with Granddad and Grandma?"

"Because Daddy and I love you and would miss you terribly." She kissed him on the top of his head.

"They love me, too."

His grandparents were part of his life since birth and living just a few steps from his back door, he got hugs and treats, sat on their laps, and snuggled as long as he wanted. They always listened to him.

"Can I come back every day and see them?"

"Ontario is a long way from Gardena." She turned his face to her. "We will come and see them, but not every day."

At the end of May, a big truck parked in front of 1561 158th Street. Biff watched men in white coveralls come in and out, and by dinnertime, every room was empty.

They moved to a Spanish style home on a quiet, tree-lined street in Ontario. The rented three-bedroom, one bath, white stucco house, had a peaked, red-tiled roof, and well-kept grass lawns front and back. A matching detached garage sat next to the small backyard.

The first weekend after they moved in, Paulo took Loucille and Biff to his new favorite Italian restaurant on Holt Blvd in Ontario, "Vince's Spaghetti". The family atmosphere and large portions suited them; Biff especially liked the giant meatballs.

Over the next six months, Biff watched his mother's tummy get bigger and bigger, and her comfortable lap disappear. Visits to his grandparents became less and less frequent, and finally stopped.

Paulo joined the Ontario Lions Club. At initiation, where he described himself as "Someone who likes to eat and sleep, and when forced to, will work." He also said he answered to the names Greek, Gabby, and Shyster, and chose not to reveal how he acquired those names. "His ambition was to be held in high esteem by his fellow men, believing there was no higher attainment."

*

At the beginning of August, confronted with an estimated one million casualties if the Allies invaded Japan, President Truman approved dropping the first ever atomic bombs.

"Little Boy" dropped on Hiroshima on August 6; and "Fat Man" on Nagasaki on August 9.

Japan surrendered unconditionally on August 14, which was celebrated world-wide as VJ Day.

*

Biff's third birthday, August 28, was a quiet affair. His parents gave him his first real wagon, filled with a can of Tinker Toys, toy planes, soldiers, and cars.

New little friends came for cake and lemonade in the afternoon. He opened their gifts that included a toy horn, books, and candy, before they played for a couple of hours in the backyard sand box.

Loucille made Biff's favorite dinner, spaghetti and meatballs. He made a wish, then blew out the three candles on his chocolate birthday cake with white frosting.

Afterwards, Paulo took them to a Mickey Mouse picture show in a theatre with air conditioning. Loucille was in the seventh month of her pregnancy and uncomfortable in the inland heat.

*

Aboard the USS Missouri in Tokyo Bay, the Japanese signed the official surrender papers ending World War II on September 2, 1945.

*

In November, before Loucille went to the hospital to have the baby, Paulo drove to Gardena to get his grandparents.

"How much longer before they come?" Biff asked.

His mother smiled. "Like I said a few minutes ago, they'll be here this afternoon. Now finish your lunch, okay?"

He took another bite of his peanut and jelly sandwich. "When in the afternoon?"

"I don't know exactly, Biff. After you finish lunch, you can wait for them on the front porch."

He took a swallow of milk and started toward the front door, sporting a milk mustache, brown bear tucked under his arm.

"Hey you! Come back here."

He turned around to see his mother holding a dishrag. As she wiped his face she said, "You're too young to have a mustache. Stay on the porch, okay?"

Biff waited and talked to his bear. "Why don't they come?" Finally, after what seemed like forever, Paulo pulled into the driveway and Biff hurried down the steps, running to the passenger side door.

His grandma waved down at him.

"Where's Granddad?" He jumped up and down, trying to see in the back seat. "Granddad? Where's Granddad?"

Paulo came around and opened the passenger-side door. "He changed his mind. Just your grandmother came."

She got out, bent down, and hugged him. "Hello, little one. It's good to see you."

Biff ran to his mother on the porch. "Why didn't Granddad come?"

"I don't know." She smiled and hugged Anna. "Thank you for coming."

"I am glad to come," she said, and went inside.

Paulo started to follow her, but Loucille put a hand on his chest. "Why didn't Raffaele come?"

"He changed his mind."

She poked him in the chest. "Why?"

"He wanted to follow me out here in his car."

"So?"

"I didn't think it was a good idea." Paulo shrugged. "When I said no, he said he wasn't coming. You know how he is."

"I know how you are, too." She frowned. "He probably didn't want to be stuck here, with no way to get around."

"I didn't want him going somewhere and getting lost. I don't have time for that."

Loucille put her hands around her belly and stared at her husband. "Your son was excited to see both his grandparents."

Biff hugged his mother's leg.

"I'm sorry, but your Granddad can be stubborn sometimes."

Loucille cleared her throat. "And you're not?"

Biff followed them into the house and flopped on the sofa, hugging his bear. He liked his grandma, but he loved his Granddad.

At dinner, the grownups talked about what had to be done while his mother was in the hospital. All he understood was his mother was leaving.

After breakfast the next morning, his mother sat with him on the sofa. "I want you to help your grandmother while I'm gone. Will you do that?"

"When are you coming back?"

"In a few days. I need to rest after I have the baby." She hugged him. "I'll miss you, my little man. You be good for Daddy and Grandma, okay?"

She took him by the hand and walked out to the porch. They watched while his father put a suitcase in the car, then come back and take his mother's hand.

She leaned down. "I love you. I'll be home soon." His father helped her into the car, and she waved at him through the windshield.

Biff watched as the car backed out of the driveway and drove away.

November 21, she gave birth to a second son, who struggled to breath after delivery.

In the delivery room, the doctor said, "Mrs. Colaluca, your baby's oxygen levels are below normal. He's in our infant intensive care unit and I've placed him on oxygen. May I have your permission to run some tests?"

Tears welled in her eyes. "Where's Paulo? Where's my husband?"

"I've sent for him. He should be here any—"

"The nurse said you wanted to see me?" Paulo said, as he came into the room.

"Something's wrong with our baby," Loucille said, tears rolling down her cheek.

The doctor repeated what he told Loucille, and added, "He's what we call a 'Blue Baby'. Their skin turns blue at birth because there's not enough oxygen in the blood."

"Yes, do whatever you need to," Paul said, as he put his arm around Loucille, and she buried her face against his neck and cried.

"When can I see him?" Loucille said, snuffling.

"In a couple of hours," the doctor said. "He's stable now. I'll come get you when we're done."

When they finally saw him through the viewing window, Loucille said,

"I want to name him Ralph, after his grandfather, okay?"

Paulo grinned. "I think he looks like a 'Buff'. That'll be his nickname."

The first thing Loucille did when she came home from the hospital was to sit on the sofa, put Biff in her lap, take his face in her hands, and kiss him on the forehead. She whispered, "I really missed you."

He smiled, snuggled into her, breathing in her familiar scent. "I missed you, too."

She rocked him and asked, "Will you help me take care of your little brother?"

"He can play with all my toys," Biff said quickly.

His mother squeezed him. "He won't be playing with any toys for a while." She put her hand on his chest. "The doctors say he has a hole in his little heart. Will you help us take extra special care of him?"

Biff nodded. He came to understand as the days passed, that whatever was wrong with his little brother absorbed most of his parents' attention.

Paulo visited Loucille and Buff every evening during the week she was in the Hospital. Once she was home, he took her to the hospital each morning, to be with him and back home in the evening. She never said so, but he knew Loucille blamed herself for Buff's heart problem.

Anna, with her daily prayers, admonitions to have faith in her baby, and sharing of her Italian cooking 'secrets', helped Loucille come out of her postpartum depression.

When Paulo brought home the December 4 edition of "The Roaring Lion" newsletter from the Ontario Lion's Club, Loucille read it aloud for Anna as they sat on the sofa after dinner.

"*Thumb Nail Sketch: Lion Paul Colaluca, recently initiated, but for some time a member, hails from Philadelphia. He was born there March 29,1912. Paul attended Philadelphia schools and lived there until he enlisted in the Navy and located permanently in California in 1938. Married in Yuma, Arizona, in 1938, the Colaluca's have one child. Lion Paul's hobby is music. He was a solo violinist in the Admiral's Orchestra prior to the war. During the war, Lion Paul traveled the world for three years while attached to the Merchant Marine. Lion Paul also answers to the names 'Greek', 'Gabby', and 'Shyster'. (That's a combination for anyone's lexicon).*"

Loucille raised her eyebrows and smiled at Paulo. "Shyster?"

He grinned and shrugged.

Loucille continued. "*How he acquired those names is not revealed. His ambition is to be held in high esteem by his fellowmen, for which there is no higher attainment. Lion Paul says, 'I love to eat and sleep, and when forced to, will work.' He is presently employed as manager of the Karakul Fur Farms, having made this association in August 1945."*

"What do you think, Anna?" Loucille said, holding up the newsletter.

"What means this word, shyster?"

Loucille laughed. "It means he can't be trusted, Anna."

Anna frowned. "No, not my bambino. Never. He's a good boy."

Loucille smiled at Paulo. "I agree with your mother. You're not a shyster."

He gazed at her and said, "Then believe me when I tell you…Buff's going to come home from the hospital, and we're all going to be fine."

Loucille put her head on his shoulder. "I believe you."

Finally, the day before Christmas, Buff came home from the hospital.

As Biff stood by the white, wicker bassinet, gazing down at his tiny, sleeping brother, Paulo knelt and put his arm around his shoulder.

"You're a big brother now, Biff, and that's special. Not everyone gets to be one, and as the first son in our family, one of your responsibilities will be to look after him."

Biff turned to his dad, a puzzled look on his face.

"Responsibilities are like jobs. I am not always going to be around and I want you to protect him and make sure nobody hurts him, understand?"

"Yes, Daddy," Biff said, his face serious.

"Good. I know you will. I love you, son."

On Christmas Day, Paulo picked up Raffaele and Anna, who cooked Biff's favorite, spaghetti and meatballs. The aroma made his stomach growl, so a half hour before dinner his grandmother sat him down with a meatball.

After dinner, Paulo, Biff, and Raffaele walked around the block.

When asked what his favorite Christmas present had been, Biff answered, "My baby brother."

To be continued.

1912,
Anna & Raffaele Colaluca
with their children.
Raffaele is holding twins
Vincenzo & Paulo, with
Clara, Angie & Emma
shown in front
from left to right

1912
Paulo & Anna
Colaluca

1914, Paulo Colaluca

1914, Anna & Raffaele Colaluca

Anna Colaluca, date unknown

Amelia Earhart, 1922 Postcard, Kissel Gold Bug Car

1925, Loucille Sweet

1923, Anna, Erina, Clara,
Vincenzo & Paulo Colaluca

1930, Back Row, Angelina & Paulo Colaluca,
Front Row, Clara Colaluca & Andrea Del Vecchio, wedding day,
children unknown

1934, Norfolk, Viginia Navy Dance Band, Paul Colaluca Director

1935, Paulo Colaluca,
Panama Coco Sola Fleet Airbase

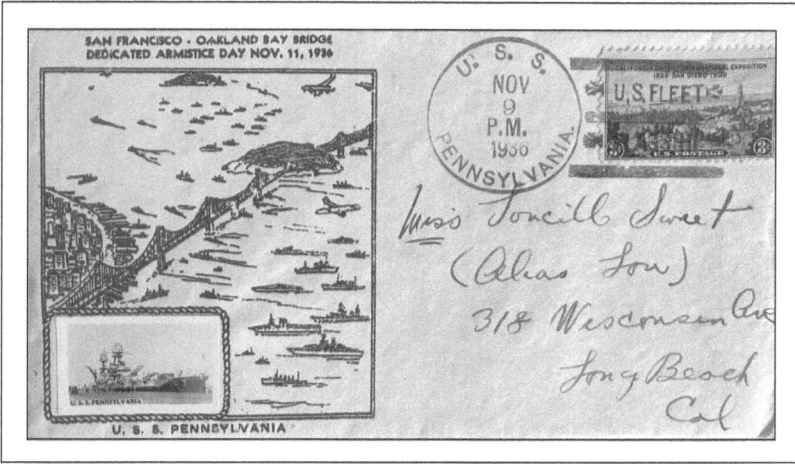

1936, Envelope addressed to Loucille Sweet

1936, Vincenzo & Paulo Colaluca
USS Pennsylvania

1937, Paulo Colaluca
USS Pennsylvania

1937, Vincenzo "Vince" Colaluca

1937 Long Beach, Almyra,
Art, Loucille, Harry & Bill

1939, Paulo & Loucille Colaluca, San Pedro

1940, Loucille Colaluca   *1940, Paulo Colaluca*

1938, Paulo & Loucille Colaluca's first home in San Pedro, CA

1940, The day the house on 158th was rented

1940, view of the back of house on 158th St.

1942 Merchant Marine Crew - Paulo Colaluca standing in front

1942, Christmas Postcard, Katsey, Bill & Billy Joe

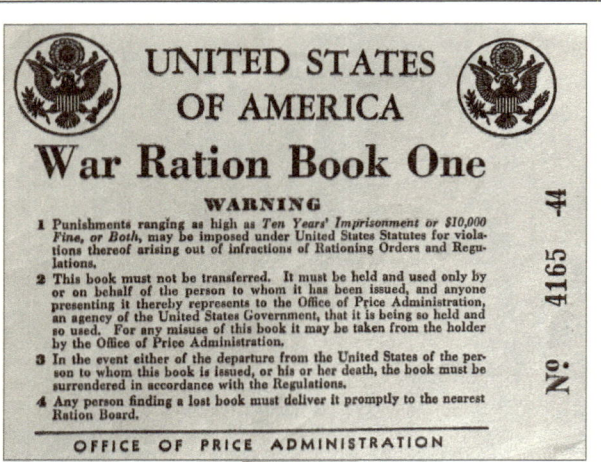

1942,
War Ration Booklet,
front view (above)
& back view (below)

1943, Paolo Colaluca, Port of Angeles, ID Card

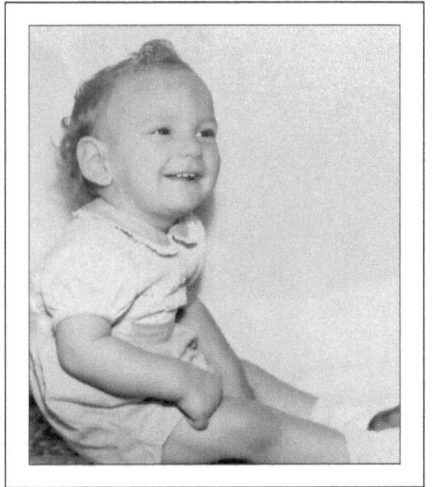

1943, Biff Colaluca

1943, Raffaele, Biff & Lady, the dog

*1943, Christmas
Raffaele, Anna & Biff*

*1944, Mary Loucille Colaluca
with Biff, 2yrs. 4mo.*

1944, The Sweet Family, Frank, Bill, Art, Loucille & Harry

1944, Anna, Biff, Loucille

1945, Loucille & Biff

*1945, Anna & Rafaela's house
on 158th St.*

ACKNOWLEDGEMENTS

The genesis of this book began with a long-held desire to share the story of my Italian grandfather coming to America as an immigrant. The narrative was subsequently expanded through the encouragement of my children, grandchildren, relatives, and friends, to tell the funny, happy, and trying family stories that have been treasured down through the years.

I gratefully acknowledge the assistance I received in my research for the book by the following organizations: The United States Department of the Navy; The Merchant Marine Museum; The Juilliard School; Curtis Institute of Music; and Philadelphia Conservatory of Music.

I want to give special thanks to Kit-Bacon Gressitt. Over the years I have attended many of her writing workshops and spent innumewrable evenings at her home participating in small writing groups. She was and is an excellent writer, teacher, and supportive mentor.

I also want to express my gratitude to four writing group friends: Elise Mack, Monica Newkircen, Kate Harding, and Marci Carri. Your kitchen table critiques, and our ongoing conversations helped me become a better writer and man.

If one is fortunate, they meet their Muse along life's path. I have been uncommonly lucky to have met two: Joyce Montgomery-Weaver and Rene Townsend. The former came to me early in my career and recently connected me to the latter, who has become my tireless copyeditor and wholehearted collaborator. Both have been invaluable guides to making the dream of this book a reality.

Turning a manuscript into a book can be a daunting task for the first-time author. It requires the experience, skills, and magic of a design/layout consultant, who will guide you through the multiple rounds of edits and proofs, obtaining your necessary ISBN, PCN, and LCCN numbers, Permissions, Copyright, and finally setting up a file for printing and submission to a publishing company. For all of the above guidance, support and more, I want to say a heartfelt "Thank you" to my magician, Olga Singer of Simply Two Design.

Finally, to Rick Perrotta, my Italian brother from another mother, and my children: Damon Colaluca, Shelley Colaluca, Lindy Colaluca-Polling, and Michelle Gilleece, for their encouragement to write down our family stories.

ABOUT THE AUTHOR

Paul was born in 1942 in Long Beach, CA. He grew up in Gardena, a small community formerly known as Berryland, for its production of strawberries, and the reputation of being the berry capital of southern California. In the 1930's it became famous as the first city to have legalized card clubs in the state.

He attended California State University, Long Beach, earning a B.A in Speech, an M.A in Speech Pathology, and an M.A. in Psychology from University Without Walls.

During his career he's been a Speech Therapist, Special Education Teacher, Preschool Director, Los Angeles County Program Specialist, Orange County Special Education Coordinator, ESL Teacher, Regular Education Elementary Principal in the Centralia and Nuview School Districts, Director of a Children's Psychiatric Residential Program, District Grant Writer, and an Adjunct Professor for the University of California, Riverside, and Concordia University.

His poems have been published in the San Diego Poetry Annual, Escondido Arts Partnership's Municipal Gallery's Art and Poetry Anthology: Summations, California State Writers Club Anthology, Inland Empire California Writers Club: Coyotes Howl, the Porter Gulch Review, and the Phantom Seed. This is his first book.

When he married Karen, he brought two children, Damon and Shelley, from his first marriage, and she brought Michelle from hers. They had Lindy to make four and have seven grandchildren. Sadly, his beloved wife of 44 years passed away in April of 2022. Paul continues to live in Riverside, CA, close to family.